D1315554

HOW TO CREATE AND USE
DECORATIVE TYPE

HOW TO CREATE AND USE DECORATIVE TYPE

MAGGIE GORDON & EUGENIE DODD

Cincinnati, Ohio

A QUARTO BOOK

First published in the USA by North Light Books, an imprint of F & W Inc.,
1507 Dana Avenue, Cincinnati, Ohio 45207

ISBN 0 89134 329 6

This book was designed and produced by
Quarto Publishing plc
The Old Brewery, 6 Blundell Street
London N7 9BH

Senior Editor Kate Kirby
Editor Richard Dawes

Design Geoff Haddon
Picture Research Sandra Bissoon/Josephine Wiggs

Art Director Moira Clinch
Assistant Art Director Chloë Alexander
Editorial Director Carolyn King
This book contains examples of graphic design work. These examples are included for the purpose of criticism and review.

Typeset by Ampersand Typesetting Limited, Bournemouth
Manufactured in Hong Kong by
Regent Publishing Services Limited
Printed in Hong Kong by Leefung-Asco Printers Limited

Contents

Introduction

3 The vigor and freedom in the calligraphic forms of Georgia Deaver's work contrast strikingly with the formality of a traditional typographic setting. The flourish of the "a" leads the eye into the main text, underlining the photographic image.

4 These decoratively modified letterforms convey the fun and excitement of both San Francisco and the fair. Color, texture, and shape add to the mood of this unusual logo designed by W. Landor and Associates.

1 A logo designed by Chermayeff and Geismar for the Museum of Contemporary Art and the Temporary Contemporary in Los Angeles. Shapes and colors are related to the basic shapes of letterforms. The inserted hand-drawn "t" mirrors the temporary quality.

2 This three-dimensional advent calendar plays with objects and people, modifying them into numbers.

"Good design and good typography are a fusion of information and inspiration, or the conscious and the unconscious, of yesterday and today, of fact and fantasy, work and play, craft and art."

Paul Rand

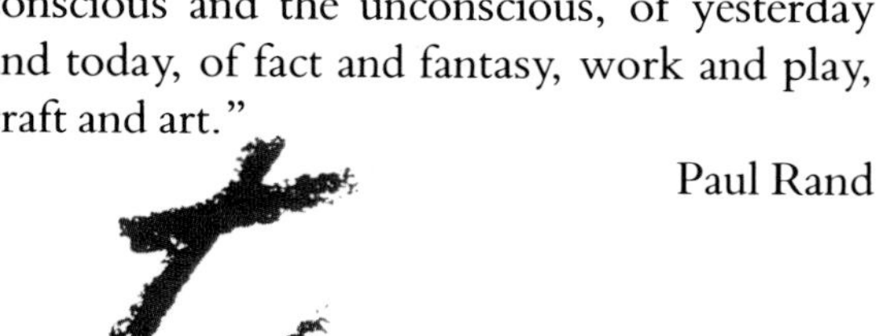

1

Decorative typography is a challenge to the conventions and uniformity of much of the "alphabet media" we see around us. It is concerned with releasing calligraphy, lettering, type, text, and ornament from the strait jacket of traditional forms. Drawn or printed, the letterform becomes an abstract shape, words assume color and a visual rhythm, text takes on a lyrical pattern in new configurations. Something of the enigmatic qualities and fascination with the alphabet can be seen in the modern art movements. This rediscovery of typography uses letters as flexible forms and marks, unconstrained by the necessity to represent. It synthesizes intuition and intellect.

The exuberance of calligraphic form, the flamboyance of the decorative typeface, and the immediacy of artwork techniques can be used to revitalize the functional word, ex-

2

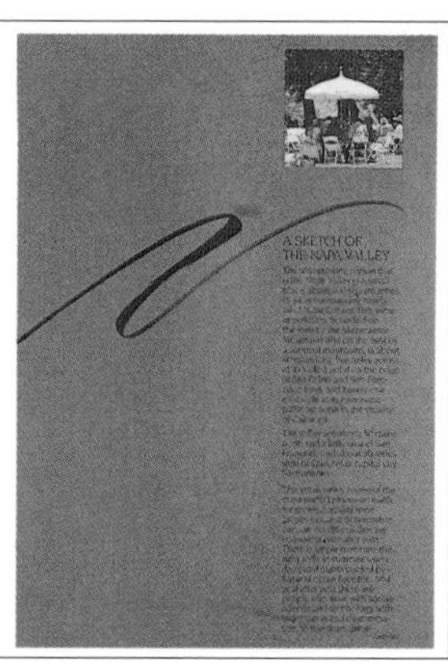

3

4

tending and emphasizing its visual impact. As designers we broadly respect the functional role of typography but are very aware of the drawbacks of this approach. A natural way of breaking down the barriers of conformity happens in our inadvertent typographic doodling, revealing the visual delights of letterforms.

As children we possess an irresistible urge to fill, decorate, and transform plain space; primitive man enhanced his environment with personal, symbolic, and pictorial decoration. This inherent desire to ornament continues to play a significant part in our lives. Witness the spray-can graffiti seen everywhere in our cities and the embellished typographic slogans and messages in a variety of media – on fascias, posters, T-shirts, packaging, book and magazine covers, on television, and cinema screens. A host of graphic contexts cajole us into lively visual dialogue.

7

7 Quarto's catalog cover hints at the comprehensive range of its publications through a lively contrast of weight, size, style, and color, although the decorative essence is not allowed to override legibility.

5

6

5 Personalized typographic confectionery packaging designed and made by Bob Gordon makes both decorative and functional use of a three-dimensional letterform. The contents make up a richly textured and delicious inner letter.

6 Many years of collecting self-adhesive printed ephemera of all kinds went into the decoration of this door. The diversity of styles and color within such a large collection merge into an animated, overall surface pattern. Visual clashes of style could occur if the display were less full.

8

8 This richly decorative letter is taken from a twelfth-century manuscript. Dragons and mythological creatures spring after each other among the foliage, yet form a balanced decoration full of vitality. Such letters were used to mark important passages in manuscripts.

1 The alphabet used in this decorative design by Anne Irwin makes inventive use of a letterform with its fine proportions developed by the Romans. The borders of alphabets and quotations from Edward Johnston's writings add interest and integrate the letter into the background.

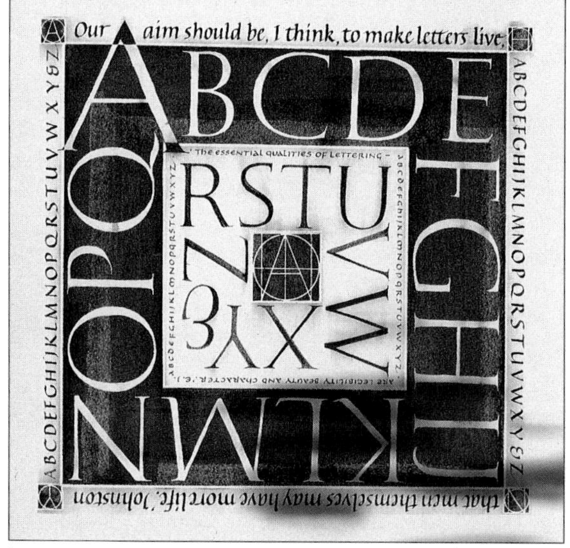

1

2 These letters decorated in national colors head up a series on Italian cookery in the *Sunday Times* magazine. In Italy food is not so much a matter of sustenance as part of the art of living, and this is reflected in the style and flourish of the lettering.

2

Before the invention of printing, the written word had a value currently unfamiliar to us. It was revered and treasured by a mainly illiterate community. The rich ornamentation of early manuscripts expressed this respect. As the hand-drawn letter gave way to printing, the character of typography and its decoration took on new forms, with greater contrasts and intricate detail.

Taste and fashion constantly bring about changes in letterforms and their use and embellishment. New methods of printing and reproduction encouraged exploitation of fresh ideas and themes. Indulgence in extravagant typographic embellishment reached a peak during the Victorian era. The twentieth century has seen a reactionary trend towards functionalism. Lavish ornamentation has disappeared, giving way to a new, clean geometric vigor in typographic form and pattern.

Today's sophisticated and accessible technology offers boundless opportunities for inventive manipulation and experimentation. As a result, a renewed interest in the art of decorative typography is emerging. The creative designer is now able to direct fresh energy into this vital art, redefining ornamentation in current terms.

3 A promotional leaflet for an American design group designed by Vaughn Wedeen Creative Inc. makes liberal use of generously sized decorated letters to highlight different aspects of its members' work. Balanced colors give a unity to the design.

3

4 Drawing letters from the outside inward is a challenge that is often rewarding.

5 This collection of multi-media type combines wood, brass, cork, ceramics, foil, and copper to form a decorative typographic relief on a wall.

6 Contrast of size, the reorientation of letters, similarity of characteristics, change of weight combined with decorative rules and bleeps of color set up a lively interplay in this unusual wedding invitation designed by Total Design.

4

6

7 Modern typographic embroidery echoing the samplers of bygone days. Ornamental rules, borders, and corner pieces enhance the period mood.

8 These stamps and miniature sheet were designed by The Partners. The pen sketch (27p) and alphabet character (32p) show the personal yet rather decorative touch of Lear's handwriting echoed in the overall sheet design.

7

8

5

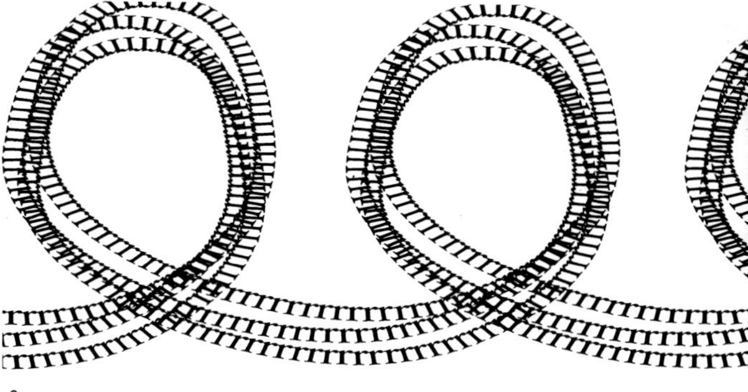

9

9 A dynamic, computer-generated typographic experiment that gives a feeling of speed and movement. Exciting patterns and textures occur where the lines of type overprint.

This book is divided into two parts. The first deals with the nature and background of decorative typography, its changing face and its uses today. The second is based on projects and deals with sources for ideas and ways in which these can be explored and developed for practical use.

1 Differences in style and weight of letterforms make the letters appear to float across a densely textured and busy background in this design by Hard Werken. The decorative treatment of the edges of the design area is strengthened by the contrasting intensity of the stark blue border, which directs the eye into the central area of visual activity.

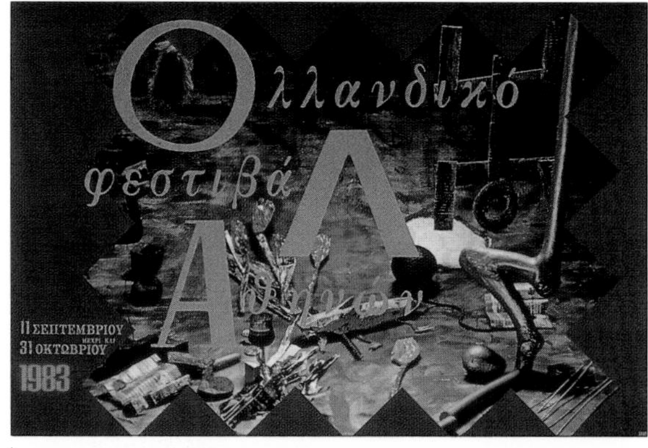

1

2

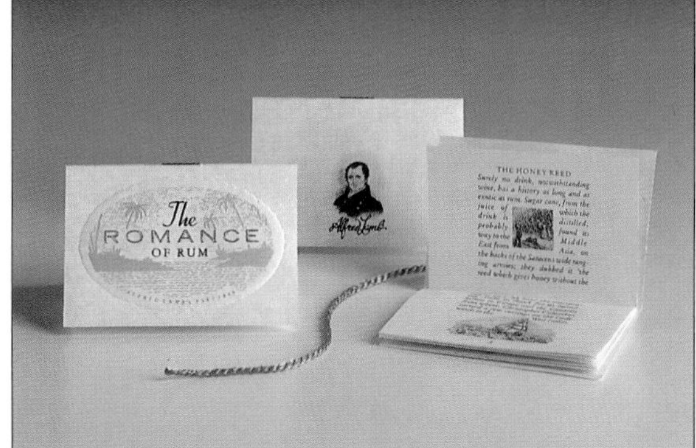

3

2 This current use of a decorated capital letter as a symbol/monogram for a real estate developer was designed by Chermayeff and Geismar. It exudes a quiet elegance and its embellishment suggests attention to detail. The proportions of the "R" within the square suggest a pleasing use of space.

3 The embossing and die-stamping used on the cover of this booklet, designed by Lewis Moberly, are techniques that are often associated with quality. The textured paper, style of typeface, and color all decoratively enhance the mood and historical connotations of fine rum.

4 An inventive use of shape and color gives an intriguing energy to this invitation designed by Total Design.

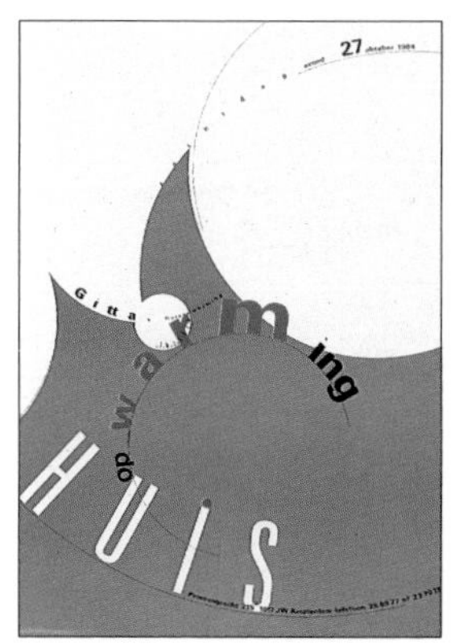

4

PART ONE

This section offers an inspirational introduction to decorative typography. It explains what it is and how it can be used effectively. Typography is looked at both as an art form and as a means of communication. Starting with a single letter, we move on to words and text, examining their decorative potential. The basic elements of typography – shape, size, weight, tone, and color – are individually explored and evaluated. Typographic pattern and texture and decorative text arrangements are introduced. Also investigated are hand-drawn letters, the richness and simplicity of modern calligraphy, and the use of graffiti in design contexts.

A section outlining the major ornamental styles provides a useful reference point for understanding the visual style of a particular period and how to re-create it for modern use. Examples of the changing interpretation of typographic ornament are shown that confirm how alive and effective the art is today. A section on how to modify letters in order to create visual interest suggests ways of enlivening type and text. Extensive examples of the current use of decorative typography demonstrate various techniques for integrating and manipulating ornament, rules, and images into decorative typographic contexts. Electronic media are shown to provide one of the most flexible, fast, and exciting tools available to the designer today.

PART TWO

This section builds on the understanding of the fundamentals of decorative typography outlined in Part One. Each project is linked to reference points in the first part. It puts the principles and ideas into action. Key areas are highlighted in which the most can be made of decorative typography. A simple method of working provides a practical foundation for tackling the projects and insuring lively results. This logical sequence, together with working visuals, traces the initial concept through to the finished product. Projects are structured to develop progressively.

This book aims to inspire and show the aesthetic pleasures that can be derived from letters and words used in new ways and contexts, to encourage the reader to discard preconceived notions of words as purely functional, to discern their decorative potential, and to enjoy the challenge of typographic illustration.

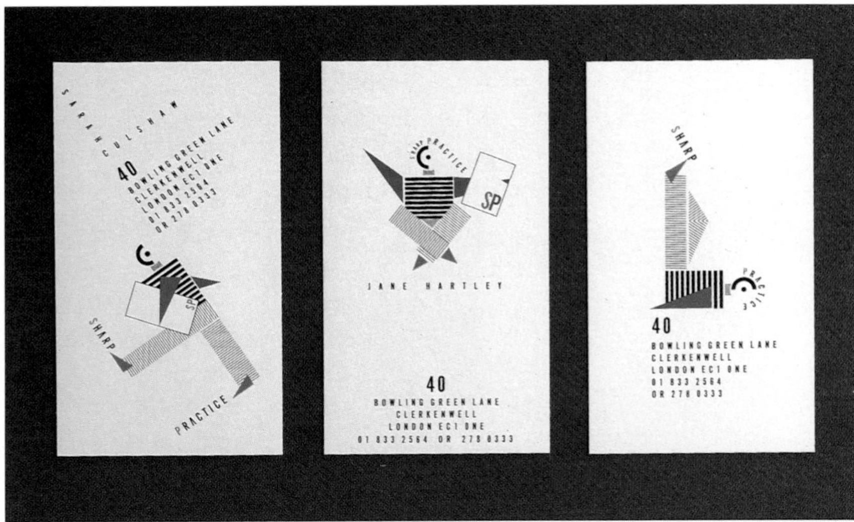

5

6

5 These three business cards form part of the corporate identity of Sharp Practice, a London illustration agency. They were designed by Lewis Moberly and make creative use of rules and shape. The information underlines the stance of the typographic person. The crisp layout echoes the company name.

6 This typographic portrait introduces a review of the work of J. Walter Thompson, London. A constantly evolving and changing agency, it is aptly represented in this inventive imagery.

7

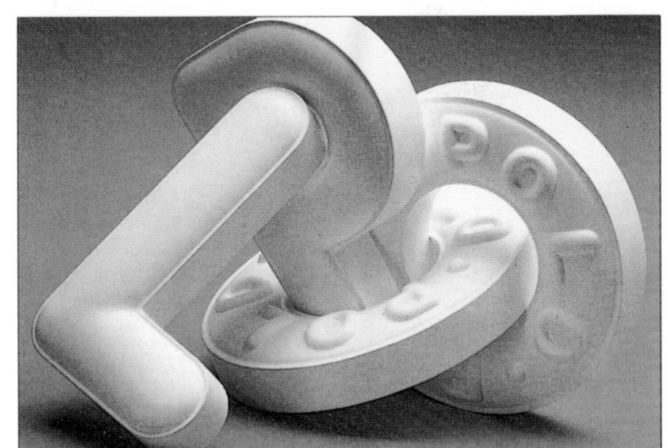

8

7 This still from a TV title sequence uses computer-generated typography to convey decoratively ideas in the form of words which merge into the title's logotype "Opinions." Designed by Bob English of English Markell Pockett for Channel 4, Great Britain.

8 An entertaining example of totally illustrative typography: the Polo poster, Britain's favorite tongue-twister, designed by J. Walter Thompson. This demonstrates perfectly how the idea can sometimes derive directly from the product itself.

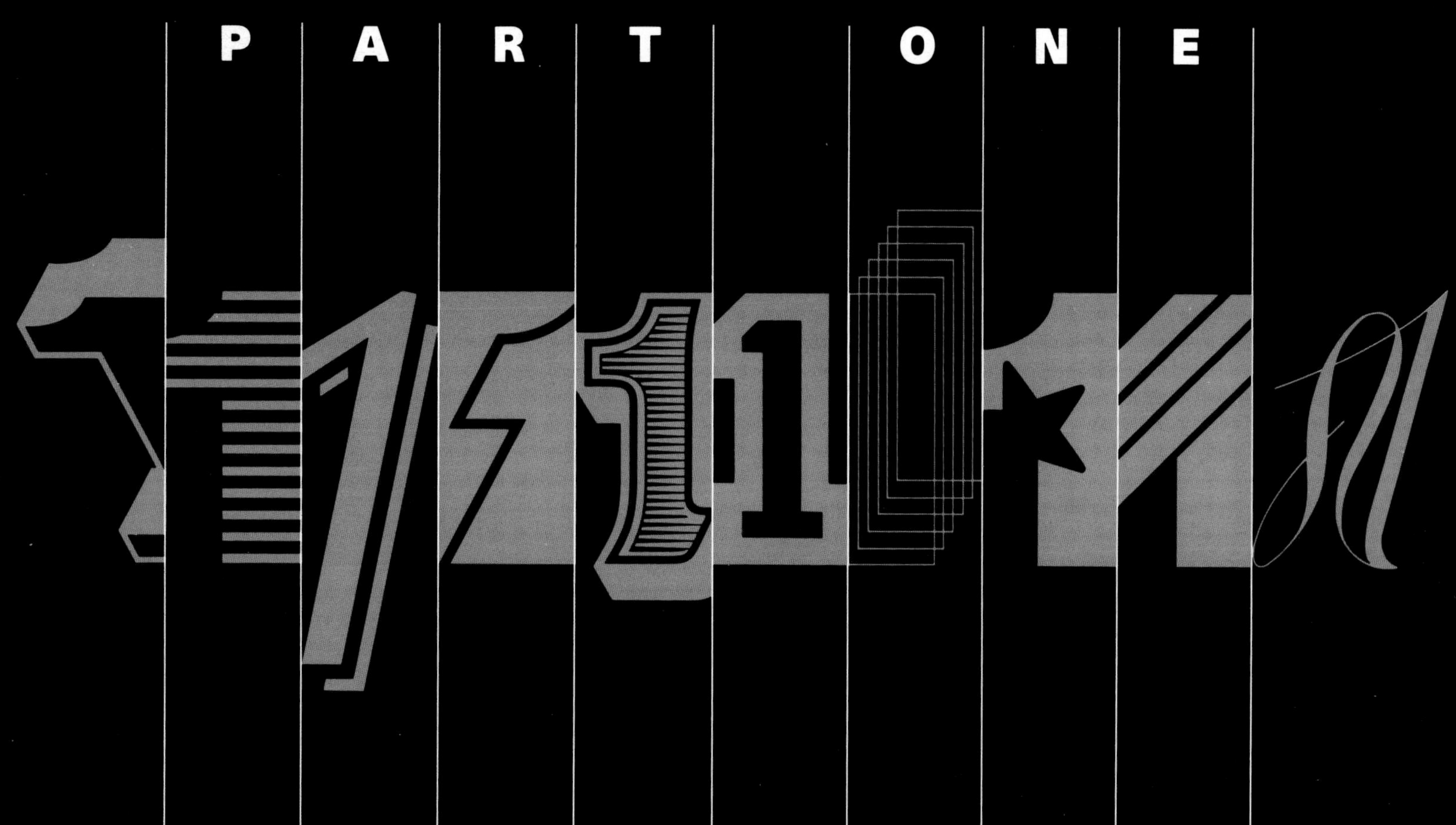
PART ONE

Letterforms ◆ Shapes

1

1 Similar shape characteristics shared by objects and letters can be fun to find.

The enjoyment of letterforms for themselves is the foundation of decorative typography. To use type decoratively requires an understanding of the shape, size, weight, tone, and color of type and of how type interacts with other elements. A simple analysis of each in turn will provide you with a rich decorative potential. You need to appreciate the vast number of different typeface designs, and which are in current use. Start by making a personal collection of different examples of a single letterform. The various typefaces fall into groups which form two distinct categories: the seriffed and the sans-serif typefaces. Serifs, or finishing strokes, are seen at the ends of the stems, arms, and tails of a letter. The structure of a seriffed letter includes both thick and thin weights. Sans-serif (or simply "sans") typefaces do not have thick and thin stresses: they are generally of an even weight without the ornamentation of serifs.

These characteristics, combined with the visual stress of the type design – vertical or diagonal – give each individual typeface its unique shape and character. Like people, letters come in different shapes, sizes, and weights, each with a personality ranging from the classic to the bizarre. To use a typeface properly needs as much attention as matching the cut and color of your clothes to your own personality.

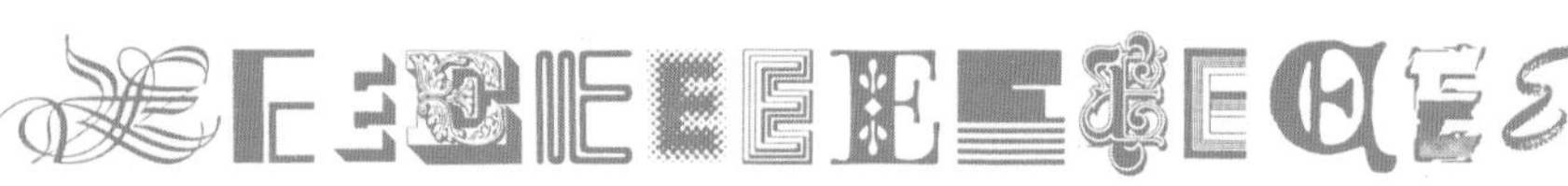

2

2 A collection of "E"s that heightens the letter's individual shape by keeping to a consistent size.

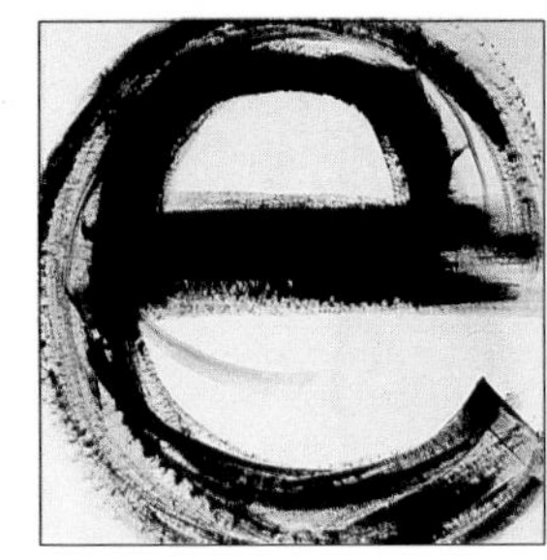

3

3 Two different ways of exploring shape through drawing. One uses a dry brush and paint, the other a soft pencil.

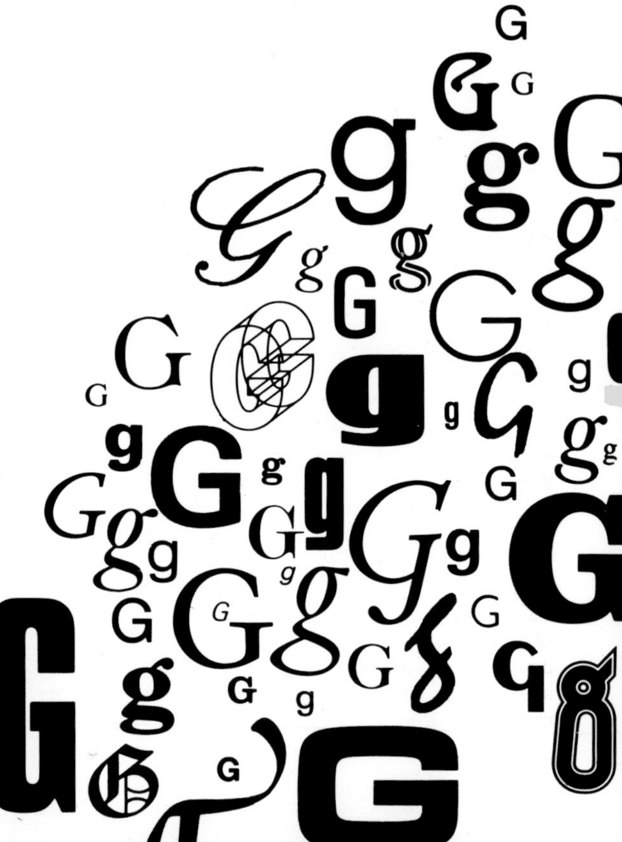

4

4 The lively, individual personalities of the same letter in different styles interact with each other. The contrasting variety of shapes, sizes, weights, and designs combine to illustrate the parallel drawn between letters and people.

5 Left to right: Hebrew, Cyrillic, Greek and Chinese characters providing intriguing examples of unusual typographic shapes. Foreign scripts can be a rich inspirational source for developing an appreciation of letterforms.

Д Ω

5

6

7

6 Shape is the essence of the Oxo logo on these packs.

7 An experiment with wood type based on shape relationships. Hand-inking the type produces a rich textural mix of colors particularly suited to large letterforms. Letters cut from card could also be used in this way.

8 The dynamic use of typographic shape and layout enhance the sense of urgency in this Russian poster. The partially concealed, receding letterforms add perspective to the drama, while the type and the image are integrated to form a strong graphic whole.

8

THE ART OF SEEING

The ability to see letterforms as abstract shapes without reference to any meaning has to be developed in order to see them as beautiful shapes in their own right. Looking at individual characters from non-Latin scripts such as Cyrillic, Arabic, Hebrew, Chinese, or Japanese, where unfamiliarity precludes any communication, allows you to enjoy their form for its own sake. It also permits a more immediate assessment of their characteristics. The decorative potential of these exotic shapes is self-evident and challenging. It is not so easy to remain oblivious to the message conveyed by the letters of our own alphabet. In order to enjoy their shape, we must experiment.

EXPERIMENTING WITH SHAPE

When we look at the ways in which artists have used type in an unexpected variety of media, we see how it lends itself, as an abstract form, countless possibilities. Such investigation makes you increasingly aware of the outer and inner shapes and of the solidity of the letterform itself. In addition to the alphabet, most typefaces include numerals, punctuation marks, and ampersands. Try turning these and the letters of the alphabet upside down or on their sides to give them a new visual identity. Draw letters freehand to a very large scale to discover their structure and rhythm. This way the personality of a letter is visually coaxed out, to assume almost human characteristics: lyrical, dynamic, stark, impassive, violent, or authoritative. Carefully cutting letters from paper will give you a crisp letterform and its perfectly matched counterform from a single cut. These inner shapes have a fascination of their own and offer many decorative possibilities. Balancing or contrasting counterforms with letterforms can enhance or hinder recognition. A more difficult exploration of shape involves drawing a letter from the outside in by blocking in the surrounding area.

1 Ampersands are derived from the Latin "et" and are the typographic symbol for "and." These Caslon and Garamond italics are beautiful ornamental examples.

2 A comparison between form and counterform cut from paper.

1

2

3

3 A decorative slab-serif letter made from terrycloth.

4 & 6 Examples of the work of a modern typographic master, Herb Lubalin. His designs delight in exploring the shape of letters in inventive ways. The "'72" on the New Year's card inverts perfectly without any loss of legibility. The combination of letters in 6, and the way they are arranged, makes dynamic use of form, counterform, and space.

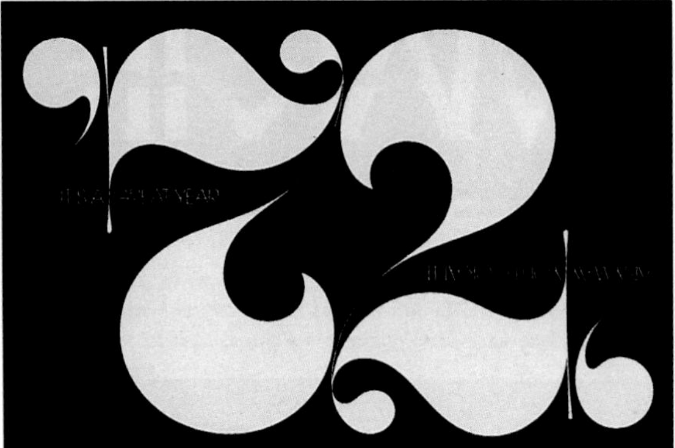

4

5

5 A section of display text that extends to the length of a book, disregarding the concertina folds, *Aba B* written and artworked by Ken Campbell. The use of contrasting expanded, and condensed wood letterforms makes creative use of shape-related words.

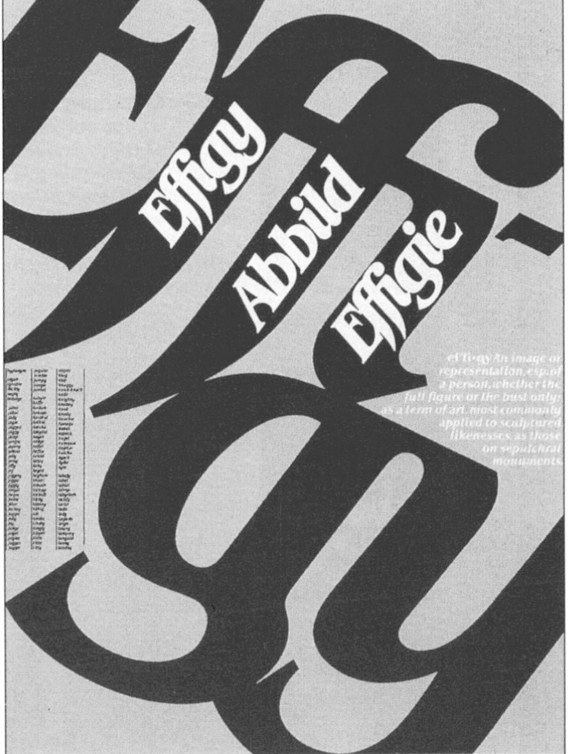

6

DEVELOPING AND USING SHAPE

These experiments in understanding shape can be further refined into creating designs for monograms. Think about forming and manipulating well-related shapes. You might, for example, interlock suitably shaped letters or amalgamate simple letterforms. Two letterforms might share a common stroke, or occupy the same area. Interesting shapes created by using only parts of a letter can also be surprisingly decorative and visually exciting. Logotype designs in which letters are brought together into a word or name also rely heavily on the shape and characteristics of type, as well as on graphic treatment, to create a particular visual identity. Integrating color into your design will add vitality and mood.

9

11

7 Modified shapes and a textured surface add a unique feel to this logo designed by Hamish Zulver.

8 This logo or monogram designed for the Victoria and Albert Museum, London, by Pentagram both creatively and decoratively merges the ampersand into the "A," forming a self-contained unit.

10 Primary colors and basic interwoven letterforms symbolize the idea of working together.

8

7

WORKING FOR LONDON

10

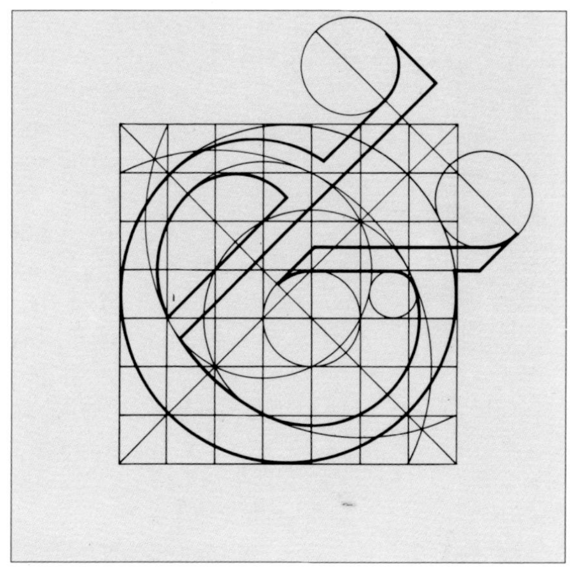

12

9 The discreet use of gray and black with elegant but contrasting typographic shapes conveys a distinctive quality in this symbol designed by Lewis Moberly.

11 This large-scale poster designed by Robin and Eugenie Dodd plays typographically with the shapes made by the words "New York." Form, counterform, and color are decoratively explored.

12 The shape and structure of this symbol designed by Peter Gill for the typesetting firm Ampersand, are based on the company name. The design's precision reflects the company's product.

Size

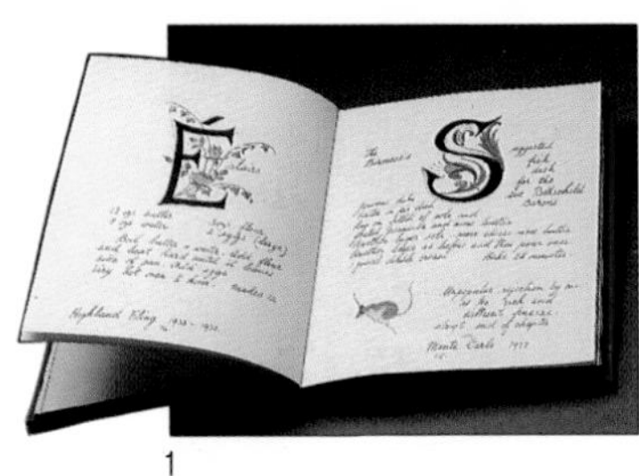

1

2

1 Decorative initial letters embellish Kirsteen Richards' recipe book, giving it a unique, personal quality.

2 This beautiful "P" shows how certain animals and objects might be transformed into decorative letters.

It is mainly through size that letters communicate. This characteristic usually takes one of two forms: "display" or "text." Display refers to large simple or decorative letters or words used in a visually arresting way in, for example, headlines, slogans, or as initial letters. Text broadly covers the smaller-sized types used for other text matter. The size of letters or words used should always be selected in relation to the scale at which you are working. Larger letters reveal the different levels of energy or lines of direction that exist within a typographic form but which are often hidden in small type. These varying thrusts can form an exciting basis for decorative experimentation.

The larger the letter the more animated and even pictorial it will appear. Large letterforms offer great scope for decoration within and around the actual strokes. A contrast of size is an almost infallible recipe for decorative purposes. It is virtually impossible to conjure up a situation where such a contrast could not be exploited. Good examples include hoard-

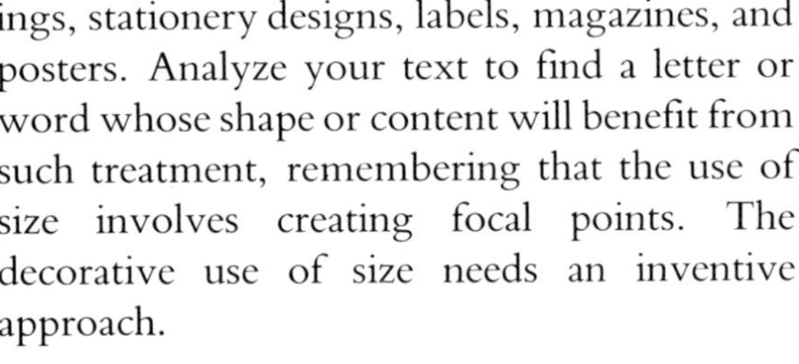

ings, stationery designs, labels, magazines, and posters. Analyze your text to find a letter or word whose shape or content will benefit from such treatment, remembering that the use of size involves creating focal points. The decorative use of size needs an inventive approach.

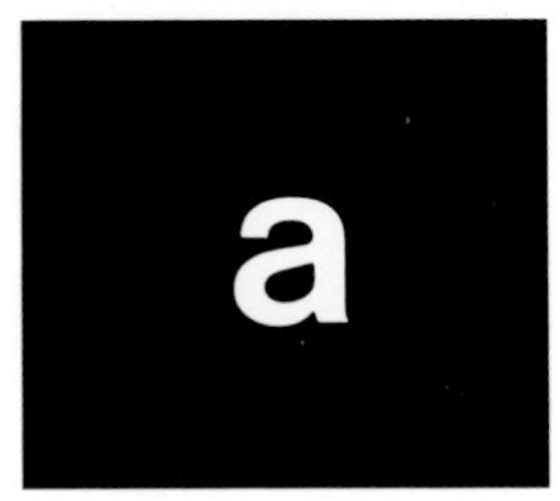

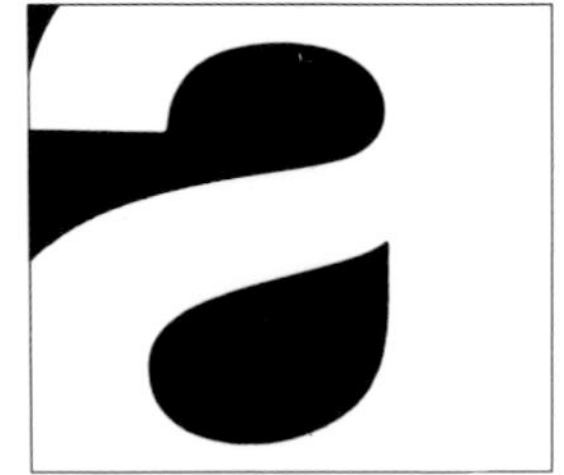

3

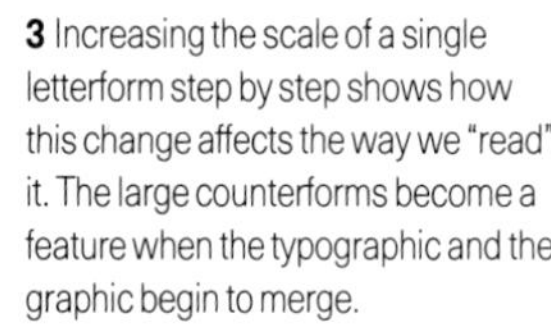

3 Increasing the scale of a single letterform step by step shows how this change affects the way we "read" it. The large counterforms become a feature when the typographic and the graphic begin to merge.

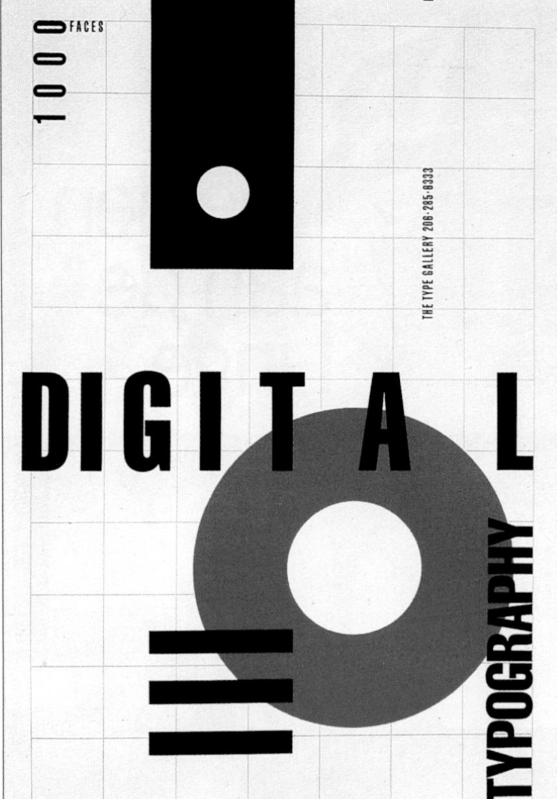

4

4 This poster for an exhibition of digitized typography designed by E. Rich and T. Draper makes exciting use of both size and shape through strong contrasts. The subtle background grid lines structure the varied typographic elements into a cohesive whole.

5 The Body Shop's product range for men called "Mostly Men" designed by the Yellow Pencil Company. The strong, simple use of the large serif "M" is easily recognizable and is remembered for its inherent imagery and associations.

6 This typographic extravaganza combines size and lavish embellishment with rich color. The underlining lettering is contrastingly simple in style, size, and decorative treatment. In this way it retains its legibility yet complements its partner perfectly.

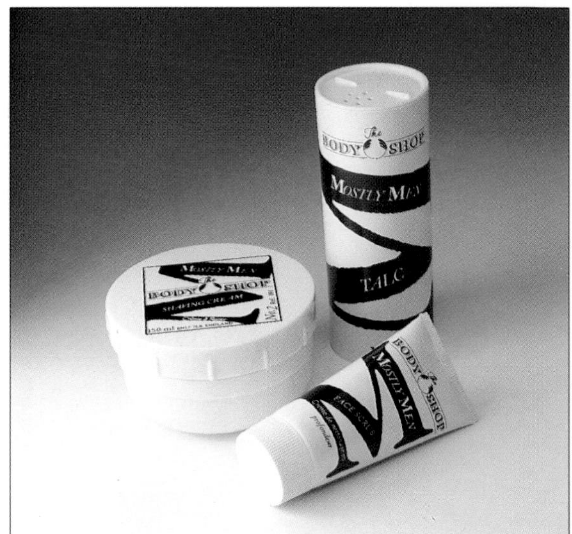

5

6

7

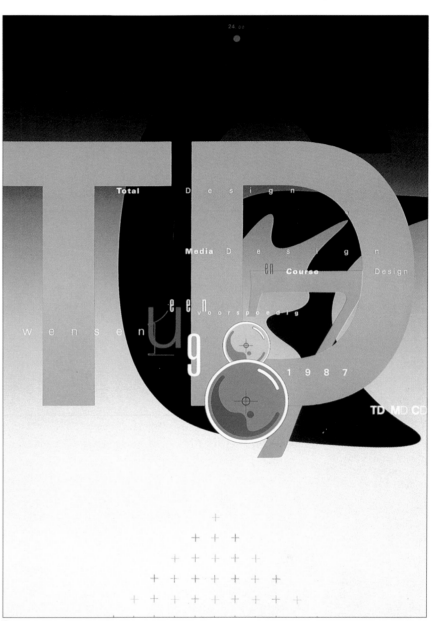

7 This design by Total Design uses tone to gently emphasize the large scale of the main typographic forms. Delicate lines of type in varying sizes animate the otherwise flat surface, suggesting a series of spatial planes. The use of spot colors and graduated background tone further reinforces this quality.

PLAYING WITH SIZE

By experimenting with the relationship of space and size you will discover how the border between the typographic and the graphic image begins to disappear. Stringing a variety of sizes together either in a line or a free composition will throw up a delightfully unexpected collection of counterforms varying in both size and shape. The juxtaposition of similar or contrasting shapes and sizes of typographic characters will create intriguing visual qualities. For example, the results might be busy and complex or quiet and spacious. Experimenting with size in a totally decorative way, ignoring legibility, allows you to break the rules and take adventurous and exciting detours.

1 Numbers and letterforms jostle for attention through the variation of size and tone in this visual parallel of Braille. The surface is given an animated tactile quality in the way the hand touches both letterforms and their Braille equivalent. Designed by Total Design.

2

2 This elegant design by Hard Werken explores the idea of overlapping the strokes of similar and varied sizes of letterforms. Great care must be taken in the way that this is done in order to retain the legibility yet add a liveliness to the whole. The change in size within words also requires careful judgement so that no one letter predominates or is overlooked.

3

3 In magazine spread design letters are frequently used at different scales to create decorative focal points within and around the text and images.

DECORATIVE FOCAL POINTS

Ornament, form, and color need to be interdependent. In early manuscripts size, form, color, and pictorial elements were intimately combined in the rich ornamentation of initial letters. These eloquent designs provided inviting starting points for the eye. Traditionally the capital letter is used as an initial, but enlarged lower-case letters, numerals, or even punctuation can be treated in the same way. The current use of raised and dropped capitals is a variation on the initial letter. Books, magazines, and advertising frequently show this decorative use of size in beginning, end, and sometimes middle positions. The structure, character, and size of the letterform or numeral are important here, and to withstand, such embellishment needs to be strong, simple, and easily recognizable. Some typefaces carry "swash" letters, which are simply more elaborate versions of conventional capitals. These decorative letters appear larger, with a part that extends in a flourish beyond the normal type size. They can add a lyrical touch to typography, their size and nature highlighting both words and phrases.

Q

R

4

4 These two Garamond italic swash characters have an almost lyrical quality. Used at a reasonable size in conjunction with text settings, they make beautiful initial letters that add a decorative flourish.

5

5 This atmospheric poster was designed by Hard Werken. It shows the traditional form of initial letter effectively incorporated into a current design context. The shape and surface decoration of the "M" reflect the feel and style of the interior. Tiny white initial letters introduce the various credits in a lively style.

The weight of letters

Weight refers to the relative solidity of a letterform, the thickness of line or surface area that goes to make up its shape. Many typeface families – Futura and Bodoni, for example – include variants in weight as well as size, ranging from extra light to extra bold. A lightweight letter is thin or delicate, has little surface area and a great deal of space in and around it. Conversely, a heavy or bold letter will appear blacker and more dense on account of its greater surface area and much reduced countershapes. These differing intensities and thicknesses of line determine to a considerable degree the visual impact of a letter. An extra-bold character is normally visually dominant.

1 Textured weight can be generated by overprinting monochrome and colored letters.

2 The weight of the strokes in these free calligraphic forms by Arthur Baker has a varying tonal value that adds a depth to the image.

1

2

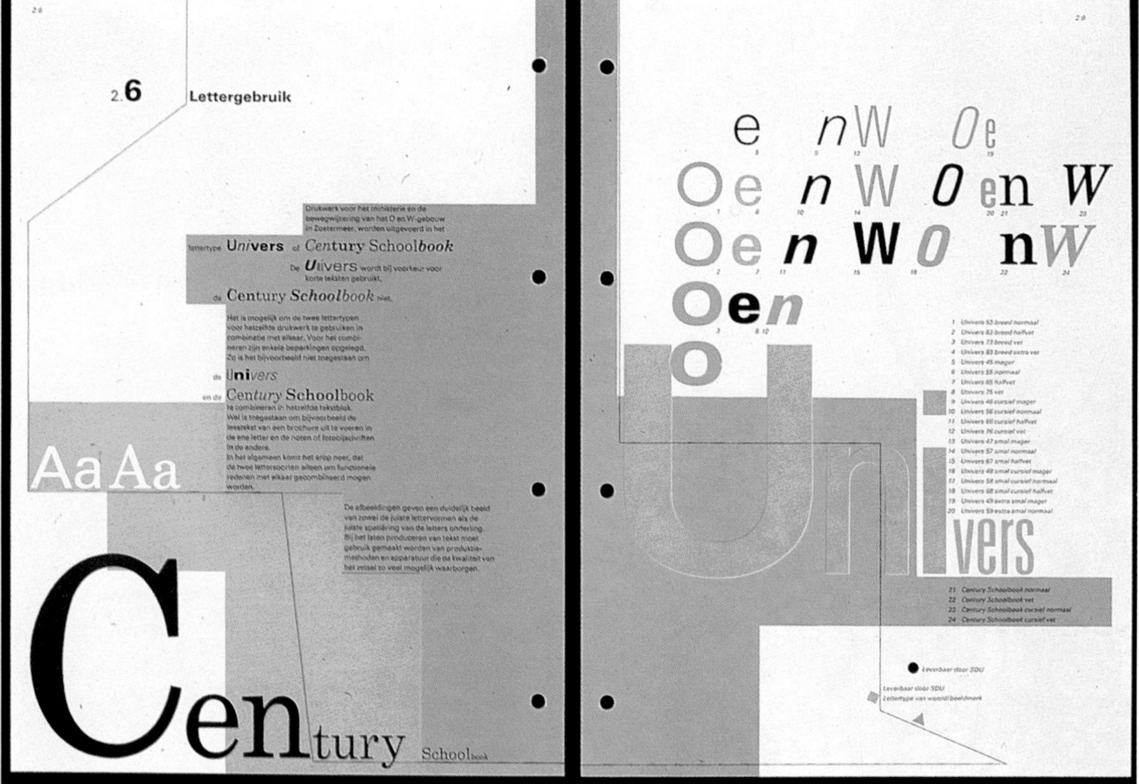

3

3 This lively publicity material promotes two quite different typefaces: Century Schoolbook and the family of Univers. The essential characteristics are highlighted through size, and the varying range of weights is emphasized by playing down the size factor.

The interaction between the figure or letter and the ground or surface on which it appears is greatly influenced by the weight of the individual letters or words. This optical balance is dependent on all the elements in a design and suggests a mood by combining contrast, intensity, and dominance and by manipulating the space surrounding the type. In this way you can mix markedly different weights of the same basic shape in an ornamental way.

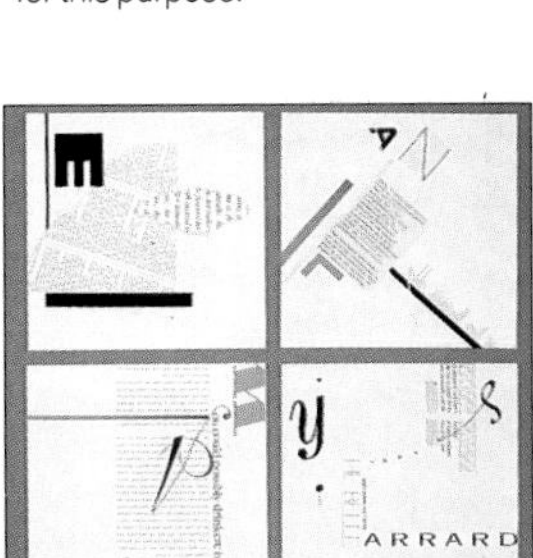

4

4 Four experimental typographic collages explore the potential of weight, size, tone, and direction. Magazines provide excellent material for this purpose.

5

5 The weight and shape of these letters visually enhance the meaning of the word.

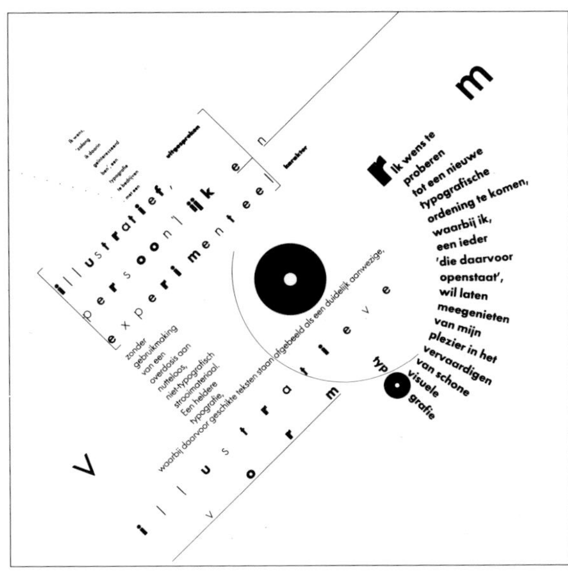

6

6 Weight variations combined with size changes create the focal points in this animated design by Total Design. The weight changes made within a uniform type size add a lively visual tempo to the words.

Radical weight changes will produce more effective results than oversubtle changes. A contrast of weight can be both useful and straightforwardly decorative as a means of emphasis or identification. This device, used extensively in catalogues, directories, newsletters, reports, and magazines, can highlight single letters, numerals, or words. Thus, the decorative potential of weight lies mainly in contrast and attracting attention.

EXPLORING WEIGHT

Try mixing different weights of the same size and shaped letter, then mix a variety of shapes, sizes, and weight together. At a relatively small scale in linear form you will produce a kind of typographic musical score. At a larger scale a freer composition with strong weight contrasts will result. Combining the use of type and rules in different weights serves to visually reinforce the impression of mass. Butt a light letter up to a heavy black rule or have a bold letter distinguished from a fine rule. Notice how this contrast underlines the dominance of weight in a decorative way.

By adding weight to the inside of a letter and reducing its countershape, you can originate you own weight variants. Adding weight to the outside contours will alter the overall proportions of a letter. Color can also heighten or soften, increase or reduce light or bold letterforms. In this way, you can make a large, heavy letterform appear light and soft. Background also contributes. Experiment with the optical differences in weight when you put white type on a black background, and different-colored letters on different-colored backgrounds as well as on black and white.

7

7 An invitation designed by J. Puisller for a series of conferences entitled "Women in Design." A strong visual impact is created by integrating elements of size, weight, and direction within a relatively small area.

How to create visual interest with type

1

You can use type both creatively and decoratively to visually express or enhance the meaning of a letter or word. Exciting effects can be achieved through graphic techniques and modification of the actual letterforms as well as by the arrangement of the letters. An inventive approach allows you to break away from the rigidity and formality of conventional usage. Generally, these techniques are best used with single letters or words; at the most in a few lines of display copy. Used indiscriminately, they result in visual confusion. Computers and electronically generated typesetting offer enormous scope in this area

2

3

1 Designed by O. Nusbaum, a typographic puzzle in the form of an apparently three-dimensional letter that changes constantly.

2 This entertaining "logotype" designed by Chermayeff and Geismar makes use of individually modified letters that celebrate specific performances and reflect the spirit of the Festival. Note how the special characters are used in conjunction with a standard typeface to avoid confusion.

3 The logotype for London's Museum of the Moving Image designed by Field Wylie & Co. is visually evocative of sequential movement in its modified letterforms and luminosity of color.

4 In this personal design for a business card Jonathan Clayton envisages the words as a whole. The individual letters are meaningless without their companions. The typographic tangle unravels itself as you look at it.

4

5 Chermayeff and Geismar designed this logotype for Design Media Inc., whose concern is contemporary furniture. The simple shadow and fine outline are used to give the name a convincing three-dimensional quality relevant to the product.

6 A Christmas-card design by Bob Gordon for a large architectural practice makes use of modified letterforms appropriate to the season.

7 Two ways of using shadow. A symbol for a TV channel designed by Chermayeff and Geismar and a "T" whose form is suggested by the shadow only.

8 These drawn letters have directness, spontaneity, and a sense of fun. The individual characteristics of each letter have been highlighted through appropriate graphic modification.

DESIGN MEDIA

5

and are quick and efficient. You can achieve equally successful results by hand, but it takes a little longer.

First, ask yourself three questions. 1. Are you dealing with a message, with decoration, or a combination of both? 2. How important is legibility? 3. Which typefaces are suitable for decorative development? The first two criteria are relatively easily established, but the third question needs particularly careful consideration. A letterform that has a strong, simple structure but not much character of its own will respond to graphic treatment better than one that has markedly different stresses and its own personality. The first type of letterform offers greater freedom for manipulation. Within the two main typeface categories, seriffed and sans-seriffed, Helvetica, Futura, Optima, Times Roman, Century Schoolbook, and Rockwell, among others, provide a good basic shape.

SHADOWS

Anything that casts a shadow suggests solidity by adding another dimension. There are both cast shadows and those that appear to be part of the object or letter itself – caught shadows. To create unambiguous shadows, let the imaginary light source come from above and the left and draw the shadows accordingly. A greater visual impact can be given to a letter by its shadow alone rather than by its actual outline. In such cases the eye is able to decipher letterforms from very few clues. Although we tend to think of shadows as being dark and the object as light, reversing this perception creates dramatic results. Atmosphere or different times of day can be suggested by changing the tone of the shadow.

6

7

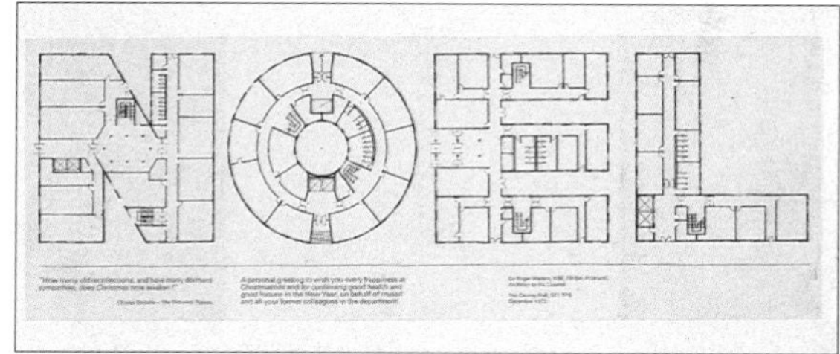

8

ADDITIVE AND SUBTRACTIVE PROCESS

The entire personality of a letter can be changed by adding to its basic inner shape, until its character almost disappears as a result of the severely reduced countershapes. Going still further, you can create completely solid letters with a strong geometric quality. Adding weight to the outside of a letterform will bring about a radical change in its general proportions. Serifs – bracketed, large, small, or triangular – allow you great versatility when modifying letters. They are one of the letterform's most distinct features and can radically transform the character of type. You can experiment with the ends of the serifs, using them curled, angled, tapered, rounded, or squared off, increasing or reducing their length. The width of serifs can also be varied or contrasted with the main body of the letter. The thick and thin stresses of type can also be increased or reduced to create a new visual quality.

The subtractive process works in reverse, by erosion. Stripping letterforms right down, leaving only the essential parts, is an interesting experiment. The eye will quite effortlessly provide the missing parts. Take a word or letter and slice it in half horizontally, dispensing with the lower portion. It is still legible. Curiously, the eye has much more difficulty deciphering meaning from the lower half alone.

1 London's Royal National Theatre logotype designed by F.H.K. Henrion and Ian Dennis. Two letters are perfectly merged into a unit through their sharing of a common stroke and serif.

1

2

2 A visual slogan used by Amex Insurance Company. It illustrates the use of subtraction, form, and counterform in a decorative fashion.

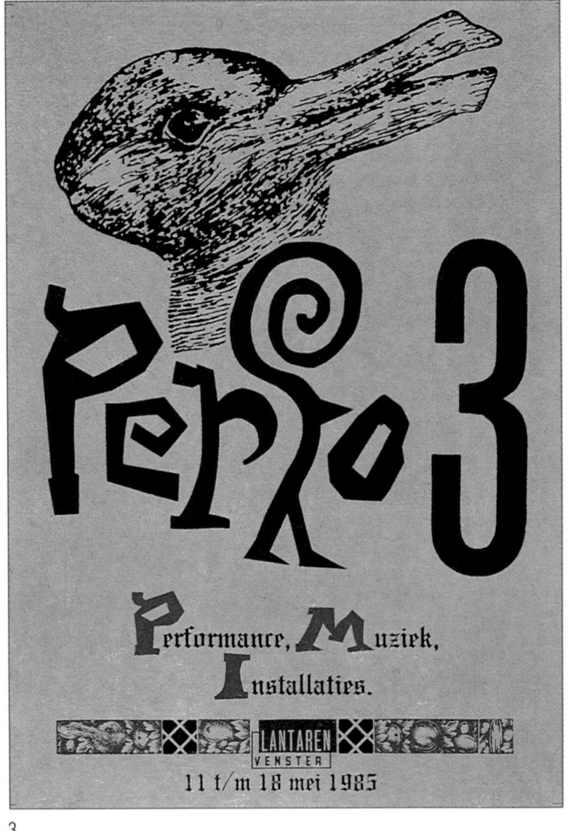

3

3 A delightfully eccentric example of the combined use of additive and substractive typographic modification. The unusual typographic image suggests the individual nature of the performances, music, and installations in question. Designed by Hard Werken.

4 The paring down of the letterforms to their absolute minimum legibility has a decorative function: it suggests visually the problems of illiteracy.

4

5 This unusual logotype designed for use on a stationery range involves the reader in an animated typographic metamorphosis. Color is used to reinforce the revealing of the name.

6 A charming typographic illustration used as a logotype for a dog biscuit manufacturer.

7 Three "E"s distorted on a photocopier suggest the potential of this technique, similar to that used in 9.

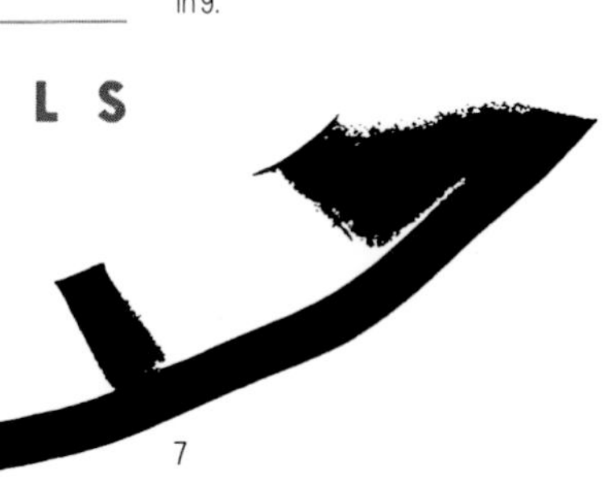

8 An inventively modified dollar sign, part of a financial report exhibit designed by Dennard Creative, is composed of carefully controlled bars of color in varying weights that result in a feeling of horizontal movement.

DISTORTION OF SHAPE

This can be as radical or as subtle as you choose, although it will be conditioned by the degree of legibility required. When working by hand it is advisable to distort by degrees, using tracing paper or film overlays, rather than attempting a major transformation in a single step. Here, a photocopier with enlarging and reducing facilities is very useful and saves time. Try out some of the following ideas on letters or words: condensing and expanding, rotating, elongating, squashing, enlarging, reducing, overlapping letters, mirroring or bending letters, creating inline, outline, box-line, double-outline letters, adding one- or two-point perspective and distorting even that! Cutting letters from paper, slicing them into vertical, horizontal, or diagonal strips, is another effective way to distort their shapes. Rearranging, removing, or varying the spacing of the strips will alter the overall effect and degree of legibility.

9 Distortion, shape, texture, and color are used to lend mood in this image designed by Hard Werken.

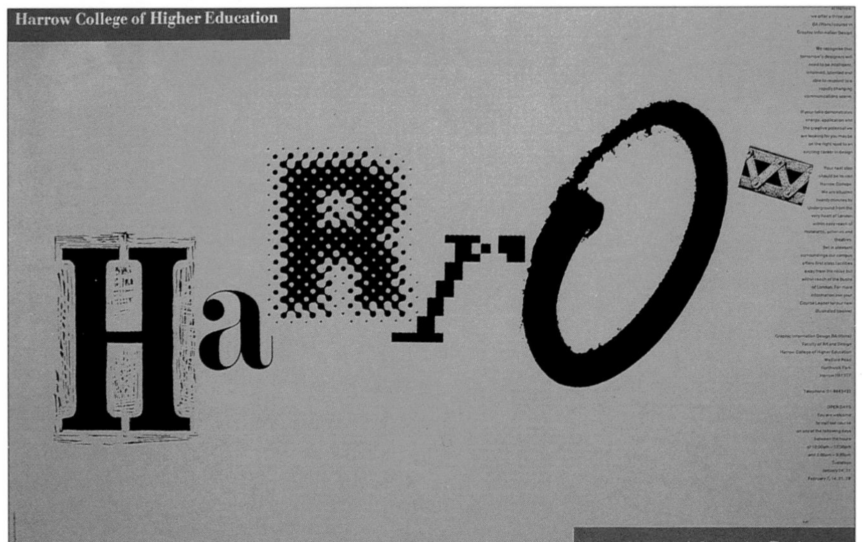

10 Creative use of various techniques, sizes, weights, and styles promotes the Graphic Information Design Course at Harrow College of Higher Education, London.

THE GRAPHIC TREATMENT OF EDGES

The edges of a letterform give it its overall visual identity. The graphic modification of these can alter considerably the impact, mood, and pace of a letter or word. Letters, freely cut from paper without guidelines, possess an edge with an immediacy quite different from that of letters torn from paper, where the edges have a ragged, natural vigor. Contrasting the hard cut with the ripped edge sets up visual tensions. Cutting out letters with a knife or scissors and treating one edge only with pinking shears lends a definite decorative feel, whereas cutting the entire letter out in this way will set up a firm association with dressmaking or tailoring. Soft and diffuse edges are best generated through sprayed or painted media on dry or wet paper. Pencil-drawn letters partially erased across the surface have a softness and translucent quality.

4 The month of May, in an exciting promotional calendar produced by the School of Visual Communication Design at Humberside College of Higher Education, England, is made up of unique computer-generated typographic images. It illustrates how the decorative potential of electronic media can be graphically explored in relation to the treatment of edges.

3

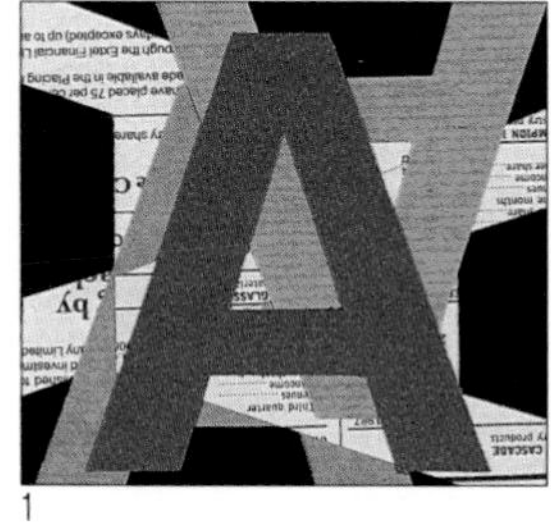

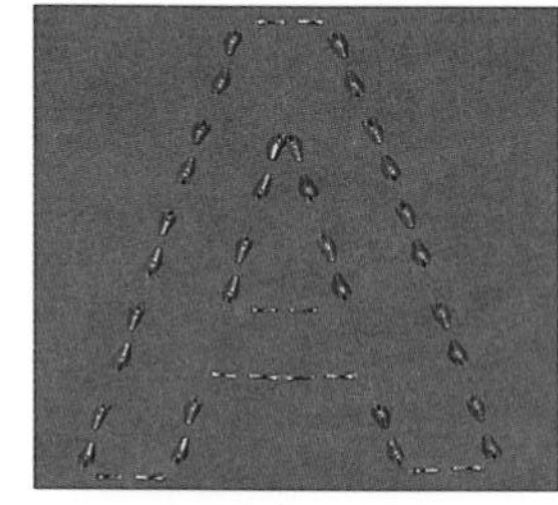

1

2

1-3 These examples show a variety of ways of treating letters and their edges to create unusual effects that can affect the way a letter or word is read. Sometimes the purpose for which you intend to use a particular letter or word, or even the word itself, will suggest appropriate techniques.

4

5 Letters cut in lino have a freshness and energy. The roughness of the edges adds character to the word.

5

THE THIRD DIMENSION

Letters can be manipulated on a two-dimensional surface and be made to appear solid. Such effects are frequently seen in comic strips. Adding one- or two-point linear perspective to a letterform throws it into sharp relief. Mapping from a head-on viewpoint, stacking the contoured layers on top of each other, results in a strong, sculptural quality. Constructing type in model form to be used in its own right or photographically as part of a design is a stimulating development of the decorative use of letterforms. A whole range of different materials be used, including paper, card, plastic, fabric, and wood. Type that is physically three-dimensional has a back and a front and an intriguing tactile quality that can only be implied on a two-dimensional surface. Uses for this technique include packaging, promotional design, three-dimensional, and pop-up greetings cards, and one-of-a-kind pieces.

CUT-OUTS

These use the same principle as stencils but are used in their own right. The letters can be free-standing or incorporated into another shape, perhaps in the form of a card, letterhead, mobile, or decorative wall hanging. Whole words can be cut out of the letterforms and joined together at strategic points. A variation on cut-outs is to outline the letter with a pin.

REVERSING OUT

Almost irrespective of shape, black type on a white background generally appears smaller or lighter than white type on a black background, since optically white advances and black recedes. White or black lettering of any transfer lettering is used for experiments with this technique. Cutting letters and counterforms from paper, reversing them from positive to negative, will produce subtle illusory changes in size and weight. Photographic reversal and photograms are also excellent techniques here, offering a high degree of control and versatility. Some photocopiers and computer graphics programs have a reversal facility, providing quick and accurate results.

8

9

6

7

6 A personal monogram designed by Lily Lee that captures the combination of spontaneity and control she has as a hand-lettering artist and calligrapher. Brush and pen movement are suggested in the image shift (reversal) from white to black.

7 Softly diffused edges can be created by painting directly onto wet paper.

8 A rich, almost tactile image for an advertising poster in Rotterdam, designed by Hard Werken. The yellow shadow on the modified word "Rotterdam" gives the lettering a luminous quality in keeping with the overall mood.

9 Three-dimensional letters designed and made from cut and folded paper. Each one folds flat. Unusual, personal greetings cards could be made using this technique.

Alphabet designs

1

The origin of letters lies in pictograms. In time these developed into a more abstract, graphic representation of ideas and eventually a set of phonetic symbols evolved – today's alphabet.

Some letters of the alphabet naturally resemble objects: for example, an S suggests a seahorse, an X a pair of open scissors. Others almost invite the reader to walk around them: to sit on the cross bar of an H or curl up inside a C. Some have an architectural quality, others a more organic feel. It is by analyzing the shape and characteristics of a letterform and seeing what these suggest that you begin to discover visual links between objects and letters. These links range from the obvious to no more than a typographic hint. To pursue this idea you might start a collection of objects whose shapes suggest letters.

The thematic decoration of letters has been a source of fascination for centuries. The invention around 1800 of lithography stimulated the development of an enormous range of visual forms and rich ornamentation. Alphabet designs based on botanical, anthropomorphic, and zoomorphic fantasy and humorous themes abounded. Today such designs are less effusive, yet retain a vigor and freshness.

3

4 A well-known current alphabet design by Mervyn Kurlansky of Pentagram, in which design and office equipment is used to mimic the shape of letterforms. The scale of the different objects has been carefully modified to give a visual cohesion to the flow of the alphabet. They work particularly well as a unit, but could, with careful judgement, be used as "initial" letters to introduce the reader to a passage of text. Individual words could also be decoratively interpreted in this way but should never be used indiscriminately as this causes visual confusion.

4

2

1 & 2 Two letters from a sixteenth-century alphabet design based on inventive letter and object associations.

3 A decorative letter from a landscape/seascape-inspired alphabet designed in the early nineteenth century. Today we still indulge in the design of fanciful pictorial alphabets.

5-7 Three amusingly decorative letters from an alphabet designed by Herb Lubalin, showing how the human form can be creatively adapted for use in entertaining typography contexts.

8 This lively logotype design for Alvia Ailey Dance Theatre by Chermayeff and Geismar uses the same theme as in 4, 5, and 6, but relates specifically to the human movement in dance.

5

8

6

9

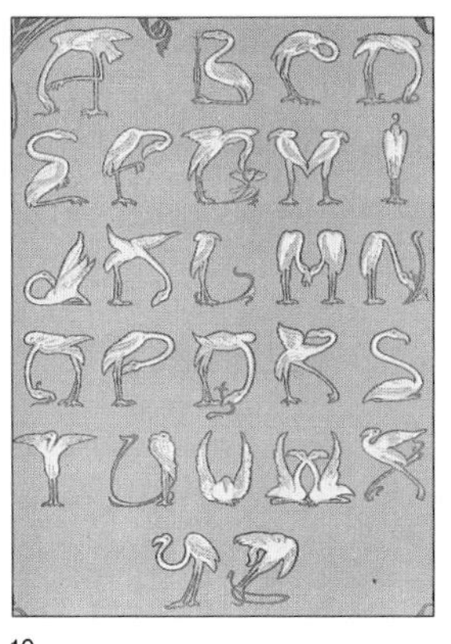

10

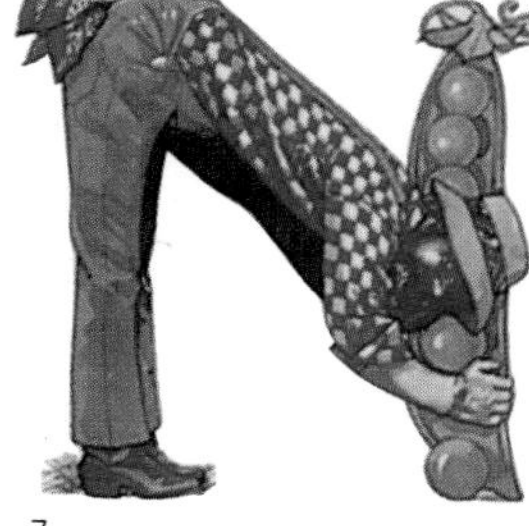

7

11

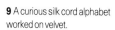

9 A curious silk cord alphabet worked on velvet.

10 A witty Art Nouveau style of alphabet manipulates the sinuous form of the flamingo.

DESIGNING YOUR OWN LETTERS

Developing your own thematic decoration will probably only involve designing a few characters at a time for a particular use. First, decide on a theme and consider how it might be interpreted. It might be representational, stylized, or abstract. The legibility and context of decoratively developed letters or words should also be taken into account. Placing richly ornamented letters in a math dictionary would be quite inappropriate. Yet incorporating a thematically decorated letter in a florist's logotype would greatly enhance its visual appeal. It is helpful to have some form of visual reference on which to base your ideas once you have decided on a theme.

It is important to select a suitable simple letterform on which to base your design. Delicate, intricate typefaces seldom provide a strong enough structure for this purpose. Even though the original letterform on which you base your thematic decoration may be superseded in the process, the resulting letterforms will retain a degree of visual conviction. Use transparent overlays to draw together the letterform structure and decorative ideas until a satisfactorily animated letter is achieved. Logotype designs in which letters are brought together to form a name rely greatly on the development and modification of their original shape and personality to give them a distinctive, possibly unique, identity.

12

11 An unusual logotype design plays decoratively with an alphabet based on a modular theme, designed by Alessandrini.

12 A simple, decorative, paper-cut alphabet.

Tone and color

When words are brought together into lines to form text, type assumes an overall tonal value through a combination of typeface, style, size, weight, and the space between words and lines. To appreciate the subtle qualities of tone in text, look at it without reference to the content, seeing it as a tonal texture rather than a message.

1

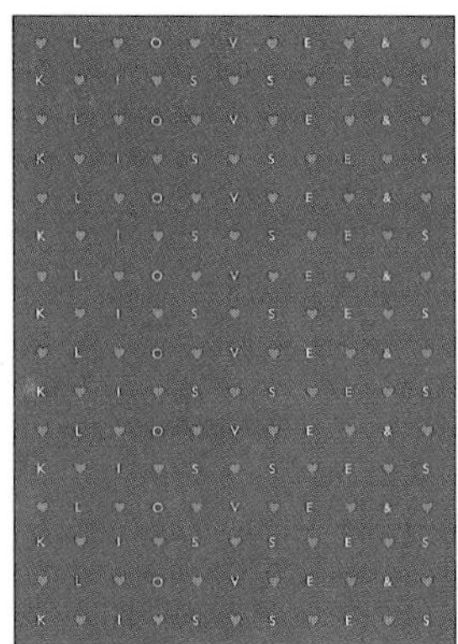

2

1 The color and tone of the typographic texture in this design by Diana Wilson contrast effectively with the intensity of color used in the individual letterforms. Notice how the white background forms an integral part of the design.

2 A soft overall tone is punctuated with points of color in this "Millimetre" postcard design by Emmanuel and Erofili. The message merges decoratively into the whole.

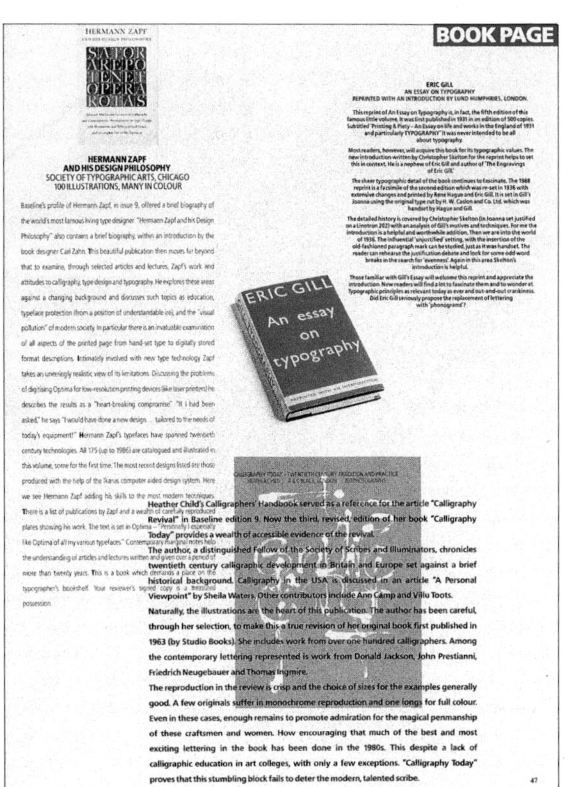

BOOK PAGE

HERMANN ZAPF
AND HIS DESIGN PHILOSOPHY
SOCIETY OF TYPOGRAPHIC ARTS, CHICAGO
100 ILLUSTRATIONS, MANY IN COLOUR

Baseline's profile of Hermann Zapf, in issue 9, offered a brief biography of the world's most famous living type designer. "Hermann Zapf and his Design Philosophy" also contains a brief biography, within an introduction by the book designer Carl Zahn. This beautiful publication then moves far beyond that to examine, through selected articles and lectures, Zapf's work and attitudes to calligraphy, type design and typography. He explores these areas against a changing background and discusses such topics as education, typeface protection (from a position of understandable ire), and the "visual pollution" of modern society. In particular there is an invaluable examination of all aspects of the printed page from hand-set type to digitally stored format descriptions. Intimately involved with new type technology Zapf takes an unerringly realistic view of its limitations. Discussing the problems of digitising Optima for low-resolution printing devices (like laser printers) he describes the results as a "heart-breaking compromise". "If I had been asked," he says "I would have done a new design … tailored to the needs of today's equipment!" Hermann Zapf's typefaces have spanned twentieth century technologies. All 175 (up to 1986) are catalogued and illustrated in this volume, some for the first time. The most recent designs listed are those produced with the help of the Ikarus computer aided design system. Here we see Hermann Zapf adding his skills to the most modern techniques. There is a list of publications by Zapf and a wealth of carefully reproduced plates showing his work. The text is set in Optima – "Personally I especially like Optima of all my various typefaces." Contemporary marginal notes help the understanding of articles and lectures written and given over a period of more than twenty years. This is a book which demands a place on the typographer's bookshelf. Your reviewer's signed copy is a treasured possession.

ERIC GILL
AN ESSAY ON TYPOGRAPHY
REPRINTED WITH AN INTRODUCTION BY LUND HUMPHRIES, LONDON.

This reprint of An Essay on Typography is, in fact, the fifth edition of this famous little volume. It was first published in 1931 in an edition of 500 copies. Subtitled 'Printing & Piety – An Essay on life and works in the England of 1931 and particularly TYPOGRAPHY' it was never intended to be all about typography.

Most readers, however, will acquire this book for its typographic values. The new introduction written by Christopher Skelton for the reprint helps to set this in context. He is a nephew of Eric Gill and author of 'The Engravings of Eric Gill.'

The sheer typographic detail of the book continues to fascinate. The 1988 reprint is a facsimile of the second edition which was re-set in 1936 with extensive changes and printed by Rene Hague and Eric Gill. It is set in Gill's Joanna using the original type cut by H. W. Caslon and Co. Ltd. which was handset by Hague and Gill.

The detailed history is covered by Christopher Skelton (in Joanna set justified on a Linotron 202) with an analysis of Gill's motives and techniques. For me the introduction is a helpful and worthwhile addition. Then we are into the world of 1936. The influential 'unjustified' setting, with the insertion of the old-fashioned paragraph mark can be studied, just as it was handset. The reader can rehearse the justification debate and look for some odd word breaks in the search for 'evenness'. Again in this area Skelton's introduction is helpful.

Those familiar with Gill's Essay will welcome this reprint and appreciate the introduction. New readers will find a lot to fascinate them and to wonder at. Typographic principles as relevant today as ever and out-and-out crankiness. Did Eric Gill seriously propose the replacement of lettering with 'phonograms'?

Heather Child's Calligraphers' Handbook served as a reference for the article "Calligraphy Revival" in Baseline edition 9. Now the third, revised, edition of her book "Calligraphy Today" provides a wealth of accessible evidence of the revival.

The author, a distinguished Fellow of the Society of Scribes and Illuminators, chronicles twentieth century calligraphic development in Britain and Europe set against a brief historical background. Calligraphy in the USA is discussed in an article "A Personal Viewpoint" by Sheila Waters. Other contributors include Ann Camp and Villu Toots.

Naturally, the illustrations are the heart of this publication. The author has been careful, through her selection, to make this a true revision of her original book first published in 1963 (by Studio Books). She includes work from over one hundred calligraphers. Among the contemporary lettering represented is work from Donald Jackson, John Prestianni, Friedrich Neugebauer and Thomas Ingmire.

The reproduction in the review is crisp and the choice of sizes for the examples generally good. A few originals suffer in monochrome reproduction and one longs for full colour. Even in these cases, enough remains to promote admiration for the magical penmanship of these craftsmen and women. How encouraging that much of the best and most exciting lettering in the book has been done in the 1980s. This despite a lack of calligraphic education in art colleges, with only a few exceptions. "Calligraphy Today" proves that this stumbling block fails to deter the modern, talented scribe.

47

3

CREATING AND CONTROLLING TONE

An even tone is created by sustained use of the same shape, size, and weight of type in, for example, the body of a newspaper. Magazines and newsletters tend to vary the tonal value of text matter to visually emphasize paragraphs, quotes, or captions, visually enlivening the text as a whole and changing the reading pace from time to time. Very subtle changes can be made by switching the style of a typeface from Roman (or upright) letters to italics, which, with their forward thrust, have a visual urgency to them. Substituting capital letters for lower-case letters mid-sentence sets up a visual interruption. A similar use of small capitals (capital letters that are the same height as lower-case letters) will change the pace in a less marked way. Mixing typefaces, serif with sans-serif for example, will throw up a curious change in texture as well as tone. The strongest

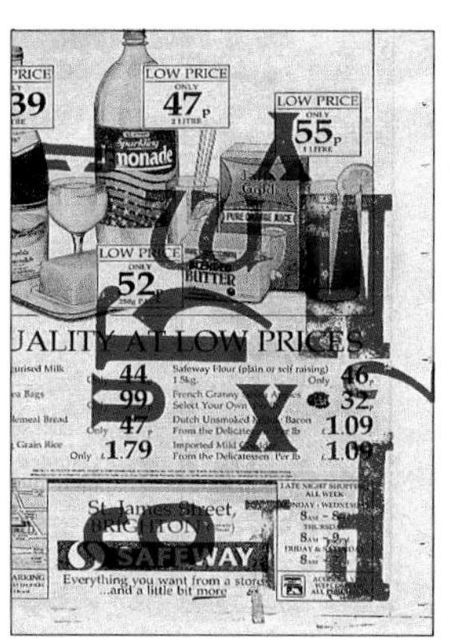

4

3 Different weights of type give an added dimension to this page from *Baseline* magazine. Typographic tonal values can also be increased or decreased by varying the interlinear spacing.

4 An experiment with wood type printed onto newspaper, showing the tonal differences caused by contrasting size, weight, and color.

contrasts are achieved through weight change alone, from extra bold to light, for example, creating the illusion of receding and advancing areas. Making a typographic patchwork of different text tones selected from magazines and newspapers will teach you how to manipulate the surface decoratively. Greater visual interest can be added by varying the direction of the printed lines from patch to patch.

SPACING

Spacing, the use of a blank area between typographic components, is an invaluable tool in creating tonal variations. Increase spacing between letters, words, or lines of type and the tone lightens; decrease it and the tone darkens.

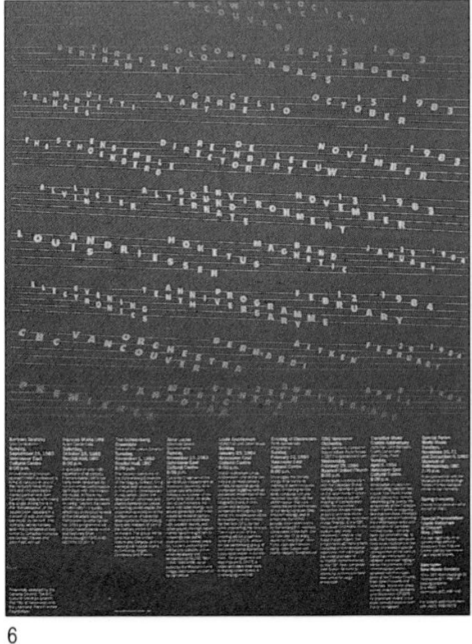

6

6 Color and tone enhance the musical use of typography in this poster designed by D. Dickson.

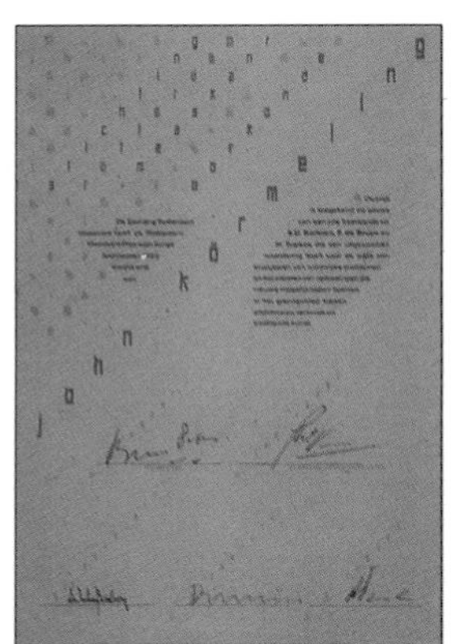

8

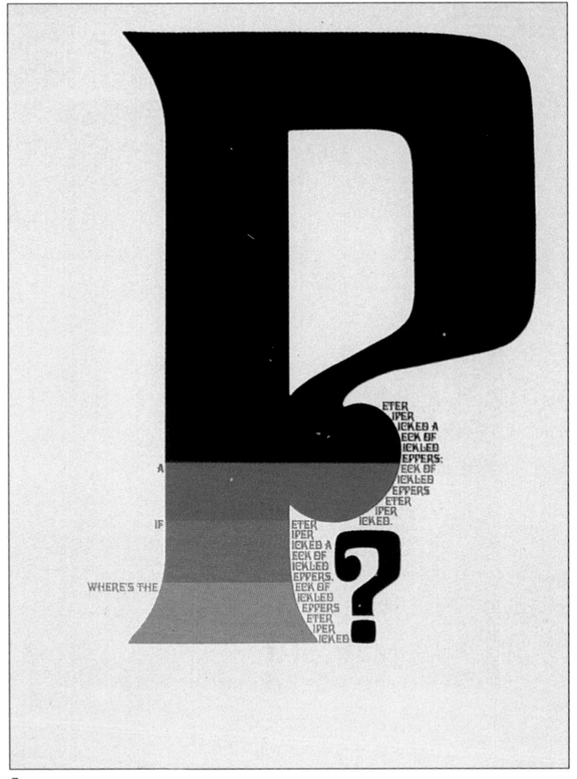

5

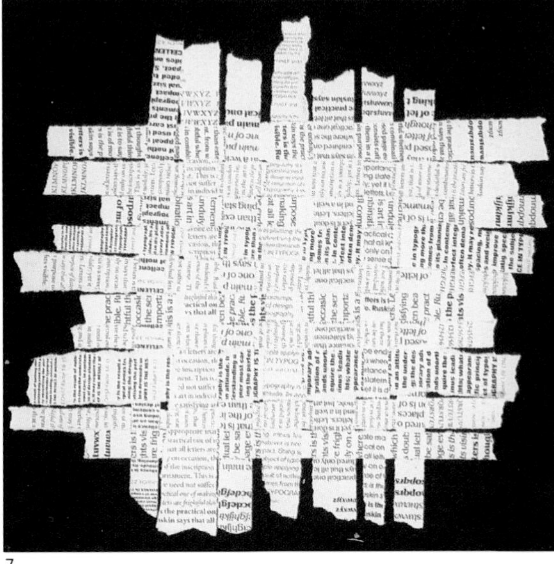

7

9

5 Herb Lubalin uses color and tonal variation to invite the reader into the text of this amusing typographic play with "P."

7 Weaving torn bands of selected weights of text matter into an abstract design where legibility takes a back seat allows you to discover and enjoy the subtle ranges of monochromatic tones that text can generate when freely juxtaposed.

8 Delicate tones are created in this piece designed by Hard Werken through the handling of inter-letter and inter-line spacing. Color changes add variation to this highly controlled use of spacing.

9 The strength of primary colors is echoed in the graphic shapes of this poster design by R. Jensen.

1 Soft colors play with the shape and graphic treatment of these letterforms. They also help to visually link the letters into the name of the magazine, *Typos* – designed by Frederick Lambert.

1

2

2 This logotype design combines the use of shadow and graduated color to reflect the company's high-quality photographic color processing laboratory.

3 The bright, fresh colors and the flourishes of the initial letters add vigor and excitement to this design by Hard Werken. It combines a calligraphic and typographic feel very successfully.

THE ROLE OF COLOR

Color adds excitement to type and ornament. It can be decorative or functional in that it heightens, lessens, classifies, or enriches.

Color also adds a spatial dimension, since warm colors such as red and orange advance,

3

while cool blues and violets recede. Colors vary in intensity, or chroma, in the same way that grays are tonal degrees of black. Yellow is the lightest in intensity, violet the darkest. Red and green are in the middle range. Large areas of color have a greater visual intensity than small areas. This is important when using colored type since most letters have a relatively small surface area unless used at extreme sizes and weights. As a result, the chroma of a color appears weaker. You can, however, compensate by using a stronger tone of color than you eventually want. Colors are rarely seen in isolation, and you will best develop an awareness of how they interact with each other through experimentation.

USING COLOR

Colors have symbolic associations as well as distinct personalities. The former could be seasonal, political, national, feminine, or masculine, or environmental, and so on. We rely on such associations to communicate in a form of universal language. Also, colors are easier to remember than words alone. Integrated into words they strengthen and embellish the visual communication. The mood or style of letters and words can also be reflected through colors. Overprinting letters in translucent colors can result in not only mixed colors but also new shapes within them. The background color is important in that it affects the legibility of type. Sympathetic colors will fuse the two together, whereas contrasting colors will generate a vibrancy that causes the type to appear to jump off the surface. Color merges and soft gradations of a single color can also be created for use as a background.

The decoration of black and white type with colored flourishes, borders, and typographic ornament softens and animates the text. The minimal use of color to highlight, classify, or emphasize selected parts of text or tabular matter lends a definite decorative feel.

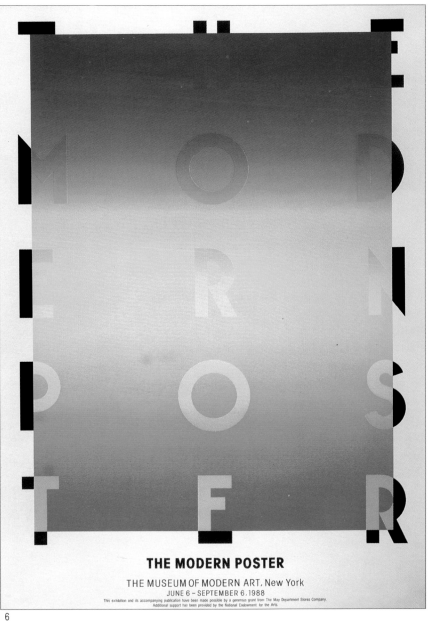

BASE
LINE
EIGHT

4

4 *Baseline*, the international typography magazine, uses stacked graduated color within each of the letterforms as the main element in its cover design. The black background and crisp white edges of the letters lend a glowing luminosity to the colors, hinting at a third dimension. Designed by Banks & Miles.

THE MODERN POSTER

THE MUSEUM OF MODERN ART, New York

JUNE 6 – SEPTEMBER 6, 1988

This exhibition and its accompanying publication have been made possible by a generous grant from The May Department Stores Company. Additional support has been provided by the National Endowment for the Arts.

6

6 This poster, a superb example of the decorative use of color and type, was designed by Koichi Sato. Color merges are used to give a rich and vibrant background that is picked up in the contrasting color of the overlaid letters. The type appears to pass behind, come out in front of, and almost disappear through, the creative use of color. The intriguing parts of letterforms printed in black form an unexpected typographic border to the whole image.

SATO, Koichi. *The Modern Poster.* 1988. Lithograph, 29 × 40″. Copyright © 1988 The Museum of Modern Art, New York.

7

7 Countershapes are used in their own right in this visual play with color and tone. The color and shape ranges extend when the letters, cut from translucent colored films, are overlaid.

5

5 Numerals made up of smaller numerals produce tonal variations against a colored background in this experiment with tone and color.

Patterns and texture ◆ Decorative possibilities

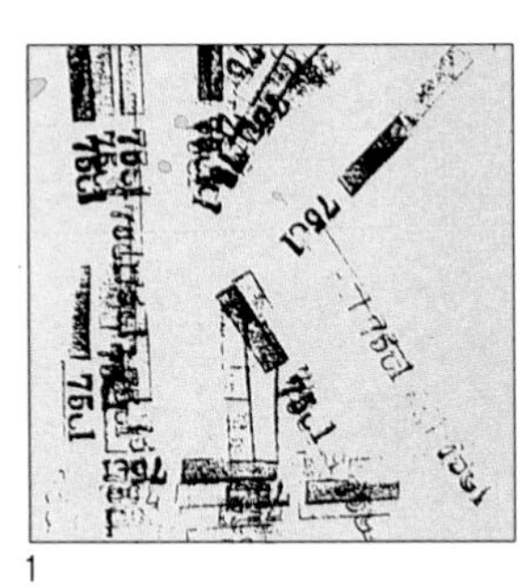

1

2

Typographic pattern and texture are closely related and cannot logically be separated since patterns have textures and textures have patterns. Both are apparent whenever letters or symbols are repeatedly printed within a specific area, where they are no longer seen as isolated shapes. Pattern is essentially repetitive and in typography relies on typographic elements in both single and modular form to set up rhythmic sequences.

Typographic texture emerges from pattern and is generated by the repetition of the main characteristics of each of the letters, numerals, or punctuation marks used. A great range of irregular, regular, and tonal textures can be created by controlling the letter spacing and interword and interline spacing. The entire surface assumes an animated quality with an almost tactile feel. Non-Latin scripts illustrate pattern and texture beautifully. Unable to understand the meaning of an unfamiliar language, the eye freely enjoys the typographic motifs which make up the richly ornamental surface.

The uses of typographic pattern are essentially decorative but can have an underlying message and a degree of legibility that further engages the viewer. Wrapping papers, greetings cards, advertisements, book jackets, packaging, murals, wall hangings, and fabrics are some of the contexts in which type-based patterns and textures are exploited.

1 The pattern surrounding this "K" allows the letters to emerge from a decorative surface.

2 This typographic pattern is part of the corporate styling for a firm of accountants, and was designed by Addison Design Consultants. It is currently used as a decorative security lining to their envelopes.

3 A textured pattern is generated by repeating the message at different sizes, which suggest different tones of voices. Color enhances the overall effect, helping to fuse the pattern.

4 A spread from a Chinese book, illustrating beautifully the quality of typographic pattern and texture. Such characteristics are not always easy to see in Latin scripts, where the content can be distracting.

3

4

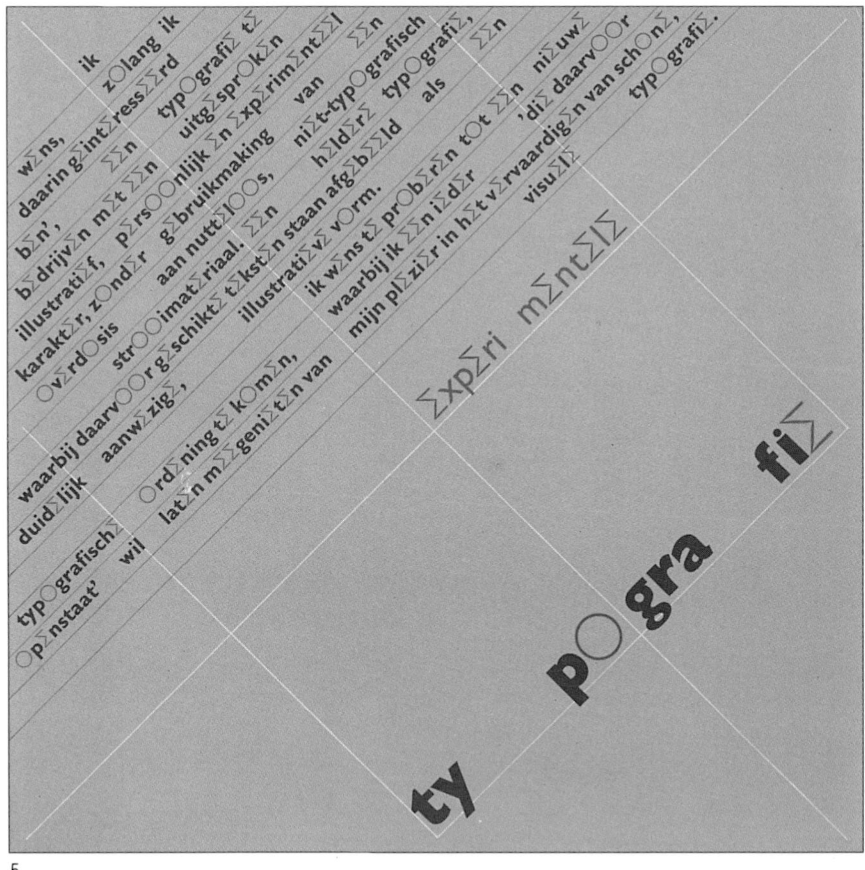

5

5 The random repetition of stylistically contrasting letters sets up a textural pattern that nevertheless retains its legibility. It also lends an appropriately experimental feel to the whole piece. Designed by Total Design.

8 A variation of typographic pattern in which the whole name of the company, including the pictorial logo, is worked into a design for in-house wrapping paper. A plain ribbon is used for contrast.

TYPES OF PATTERN

Pattern can be overall or made up of full or half-drop repeats. Geometrically based shapes can be echoed through regular, designed arrangements, while more organic forms respond well to a random, carefree arrangement. A challenging experiment is to mix the two together to create a densely busy, animated feel. Carefully selected color will then add contrast or balance and appropriate light and mood.

Since patterns are always based on repetition, a grid offers a useful basis on which to work. The grid allows a great deal of manipulation, movement, and variation to take place within its framework. This skeletal structure allows you to rearrange a whole variety of units, giving them a new, lively cohesion. Absolutely even textures and patterns can be originated with the help of grids.

Overall patterns using an abundance of elements will become textural, whereas a sparsity of motifs or grouped units will give a more open, scattered feel whether the components are randomly or formally organized.

6

6 Typographic ribbons made up of letters and numbers add decorative detailing to the plain gift wrapping.

7

7 The Waitrose range of toiletries for men uses a serif "M" in a repeated monogram style to form a background pattern on the packaging, giving it a look of quiet distinction.

8

ORIGINATING PATTERNS AND TEXTURES

The shape, size, weight, and color of type are drawn together here, so an analysis of the characteristics inherent in a typeface is necessary, including evaluating any idiosyncrasies that could be ornamentally exploited. Such things as the contrast of thick and thin stresses, bracketed, triangular, or minimal serifs, Roman, italic, or script type styles, countershapes, or the interletter spacing itself can provide the catalyst in decorative developments. Certain typefaces suggest types of pattern through their basic shape: Caslon, for example, with its flowing, lyrical, flourishing personality or Serifa, with its clean, fresh geometrical lines. The visual rhythms that are set up by the repetition of such characteristics can be used to create a wide range of effects through contrast and balance.

Parts of letters that have hidden pattern potential can also be used. Experiment with a large number of photocopied letterforms, numerals, or punctuation marks, cutting them up and rearranging them into unusual and exciting type-based abstract patterns. Playing with the optical shift between form and counterform in black and white or color combinations will produce a constantly changing pattern where the eye is never quite sure which is surface and which is background.

When you vary the tone and color of type within a pattern, you begin to generate a spatial illusion, bringing depth to the surface. Pattern composed of shadows or parts of shadowed type implies a third dimension that throws the surface into relief. Letterforms can be turned upside down, inside out, reversed, mirrored, or interlocked to originate patterns. Eliminating the space, or kerning, between letterforms generates new typographic shapes that form naturally into patterns. You can punctuate pattern by introducing additional ornaments in the form of typographic devices. Overprinted type or overlapped letters generate decoratively rich textures. Collage is a technique with enormous and exciting potential.

Handwriting, calligraphy, and hand-drawn type have an energy and uniqueness in their

2

3

2 & 3 By simply cutting and repeating these capital letters a dramatic pattern is achieved, while a softer pattern emerges when using lower case "e"s that have been cut and rearranged.

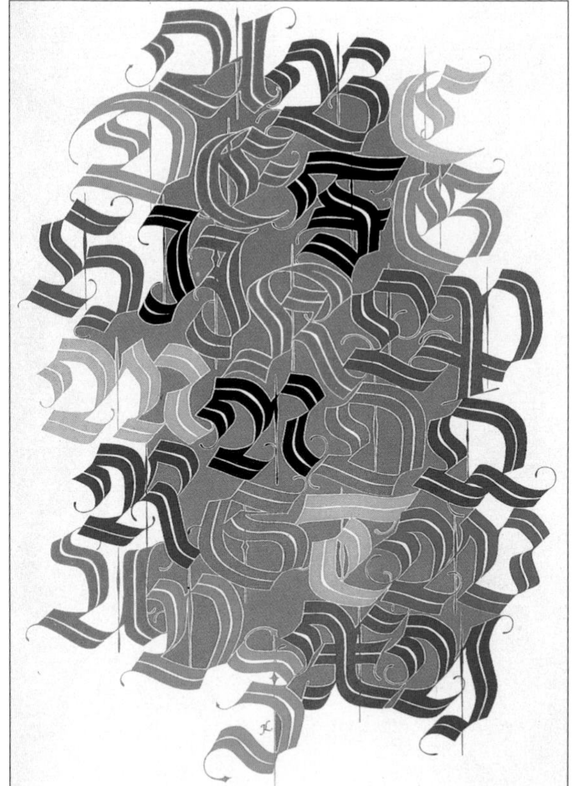

1

1 This modern alphabet pattern by Jean Larcher is of Gothic capitals based on early German manuscripts. Its decorative quality comes from the double pen strokes, the freedom of arrangement, and the use of bright colors on a gold and silver ground.

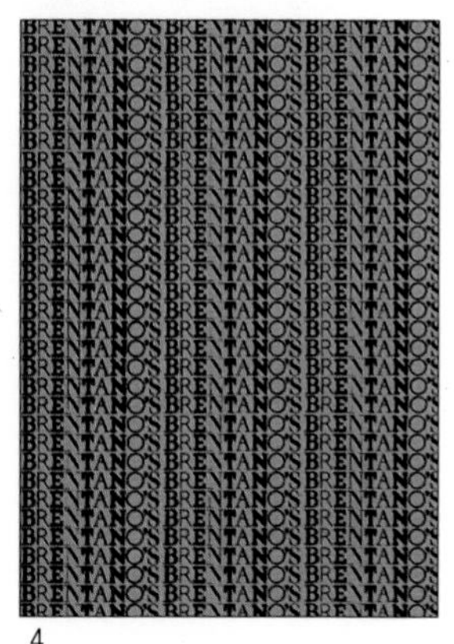

4

4 This mechanically generated repeat pattern creates strong vertical rhythms. Weight and style changes in the type also add a tonal variation to the surface. This kind of textured pattern retains total legibility.

spontaneity and natural irregularities, combining repetition with individuality. Lino cuts, stencils, cut paper, typewriters, typesetting, rubber stamps, and potato cuts are excellent ways of repeating letterforms and words for pattern-making. A photocopier is invaluable here. Further decorative development can be hand done and then re-photocopied until the design is complete. Combining electronically generated typographic textures with manual techniques and the enlarging or reducing facilities of a photocopier extends this technique still further. Adding color by hand and color copying the final design gives a professional finish as well as producing multiple copies for creating larger areas of repeat pattern and for varying color ways.

5

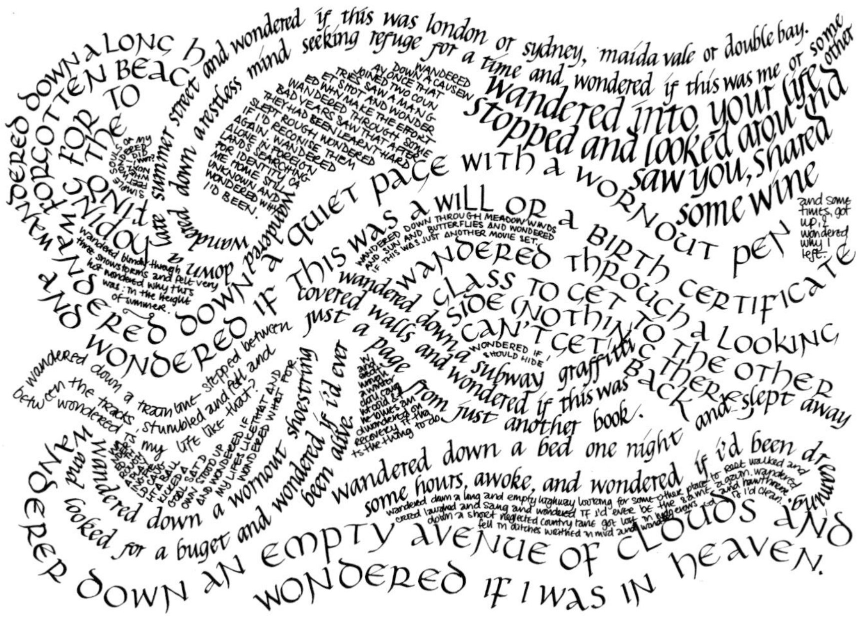

6

7

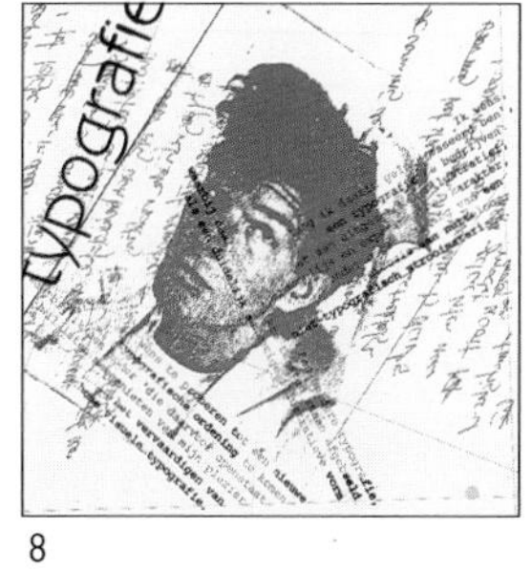

8

5 A freely drawn mixture of capitals and lower-case letters emphasized with transfer mechanical tints, tones, and color, explores the pattern potential of playing positive against negative. The work, entitled "Alphascape," is by John Smith.

6 Rich textural patterns are created by the way that the text meanders across the page unconstrained by typographic convention. The variations of style and size embellish the whole effect. Created by Diana Wilson.

7 The random pattern of the main heading in this moving announcement by Total Design echoes the atmospheric texture and movement of the image, which is also relevant to the message.

8 The contrast between the freedom of handwriting and the mechanical nature of typewritten text overprinted across an image suggests a layered texture in this lively design.

Shaped text

1-3 Three variations on the typographic interpretation of Christmas-tree shapes ranging from the random to the carefully controlled. Each shaped text captures the festive spirit in its individual way.

4 In this design by Total Design the architectural character and size of the "T" is underlined in the configuration of the main body of text. A dynamic contrast in the curving line of text adds movement and depth.

Typographic illustration or shaping text is essentially light-hearted and fun. Over a thousand years old, the technique first appeared as figured compositions or calligrams. It turns straight typography into graphic configurations with a degree of legibility, informing and entertaining the reader in an emotive way, as well as relieving the formality of conventional text.

Most traditional text settings are based on symmetry and asymmetry. Although you will be primarily concerned with legibility, you can, through careful selection of justified, centered, ranged-left, or ranged-right setting styles, hint at the mood and echo the content of the text. It is possible to set text into regular shapes such as squares, triangles, diamonds, and circles as well as irregular ones. In such cases legibility is necessarily secondary to the visual impact. The text need not cover the entire surface, for words, letters, or numerals can be used in a linear fashion, bending and curving to describe the contours of a particular form. Text can be shaped, or wrapped around images, defined spaces, or silhouettes, as well as forming an image itself. Controlled changes of typeface weight within the main text area will create subtle secondary typographic shapes or images. However, shaping text into representational objects associated with the meaning of the words throws caution to the winds. It pulls together text written, printed, or drawn, and design and image into a direct and decorative expression of content. The eye is driven by curiosity to accept this caricature of text in which humor, wit, and inventiveness provoke an inner smile.

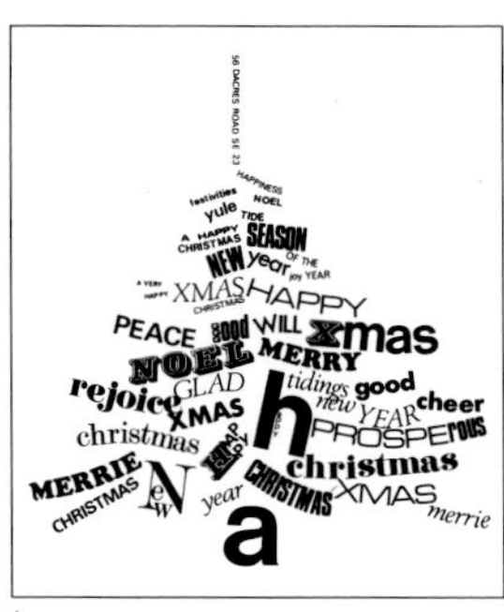

1

The wood-cutters came with the first snows and felled some among the largest of the trees; this happened every year and the Fir-Tree, who was by this time a tolerable height, shuddered when he saw those grand, magnificent trees fall with a tremendous crash, crackling to the earth. They were laid one upon another in wagons, and horses drew them away, far, far away, from the forest. Where could they be going! What might be their fortunes? When Christmas approached, many quite young trees were felled – trees which were some of them not so tall or of just the same height as the young restless Fir-Tree who was always longing to be away; these young trees were chosen from the most beautiful, they too were laid into wagons, and horses drew them away, far, far away, from the forest. 'Where are they going?' asked the Fir-Tree. 'They are not larger than I am; indeed, one of them was much less; where can they be gone?' 'We know! We know!' twitted the Sparrows. 'We peeped in through the windows of the town below! We know where they are gone! Oh you cannot think of what honour and glory they receive! We looked through the window-panes and saw them planted in a warm room, and decked out with such beautiful things – gilded apples, sweetmeats, playthings, and hundreds of bright candles!' 'And then?' asked the Fir-Tree, trembling in every bough; and then, what happened then?' 'Oh, we saw no more. That was beautiful, beautiful beyond compare! – An excerpt from the story of 'The Fir-Tree' by Hans Christian Andersen.

2

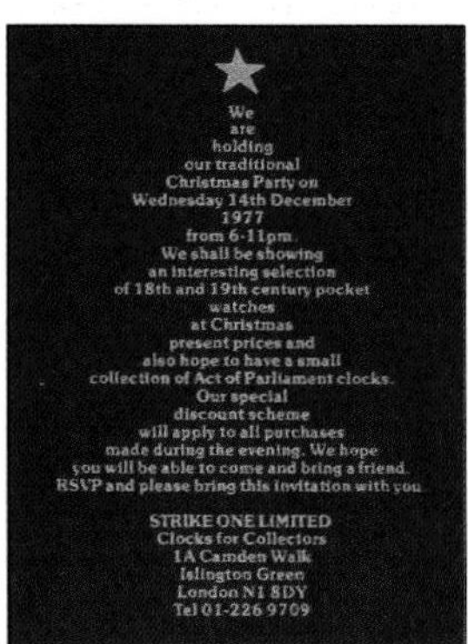
We
are
holding
our traditional
Christmas Party on
Wednesday 14th December
1977
from 6-11pm.
We shall be showing
an interesting selection
of 18th and 19th century pocket
watches
at Christmas
present prices and
also hope to have a small
collection of Act of Parliament clocks.
Our special
discount scheme
will apply to all purchases
made during the evening. We hope
you will be able to come and bring a friend.
RSVP and please bring this invitation with you.

STRIKE ONE LIMITED
Clocks for Collectors
1A Camden Walk
Islington Green
London N1 8DY
Tel 01-226 9709

3

4

5 Convincing typographic portraits can be generated by digitized phototypesetting systems. Facial features can be effectively described by making subtle changes in weight, style, and size.

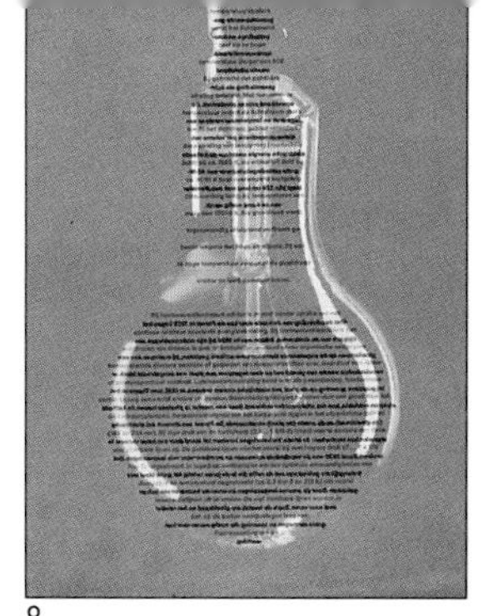

8 This shaped text printed on tracing paper forms part of a design by Total Design and typographically mirrors the photographic image to which it relates.

9 A single line of text traces the flight path of a ladybird in a decoratively informative way. Single lines can be designed into shapes equally as well as areas of text, depending on the degree of legibility required.

10 The dense texture of printed letters in this typographic illustration by Armando Testa visually parallels the feather pattern of the chicken.

Our Latin alphabet, composed basically of straight lines, circles, and part circles, has to be resourcefully manipulated to be effectively used in this way. Scripts such as Arabic, which are flowing and organic, lend themselves more readily to such graphic decorative techniques.

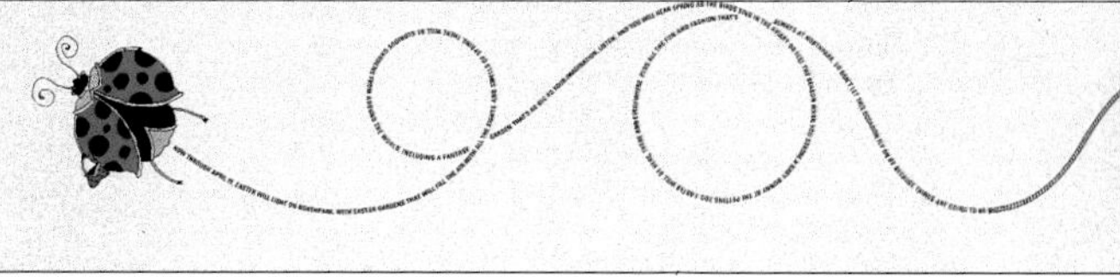

The decorative nature of shaped text transforms reading into a visual experience. Advertising uses this technique to give slogans or short pieces of text an embellished form with the visual impact to convey a message. Logotype designs also make use of this device. Text might be composed into the shape of shoes, wine glasses, bottles, heads, complete bodies, animals, birds, fishes, trees, or whole townscapes. Usually, the idea for shaping text stems from the content.

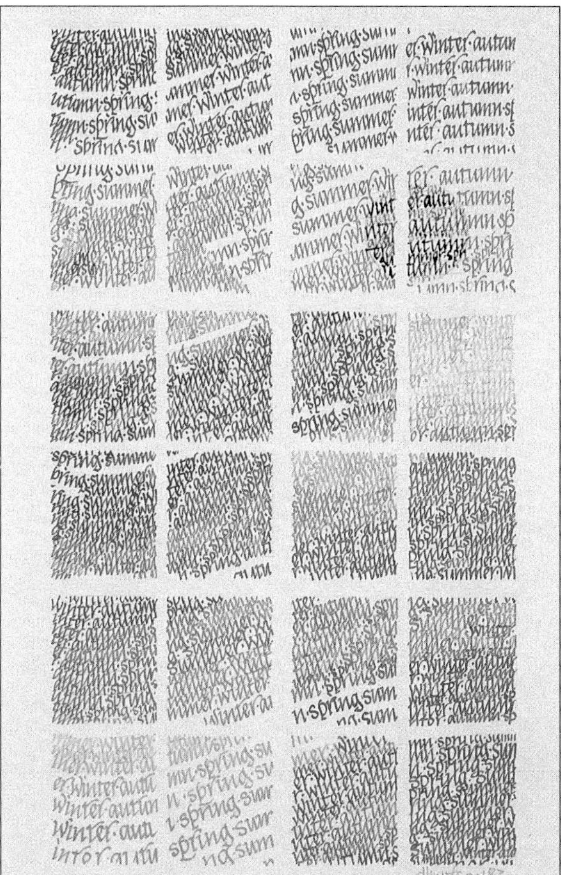

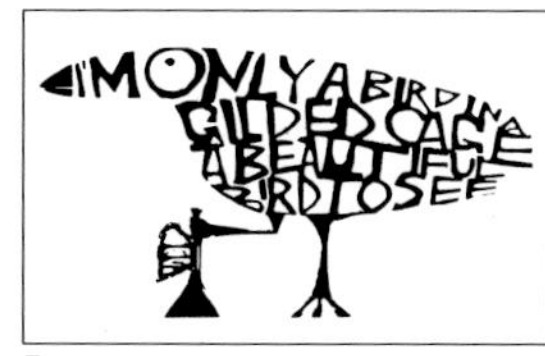

6 Diana Wilson captures the moods of spring, summer, autumn, and winter in windowlike areas of drawn text through color, rhythm, and texture.

7 This charming anonymous design demonstrates the flexibility of hand-drawn letters when used for shaped text.

Written portraits created through the texture and tone of words, where virtual photographic likenesses of the subject, human or animal, can be achieved through an inordinate amount of dexterity and skill, are feats of decorative typography. Digitized portraits or pictures can be much less arduously originated on a computer that allows you to experiment freely with typographic shading by changing the weight of the relevant parts of the text. Typographic illustrations generated on a computer tend to have a curious tapestrylike decorative quality to them, whereas handwritten ones retain the individuality of the designer's lettering with its more subtle texture.

Apart from direct representation, you could base your design on associated themes. Whatever the idea, obvious or subtle, working from a drawing or photographic reference will help insure the end result is visually convincing. The actual rendering of the image, representational or not, can be done using a mechanized, freehand or electronic system which might be careful or carefree but will in any case call for a degree of precision as well as permitting spontaneity. The different characteristics of handwriting, using a typewriter or a computer, or cutting and pasting typesetting, all give very different effects and invite experimentation. Part of a drawing or photographic image can have appropriately shaped text superimposed on it, or substituted for part of it. Lino cuts can be made from simple typographic figured texts and be printed or repeated for further experimentation with pattern and texture.

1 An example of informative text cleverly shaped to form a "parking bay" that echoes the neat proportions of the Mini. Careful handling of the copy has prevented unsightly hyphenation from disrupting the shape, and the absence of capital letters lends an even overall texture to the type.

chartered society of designers
conversations : a series of
five discussions
on the twentieth
century british
design classics to
take place on the
first saturday of
each month at 7.30
tickets £5 from the
chartered society of designers
29 bedford sq. london WC1B 3EG
7th january product design ·
4th february penguin books ·
4th march in fashion · 1st april
monotype classics · 6th may
corporate identity and style

1

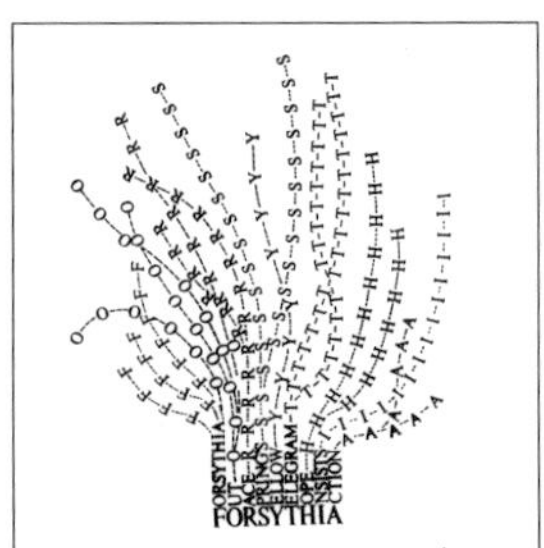

2

2 This typographic play with the word "Forsythia" is essentially experimental yet conveys a sense of unity. The components are all visually related so as to give the impression of a homogeneous whole.

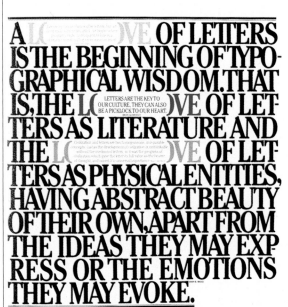

A LOVE OF LETTERS IS THE BEGINNING OF TYPOGRAPHICAL WISDOM. THAT IS, THE LOVE OF LETTERS AS LITERATURE AND THE LOVE OF LETTERS AS PHYSICAL ENTITIES, HAVING ABSTRACT BEAUTY OF THEIR OWN, APART FROM THE IDEAS THEY MAY EXPRESS OR THE EMOTIONS THEY MAY EVOKE.

LETTERS ARE THE KEY TO OUR CULTURE. THEY CAN ALSO BE A PICKLOCK TO OUR HEART.

3

3 A subtly inventive example of shaped text by Herb Lubalin. The left-hand section shows how the character of individual letters can be creatively explored. Tiny hyphens serve to retain the legibility and overall shape. The right-hand section uses rules and headings to give form to the text. Textural tones and color nuances are used to suggest different spatial planes.

4

4, 8 & 11 Numbers are playfully arranged to form amusing "figures" that suggest relevant notions of teamwork and competition and enliven Addison Design's publicity for Grant Thornton.

6 Simple lines of type curl and twist effectively as part of a Channel 4 title sequence by Bob English of English Markell Pockett.

6

9 Armando Testa skilfully manipulates conventional text setting and scriptlike flourishes into an amusing and convincing illustrative context.

10 The experimental arrangement of these foil-blocked words visually echoes a flourish of trumpets.

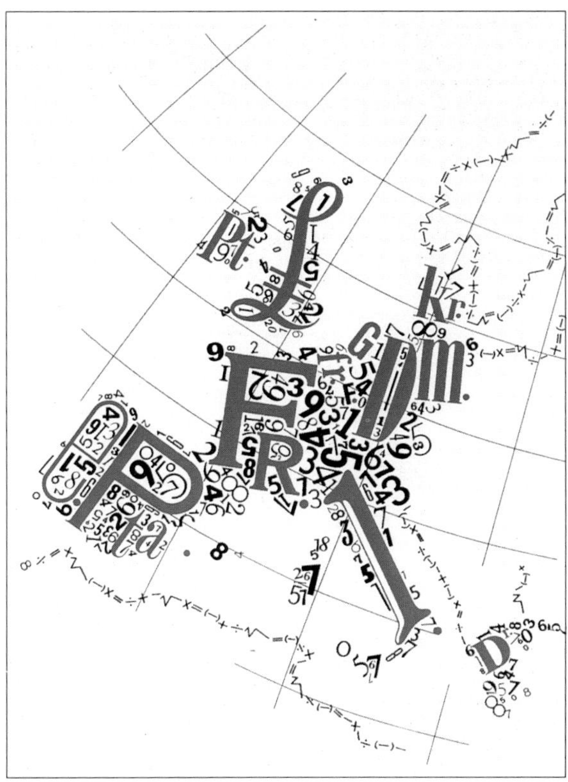

5

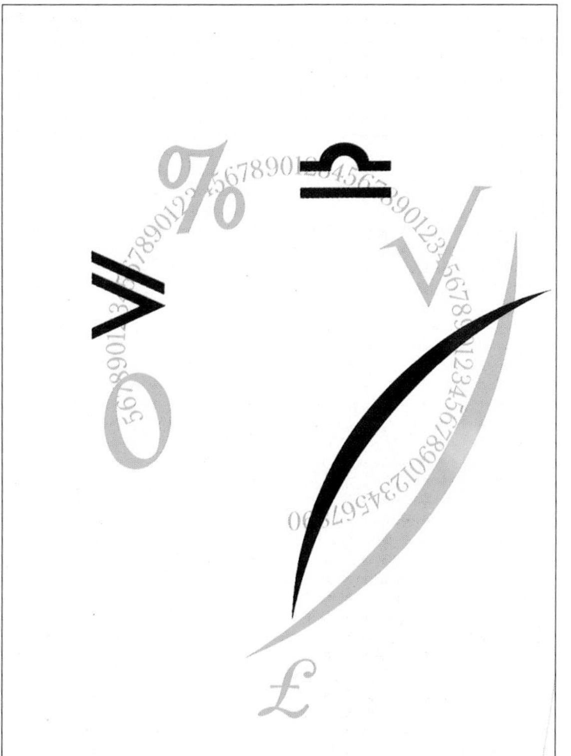

7

9

10

5 As a large firm of chartered accountants, the Grant Thornton group meet the European challenge with this entertaining "financial" map in which the countries are further identified by their individual currencies.

8

7 Corporate finance raises many questions, as symbolized in this cover design by Addision Design for Grant Thornton.

11

Textured letters and words

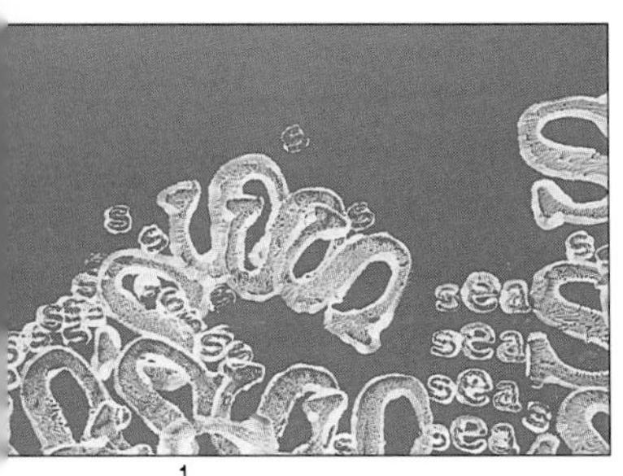

1

2 The cover for the catalog of the Mexico Nuevo project designed by Vaughn Weeden Creative Inc. uses intense color and texture to evoke the feel of that country. The vibrancy of color, together with the tactile surface quality of the textured numeral, makes a strong decorative impact.

3 Large-scale lettering provides a substantial surface to carry a photographic image without obscuring the emotive content. This design by Herb Lubalin was produced to accompany an exhibit in New York.

3

1 A typographic experiment inspired by the sea. The textured surface of the printed wood letters imitates spray and surf.

2

This technique allows you to create a mood by applying decoration to the surface of display type. The development of pictorial decoration, texture, or pattern can stem from virtually any source and the task should be approached with an open mind. Themes such as travel, or seasonal, political, musical, architectural, and literary sources, can be richly interpreted and used in magazine or newsletter headings, book jackets, posters, or promotional brochures.

CREATING DECORATIVELY TEXTURED LETTERS

The suitability of the letterform's shape, size, and weight is very important. The surface area (weight) should be such that any surface treatment will carry visual impact. (Thin or light characters are not suitable.) Counterforms of both bold and light letterforms can be embellished and, in contrast, the letter itself left plain. The scale of the texture, pattern, or image to be used must also be appropriate to the size and weight of letterform for the result to be legible.

4

6

7

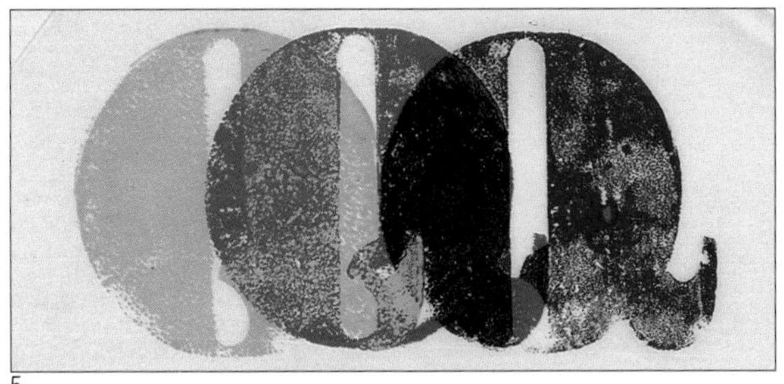

5

8

9

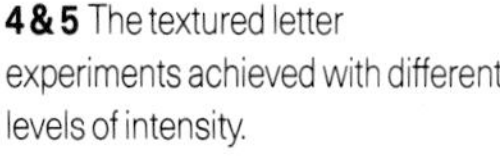

4 & 5 The textured letter experiments achieved with different levels of intensity.

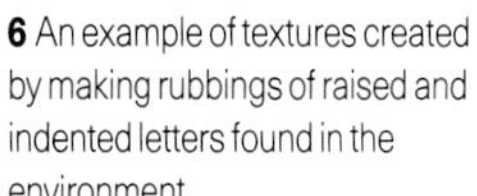

6 An example of textures created by making rubbings of raised and indented letters found in the environment.

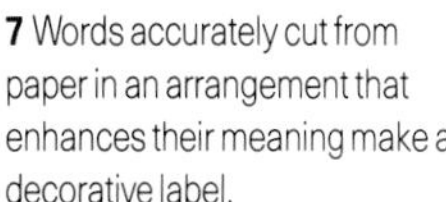

7 Words accurately cut from paper in an arrangement that enhances their meaning make a decorative label.

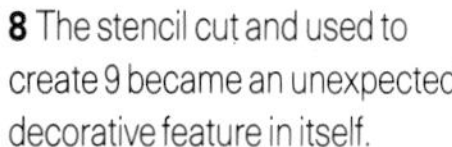

8 The stencil cut and used to create 9 became an unexpected decorative feature in itself.

9 Colored chalks were fused to create the color merge in this "K."

GENERATING TEXTURED LETTERS

Experimenting by hand will provide a good visual basis from which to make innovative use of electronically generated textures including many of those listed below.

PRINTING

Broken surface textures can be achieved by printing from partially inked wood type or type cut in lino. Heavy inking will produce a dense, stippled effect. Letterforms for printing can be drawn and cut from potatoes, card, lino, or wood.

RUBBING

This very simple technique generates a rich texture very quickly and can be achieved with newsprint and large wax crayons.

STENCILS

A range of stencils varying in both size and shape is commercially available. You can make your own by drawing and cutting letterforms or words from thin card or stiff paper, remembering to join the countershapes to the letterform at strategic points. Stencils used with a stencil brush, spray diffuser, spatter technique, or scribbling with a crayon give a wide variety of textures. With color, very exciting effects are possible. Reverse stencilling results in a plain letter with a textured surround. Stencilling can be used on a variety of surfaces, including wood, metal, plastic, and ceramics. Images can be photographically applied to letterforms using a master or stencil cut to the shape of a letter or word.

USING OTHER MATERIALS

Letterforms can be cut from a wide range of textured materials. These include corrugated card, grained paper, glossy and matt papers, tracing paper, clear or colored film, sandpaper, newspapers, pictures in magazines, and fabrics patterned or textured. Translucent letterforms can be overlaid on an imaged background to give an added dimension.

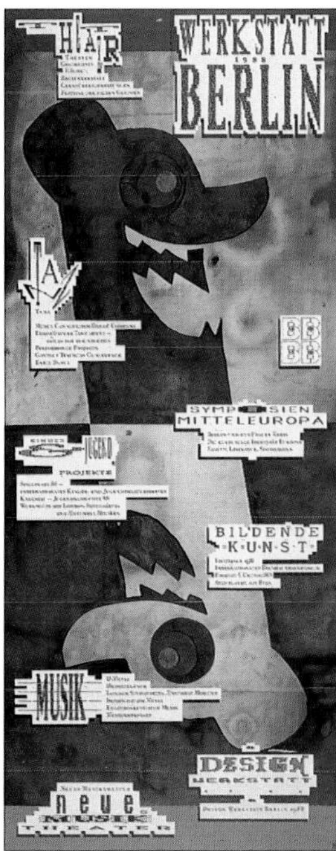

10

10 A few of the many possibilities offered by electronic media for adding textures to letters and words are explored here by Hard Werken.

1

1 Black dry-transfer lettering and small shapes of adhesive paper were used to mask off the white areas. An inexpensive airbrush system using canned compressed air and markers were used to decoratively color the background. Adhesive tape was used to remove the "masks," revealing crisp white shapes.

3

3 This embossed "E" was created by the method described in the text below.

SPRAYING

An airbrush is expensive, but is possibly the most versatile tool, and gives the greatest degree of control for generating soft-edged or diffused lettering. Airbrushing requires a degree of skill that can only come with experience. Other spray mechanisms, such as fixative blowers and aerosol paints, are more accessible and will produce a similar effect. Whichever you choose, allow yourself time to experiment. Wonderful layers of translucent color can be built up using colored drawing inks and a fixative diffuser. It is advisable to use an absorbent paper in order to minimize the risk of paint dripping and running. Varying the distance of the spray source from the surface will give either a clean or a diffused edge.

EMBOSSING

Embossed type has a beautiful subtlety to it, both in its original form and reproduced photographically. You need first to make a mold of the required letter from a rectangle of thin card or stiff paper. To do this, cut out the letterform and stick the various parts of it into the correct position onto another rectangle of card. Fix a sheet of paper over the top and rub over the letterform mold using an embossing tool, a small flat piece of wood, or a fingernail, working carefully in and around the raised shape until the letterform appears in relief. The edges will be either sharp or rounded according to the pressure applied.

2

2 Individual hand-cut paper stencils were used for this experiment. The same airbrush system as used for 1 applied the even color. Each stencil was overlapped on top of the preceding number before spraying.

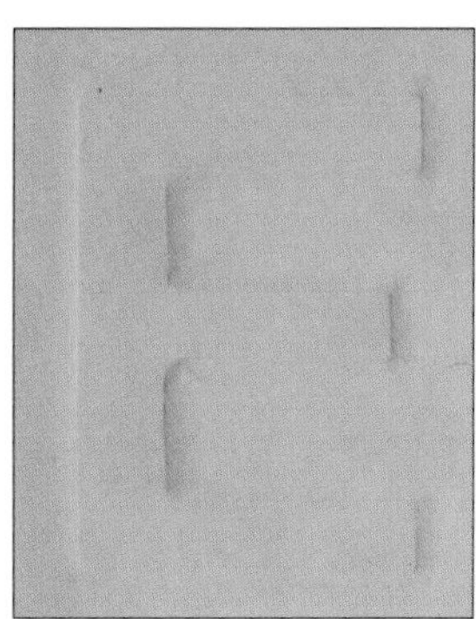
4

4 An alternative to embossing is to indent the surface. You simply use the card cut-out stencil left over from the original embossing mold and carefully work the paper into it.

7 Dry-transfer sheets of mechanical textures can be effectively used to create textured letters.

5 A highly individual feel is generated in this decorative collage that explores the possibilities of the medium through a selection of type, images, pattern, texture, and color. The images are further enhanced by the surrounding text made up entirely of found letters.

6 A different approach to the same technique in which squared-up generated areas of type, texture, and image are assembled into a lively design with a strong visual impact.

MECHANICAL TEXTURES

Square grids imposed on display-sized type break up the surface and background into even-sized "bits," giving a mosaic effect which can be decoratively manipulated. Circles, triangles, hexagons, and irregular shapes can be organized into grids to create different textures. The surface of letters can be enhanced or transformed with dots, lines, half-tone screens, textures, tints, or tones at a variety of scales to produce a wide range of results. Dry-transfer lettering systems offer a wide range of mechanical textures suitable for use on letterforms and a great number of effects are available on graphics computer programs.

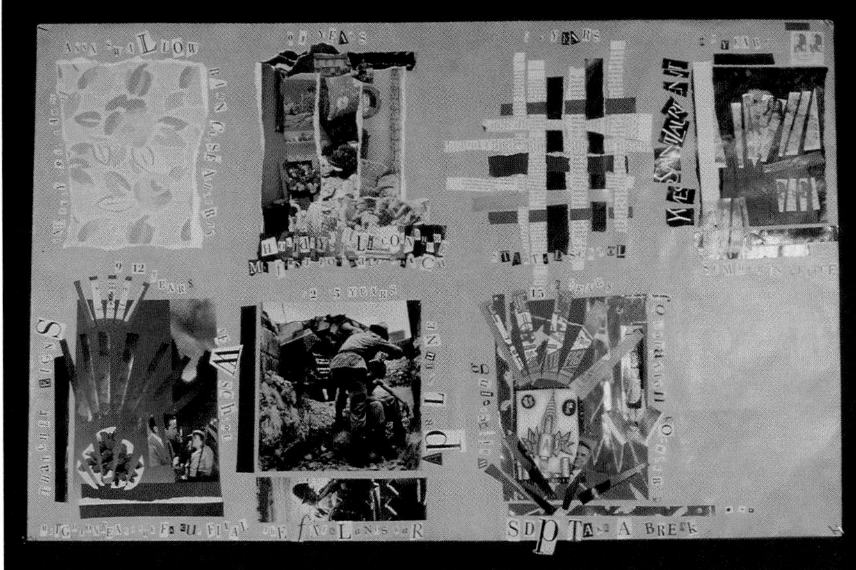

5

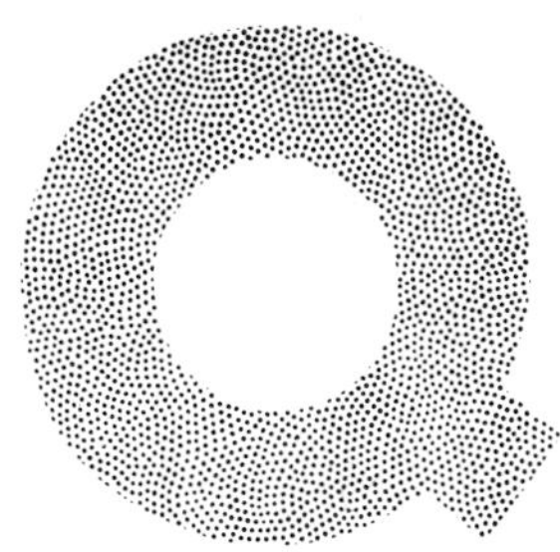

7

COLLAGE

This is one of the most versatile techniques, with a strong tactile quality. Collage allows you to combine any number of different media in any shape or form, contrasting or harmonizing colored, textured, printed, cut, torn, found, originated, photographed, photocopied material, in layers both opaque and transparent, controlled or random. Its many uses include the creation of a unique piece of decorative art, posters, cards, stationery, and magazines, in the latter it might be decoratively combined with or integrated into the text.

6

Hand-drawn techniques ◆ Letters

1

2

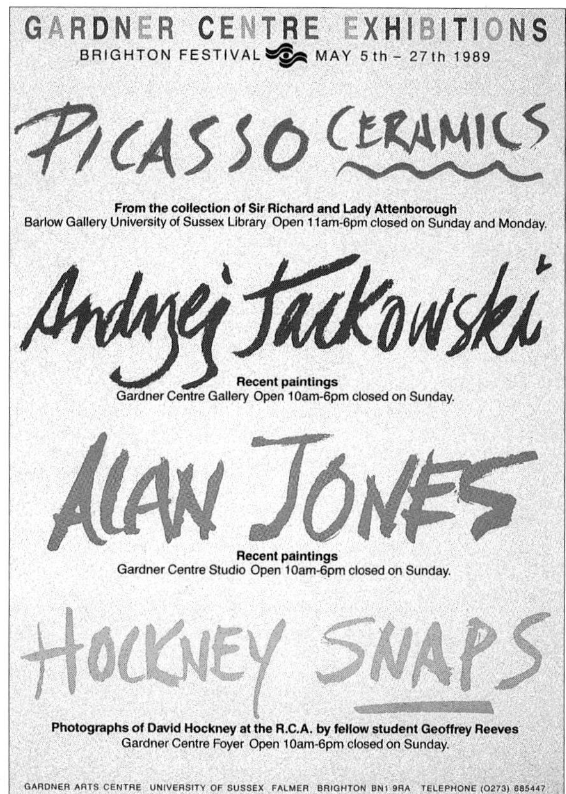

3

1 The vital, almost calligraphic nature of the hand-drawn lettering aptly captures the character of a communications and public relations magazine.

2 The haunting quality of the facial decoration in this design is carried through into the titling in both line and color. This and 1 were designed by Georgia Deaver.

3 This poster designed by Andy Gammon mimics styles of signatures, hinting at the individuality of the exhibitors' work without giving anything of their identity away.

4 Freely drawn, flowing letters embellish the minimal typography on these packs designed by Lewis Moberly. Notice how a decorative link is formed between the packs.

4

Decorative hand-drawn letters, ranging from the primitive to the exquisite, surround us in both the urban and the rural environment. Amateur and professional examples can be seen in greengrocers' signs, blackboard memos, fairground lettering, shop fascias, stone inscriptions, decorative ironwork, embroidery, and etched glass, all of which spring from the hand. The materials, medium, and style of these letters reflect the spirit of the message, whether celebratory, solemn, frivolous, or essentially informative. In the context of decorative typography, hand-drawn type can be appreciated and enjoyed in its own right. Unlike its printed counterpart, the drawn letter carries a sense of freedom and personal involvement, and does not attempt to mimic precision. Printed type by its nature can never achieve this unique quality.

Drawing letters is a personalized rendering of the essential characteristics of a typeface. In the same way as drawing anything else, it requires visual selection and judgement. The apparent freedom of drawing in fact conceals intense observation of structure, shape, size, and weight. Hand-drawn letters can be used as initial letters or headings, contrasting strongly with the uniformity of printed text. They can be combined with illustration on labels and covers or formed into logotypes, monograms, or watermarks. Greetings and invitation cards or posters can be effectively hand drawn and

5 A hand-drawn logotype created by Chris Bigg for Salute, a design-conscious fashion shop in Brighton, England. It reflects the unusual interior styling which, in contrast with the currently more familiar high-tech approach, uses man-made and natural materials in an undisguised way.

6 This one-of-a-kind hand-made package based on the theme of Time shows how words and images can be decoratively integrated when both are hand-drawn and color is allowed to flow from one to the other.

5

6

7 & 8 Two examples that show how drawing can capture the contrasting character and spirit of letters. Letters rendered in this way become decorative elements in their own right. But in order to achieve convincing results it is essential to draw from reference.

enhanced with color. Letters and numerals provide a wonderful vehicle for humor and wit, particularly when hand drawn, since they integrate extremely well with pictorial elements. The letters themselves can suggest humorous ideas by their shape when set in unexpected situations or grouped together to look like the word they represent.

DRAWING LETTERS

More often than not, we draw what we think we see rather than what is actually there. It is useful to work from existing examples to strengthen your awareness of structure and form and to sharpen your observation. Working with a favorite letter or numeral strengthens your personal interest and makes the drawing more fun. Experiment with a variety of media: chalk, crayons, soft pencils, markers, brush, and ink or paint. Different combinations of media and surface will produce exciting results. Start by drawing the basic structure. Gradually build up a letter, using overlapping strokes to evolve the thick and thin stresses of the type design. Adding these by degrees and constantly referring back to your example will develop your visual judgement.

Weigh up overall proportion, what proportion of a square the letter would occupy, the relationship of height to width, whether the letter is wide, narrow, thin or fat, and the character of the serifs. Look at the proportions of the individual strokes. Study the orientation of the letters and their inner directions. Combining these observations, you can make a visual improvisation of the family characteristics of the letterform. The result will have an individual freshness and bear a direct visual relationship to the source typeface.

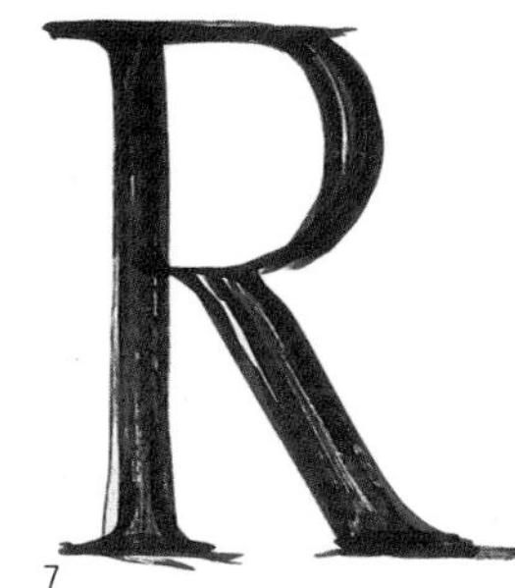

7

8

9

9 This spirited piece by Total Design communicates a dynamic sense of movement that speaks for itself through color and spontaneity.

10 Another example of text and title forming part of an image. The conventional barriers between type and image have been totally removed. The shape of the numerals and letters successfully echoes the line and pattern in the abstract imagery.

10

Calligraphy

Calligraphy is the art of handwriting. The precursor to type, calligraphy was more flexible, yet had its own structures and formalities. The term evokes the formal script used in early manuscripts and scrolls, where it was often lavishly illuminated with ornaments and designs in brilliant colors. The cursive penmanship of ledgers, deeds, bills of sale, and correspondence also comes to mind. In both spheres skill and craftsmanship are required. Alongside these traditional applications of calligraphy is its modern use as a free-form rendering of the alphabet.

Combining calligraphy with an inventive approach to media and materials offers much scope for decorative use. The vigor of calligraphic strokes is extremely emotive and has tremendous visual impact. There is a visible spring to both formal and informal calligraphic letterforms, giving a rhythmic quality to the thick and thin stresses. Each piece of work is unique in itself, spontaneity and fortuity play-

1

2

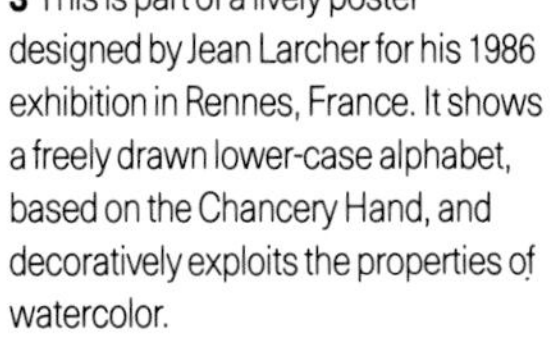

3 This is part of a lively poster designed by Jean Larcher for his 1986 exhibition in Rennes, France. It shows a freely drawn lower-case alphabet, based on the Chancery Hand, and decoratively exploits the properties of watercolor.

3

4

5

1 The celebratory nature of this design by Georgia Deaver is reflected in the calligraphic flourish of her interpretation of the title. It conveys a sense not only of quality but of inviting fun and enjoyment.

2 The unusual use of free-form calligraphy to promote a range of cabinets gives a unique identity to the series. Georgia Deaver's calligraphy reflects the color range, as well as intriguing the potential buyer.

4 A calligraphic hand and arrangement of text used by F. Gaunt to both inform and entertain the recipient of this highly individual letter. Calligraphy can add a personal embellishment to conventional contexts.

5 The fun, excitement, and sense of occasion associated with champagne are mirrored in Georgia Deaver's label design.

6

6 An automatic pen was used to achieve this rather formal calligraphic effect. Notice how the pen widens or narrows the strokes according to the pressure applied. The ink's tone can also be darkened or lightened in the same way.

7 Another example of work done with the automatic pen, but quite different in character. There is in the strokes a strong rhythmic quality akin to the meaning of the word. The surface quality of the paper also affects the letterforms. A roughness will add texture, while a smoothness will result in a crisp, clean edge.

ing a very important part. Open-minded experimentation will produce exciting and often unexpected results, particularly if minimal planning has been done. "Mistakes" need not be discarded but may lead you to other approaches and ideas.

Free-form calligraphy can be successfully incorporated into a variety of areas such as logotypes, posters, packaging, and cards. A more formal approach could be used for certificates, book plates, or commemorative commissions. Calligraphic flourishes added to individual letters or typeset text lend a decorative touch.

MAKING A SIMPLE START

You will need a direct, spontaneous approach combined with lots of practice, although most of these experiments will give a feeling of success and fairly instant results. Basically, calligraphic experimentation starts with a carpenter's pencil, square-ended pen, or chisel-tipped marker. The distinctive thick and thin calligraphic strokes will automatically appear if you write with the implement at a fixed angle. You can vary these thick and thin strokes by changing the angle. The emphasis or weight of the strokes can also be varied by applying or relieving pressure on the writing implement or brush.

Another technique is to tape two different-colored ballpoint pens together and draw letters with them. In this way you can successfully produce letters quickly and freely. As you gain confidence, strokes and serifs can be decoratively extended, flourishes added, and different color combinations tried.

8

8 This slight quality, almost like handwriting, is achieved by using a chisel-shaped brush, which lends yet another dimension to calligraphic forms. The paper texture can be more clearly revealed with brush calligraphy than with a pen because of the comparatively light pressure needed.

9

10

9 The exuberance of this free calligraphy by Georgia Deaver is totally relevant to the birthday greetings on this card. The integration of small, traditional type helps to lead the eye across the message.

10 This richly decorative wedding invitation benefits from entwined flourishes that echo the motion of calligraphy and betoken the occasion. By Georgia Deaver.

The overlap of hand-drawn letters and calligraphy

When calligraphy and lettering are used as a free-form expression, it is almost impossible to draw a distinction between them. Both are "one-of-a-kind" and hand originated. Everyday handwriting also belongs in this category, being neither true calligraphy nor real lettering. Used as a decorative element, it can convey the message in a personal, unconstrained way. The style of writing used will suggest a mood – thoughtfully, purposefully, urgently, or instantly. Color and the medium can add vitality and depth. Objects that resemble letters can be made to do so even more strongly through drawing, where the object and the letter become one. Calligraphically interpreted letters or words offer even greater flexibility in this area. Modification of letterforms is satisfactorily done by drawing. Typographic or calligraphic doodling is an entertaining way of generating ideas for this purpose, allowing the freely formed letters to suggest shapes and arrangements to which flourishes and ornaments can be added.

Calligraphy and hand-drawn letters are extremely dependent for their success on effective arrangement or layout. A single letter has endless possibilities for arrangement. Alphabets, words, and sentences can also be arranged in many different ways in relation to each other as well as to the page. Care must be taken in the optical spacing of letters – too

Belle Tournure

B Y A N N A W I L L I A M S

1

1 Based on handwriting, this design nevertheless reveals certain calligraphic characteristics, particularly in the "T."

2

2 Part of a poster design where all the text and headings were hand-drawn. An inner rhythm is set up by the random use of bold letters within the text. There is a strong tonal correlation between image and text.

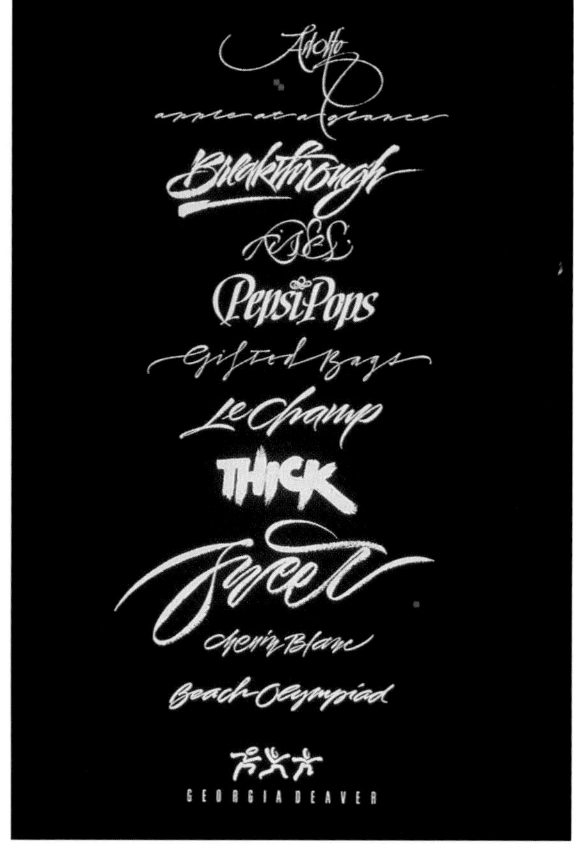

3

3 A vigorous combination of hand-drawn letters and calligraphy by Georgia Deaver that demonstrates the difficulty of distinguishing between the two techniques.

much or too little will impede the visual flow and affect the legibility. Inspiration for layout should spring from the message, the shape of the page, and the number of words involved. The arrangement on the page should not only enhance the content but be a delight to look at. It does not necessarily have to be parallel to the page. Though the success of hand lettering, calligraphy, and handwriting hinges on a degree of immediacy, if you are working with more than a couple of words it can be helpful to draw a faint pencil framework to help position your lettering and determine approximate positions and line lengths. In this way you are free to channel your energy into the joy of creating the letters themselves.

FURTHER TECHNIQUES

Monoprinting allows you to work into the surface rather than on it and can give excellent results with lettering and calligraphic approaches. An inking slab or any flat, non-porous surface is covered with an even layer of printing ink, and letters are freely drawn into it using a piece of square-cornered card or balsa-wood as a "pen." A print is taken from the design by placing a sheet of paper on the surface. Inking the surface in with merged colors gives vibrant results.

Drawing letters with a soft brush in paint or drawing ink onto a wet surface results in beautiful diffused edges. Changing colors will create exciting, unpredictable mergers. The bleach technique shown in the example far right also produces interesting results in calligraphic and lettered forms when carried out with either a brush or a pen with a reservoir. Gold and silver can be dusted onto letters drawn with a tacky medium.

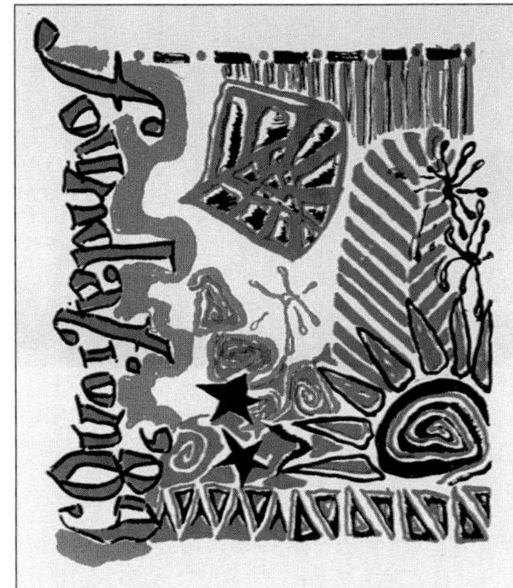

4

4 A promotional T-shirt design in which the lettering is used as part of a decorative border.

5 An example of monoprinting. Remember to draw the letters in reverse into the ink.

6 A book jacket designed by Hard Werken in which the hand-drawn character of the lettering evokes the historical period. The decorative border further embellishes the whole.

5

6

7 A hand-lettered wordcard by Diana Wilson in which calligraphy and hand drawn letters overlap decoratively.

8 The calligraphic nature of this alphabet drawn in bleach on colored paper retains a definite typographic quality despite its free interpretation.

7

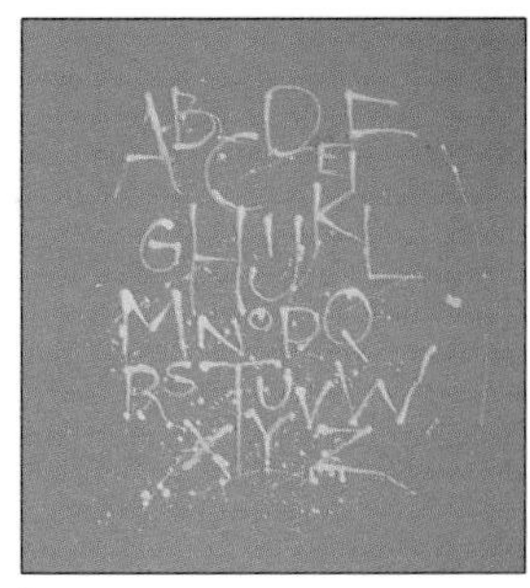

8

Hand-drawn text

Text that is hand drawn has a gentle, personal quality. Since it is not a mechanical process, it cannot be perfect or even accurate, whether it is based on a typeface or freely written. The unintentional slips and irregularities that occur within it lend a richness quite different from the uniformity of typesetting. When selecting a suitable text it is important to consider the message and tone so that these can be echoed visually. The mood of the text can be hinted at by a symmetrical, asymmetrical, or eccentric arrangement, and bold and light letters can be brought together functionally or decoratively and enlivened with color. Generally, this kind of text interpretation benefits from retaining

1 A delightful example of the applied use of hand-drawn text entirely appropriate to the contents, hand-collected wild flower seeds.

2 "Seascape Circle" created by Diana Wilson uses hand-drawn text as a unique typographic illustration in which color is employed to reinforce the subject matter.

1

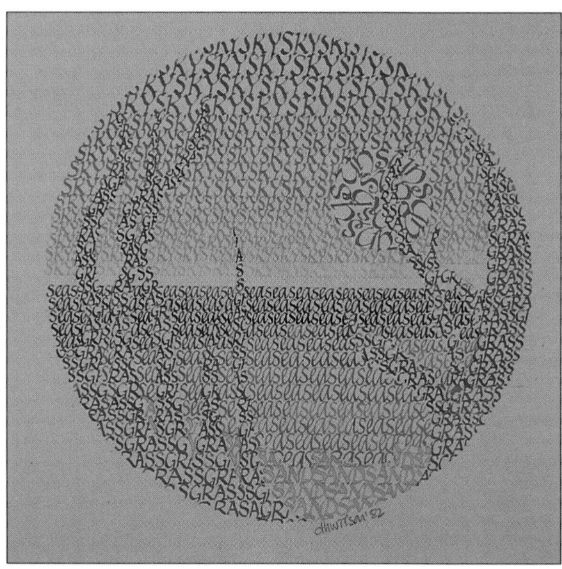

2

3 This rich-textured woodcut lettering is by Ernst Ludwig Kirchner. It shows how, with careful planning, a text can be designed into a visually satisfying unit complete with an initial letter. Interestingly, the text remains wholly legible.

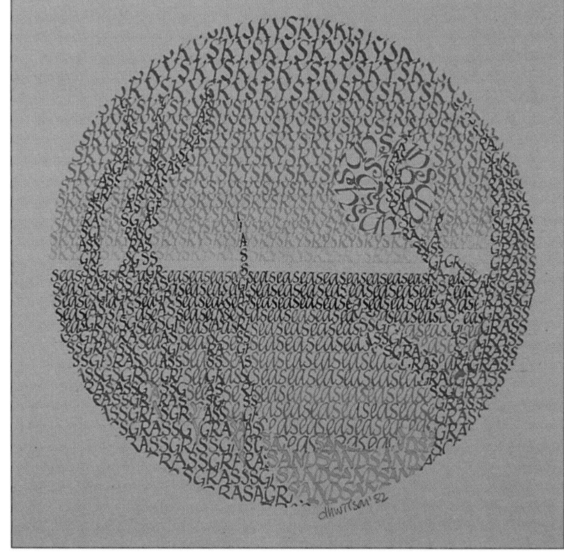

3

legibility and is not happily forced into tight shapes.

In working with text you are confronted with lines of words that need arranging or rearranging. To some extent hand-drawn text behaves like text setting. Certain texts suggest a random wandering across the page, while others need more ordering. You will need to estimate the line breaks in your text, which might be arbitrary or related to the sense of the content. A useful technique for modifying over-long lines is to slightly squeeze the letters together. Lines that fall much too short can be optically adjusted by adding an ornament or flourish at the end. A dip pen and ink are flexible tools for drawing text and give a rhythm and texture. Colored inks, if used without cleaning the pen in between changes, will give subtle color changes throughout the entire text. Embellishments, pictorial or calligraphic, can be added when the drawn text is completed.

7

7 A structured yet free design and drawing of an alphabet and text. Lines and rhythms are mirrored in both letters and image. The more mechanical nature of the wood type enhances the directions of the handwork.

4

4 The lyrical interpretation of this poem inventively combines hand-drawn text with delicately colored calligraphic flourishes and minute typographic characters in a decorative yet legible style.

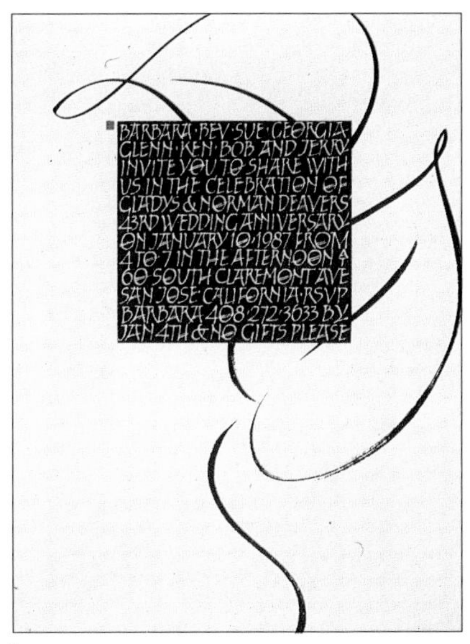

5

5 An appropriately formal treatment of hand-drawn text contrasts dynamically with the simple, rhythmic movement of freely drawn line.

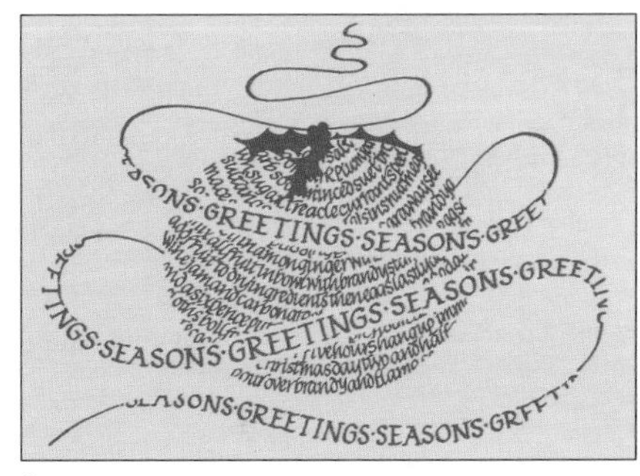

6

6 In this card design by Diana Wilson a typographically illustrative Christmas pudding recipe, complete with tantalizing steam, hints at the delights of the season.

Decorative contrasts

The vigor and directness of calligraphy and hand-drawn letters convey a mood that contrasts sharply with the quieter, more neutral quality of typeset text. Yet each visually reinforces the other. The theme of contrast should be explored through the size, shape, weight, structure, color, texture, and direction of letters and words. Used in combinations, they add energy and excitement. Size is an almost essential ingredient in whatever combination of contrasts you use. Dramatic contrasts are probably most successful in display type or headings. On a smaller scale, they can be used to create focal points or as a means of decorative emphasis, as in hand-underlining or calligraphic flourishes within and around the text.

To freely explore the contrast between mechanical type and calligraphy, experiment with unusual combinations of lettering and typewriting, rubber stamps, instant lettering, or computer printouts, playing with the textural contrasts. For pure enjoyment a composition of calligraphic forms might be freely drawn in color on a surface of different typographic textures collaged together. Applications of these ideas include posters, announcements, greetings cards, and an unusual way of enhancing personal correspondence.

1

1 The formality of set text, the photographic image, and the decorative "flavor" of the coffee are a perfect visual complement to each other. A rich, inviting aroma and mood are evoked by this effective contrast.

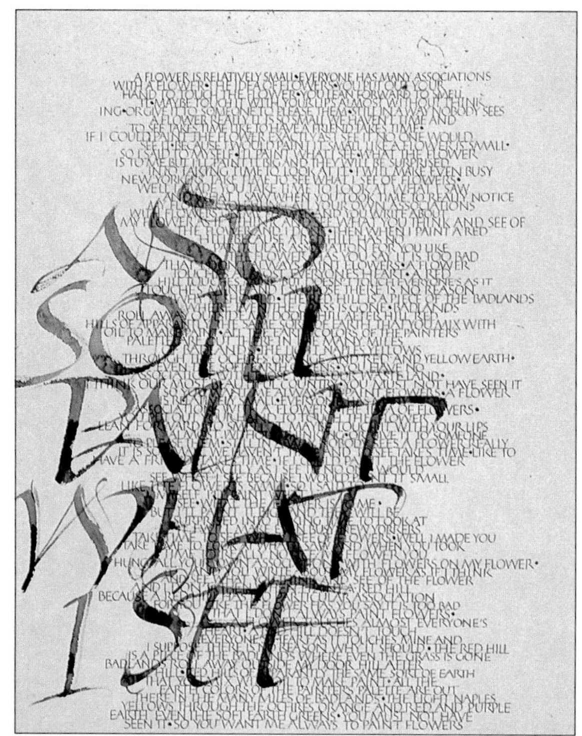

2

2 The evocative, flowing movement of calligraphic form is underlined by the smaller-scale, more controlled rendering of the background text. The tonal change and occasional text that can be seen through the translucent forms add subtlety to this work by Georgia Deaver.

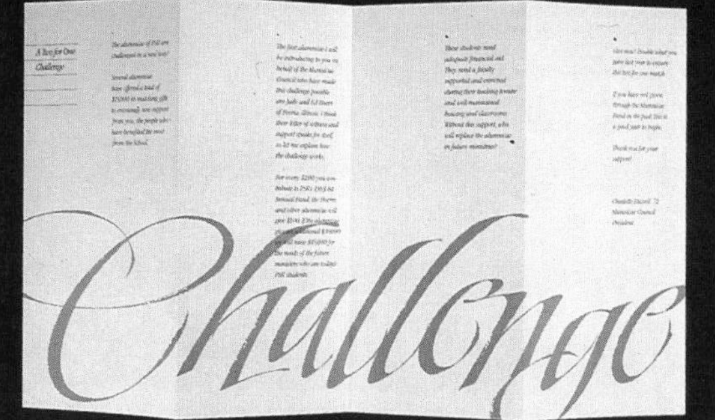

3

3 An example of the exciting contrast that can be set up between typesetting and calligraphy.

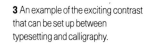

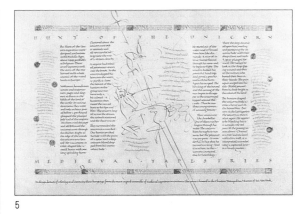

4

5

5 This design is full of varied decorative devices and contrast, ranging from the obvious to the subtle.. The overall textured quality relates well to the tapestry that is the subject matter.

"Mmm, a hole and it's empty, no wonder I felt light headed last night." He never once had seen a doctor or a barber or a treetrimmer & he was not about to start now. So he went around collecting rent with a hole in his head. The summer rains soon filled the hole with water. "Now I'll have to sleep sitting up. If I don't there'll be puddles all over my bed," said the landlord. Fish began to swim in hole though. The fish got big and the landlord looked rather pleased with all of the carp.

"Why now I won't have to buy another carp from the fishmonger. Less money to spend. More money in the bank." He came close to chuckling. The landlord looked forward to his afternoon naps in his garden. He always sat straight up so as not to lose any fish. And while he slept, the villagers enjoyed very peaceful afternoons. That was the only time the wicked man was not complaining. Tabo, the bravest boy in the village, snuck up to the landlord's old house one afternoon.

6

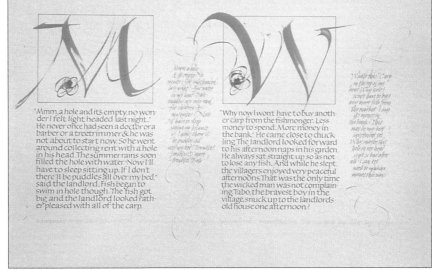

4 A type of calligraphic and hand-drawn sampler decorative in its contrasting content, styles, and arrangement. Minute dots of bright color add a visual structure and pace to the whole design.

6 Two vigorous letters overlook their box rules and head up more disciplined text in a spirited manner.

7 Two complementary colors are effectively a calligraphic shadow.

7

Graffiti

1 The overprinted signatures of students make a contrasting, decorative and highly relevant image in this poster.

2 A sense of urgency and directness is conveyed in this "window writing" used as a record cover design.

3 Another record cover design uses stencil-like letters and strong color to create the visual spontaneity associated with street art.

1

2

3

4

Undoubtedly graffiti is a contentious subject. In our cities graffiti messages daily inform, entertain, offend, or protest to a captive audience. Depending on your viewpoint, graffiti is either vandalism, a vehicle for releasing pent-up feelings, or a source of enjoyment. Since time immemorial, man has left his personal message in this way, surreptitiously scrawling or carving it into any vulnerable surface. Wanton damage to our urban environment can never be condoned. Yet graffiti has an intense energy and wit fired by rebellion, frustration, and self-expression. In recent years a slick, highly colorful art form has evolved from the earlier crude graffiti of underground movements, although it has moved away from the purely political and topical themes. The designs have taken on a vigorously decorative quality. Letterforms, shapes, and pictorial elements are fused into an overall dynamic graphic image where legibility can take a back seat and the working area can be filled to capacity. A wealth of graphic devices obliterate any remaining spaces.

Speed, vigor, and excitement are inseparable from graffiti art. This is because it is

4 & 6 Two different interpretations of the same "tag," or highly stylized personal trademark, of the graffiti artist. Full legibility has been retained – not always the case in this field.

5 This work defies recognition by the uninitiated yet its own visual language offers vigorously patterned shapes and a sense of excitement.

6

7 A highly decorative work with a curious three-dimensional effect created through the use of modulated tones and typography-based shapes, rather than color.

5

usually an illicit activity. Its clandestine nature is in itself a motivating force and dictates the type of equipment used: spray cans or broad-tipped markers – easily carried, effective, and fast. These tools of the trade produce a unique, fluent, animated, and well-integrated visual vocabulary. Fat outline letters overlap each other with stars, highlights, specially designed ornaments, and flourishes, and pictorial elements are combined to lend a mural-like, highly decorative, lively feel belying any illegality. The rich visual dynamism of designed mark-making conveys a great sense of enjoyment, which may well be echoed in the viewer.

There are uses and applications for this questionable street art. Urban locations have been designated for this very purpose. Record covers, posters, comics, and badges use this medium to capture the essence of a message and convey it in an arresting and powerful way. Individual letters can be quickly drawn in this direct style or more conventional ones modified and decorated in a similar style. Used in design contexts, graffiti provides an animated contrast and a powerful visual impact.

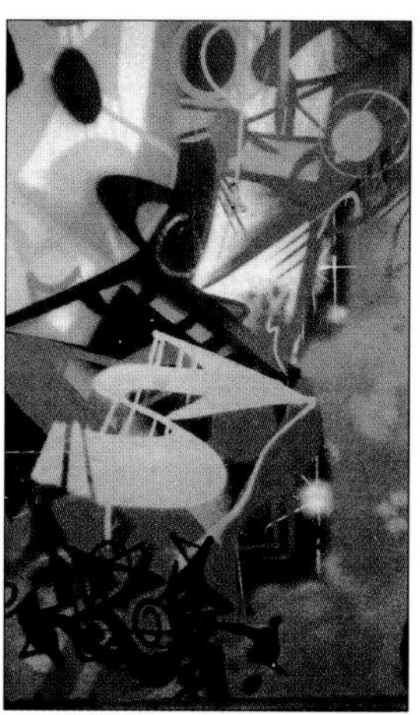

7

Ornament ◆ Typographic

A celebration of ornament in scrapbook form that shows the earlier delights of decorative typography, so evocative of their times in style and color. This heritage provides us with a rich source of inspiration.

ARMIES OF THE EAST AND WEST.
US

INGREDIENTI
ZUCCHERO - MANDORLE
NOCCIOLE - MIELE
OSTIE - ALBUME D'UOVO
AROMI NATURALI
PESO NETTO GR. 14

Mediolanum
Castrum
Galeazzo Maria Sforza
NOUGAT CANDY
TORRONE CLASSICO DI CREMONA
NET WEIGHT 1/2 OZ
PRODOTTO E CONFEZIONATO
DALLA DITTA
Dondi Lorenzo
CREMONA - ITALY
INGREDIENTS
SUGAR - ALMONDS - HAZELNUTS
HONEY - WAFERS - DRY
EGG ALBUMEN - NATURAL
FLAVOURING EXTRACTS
NET WEIGHT 1/2 OZ.

VENTE
au
Comptant

QUINAULT

pears'
Soap
OXO

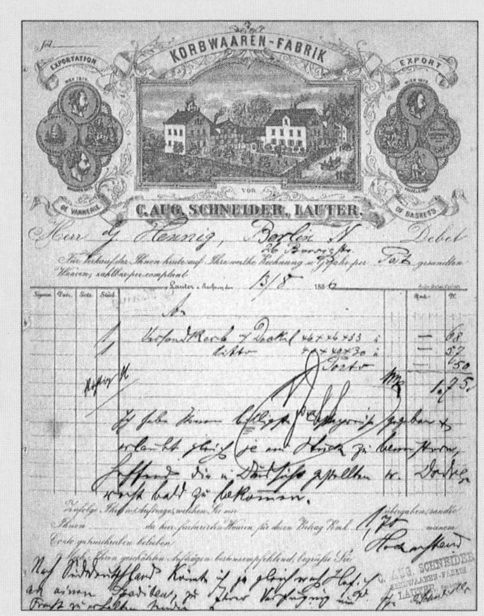
KORBWAAREN-FABRIK
EXPORTATION
EXPORT
C. AUG. SCHNEIDER, LAUTER.
Debet

A · JOLLY
CHRISTMAS

Ornament draws attention, softens, enhances, or enlivens. It suggests a richer, more leisurely way of life and is in itself a source of delight. We naturally turn to decoration and ornamentation to embellish our surroundings. Climbing plants disguise bare walls, others lend flourishes of color, and buildings and interiors support decorative details. Pictorial material, styles of type, and decoration can be used to evoke the spirit of times past. Alternatively, by looking around and borrowing from different areas and styles you can originate new and innovative designs yourself.

Alongside the formal letters, numerals, and punctuation of a type family exists a range of decorative typographic components. These include ornaments, pictorial devices, borders, and rules, all of which lend style and flourish to typography. Whether used extravagantly or sparingly, they can create moods, decorative focal points, visual emphasis, or signposts and can be used to enliven and clarify information.

ORNAMENT TODAY

Far from belonging to a bygone era, ornament is very much alive today, and finding new forms. Fashion determines a cyclical resort to pastiche, but a whole range of different ornamental styles is currently in commercial use. Ornament of today echoes the increased

1 A commemorative menu cover design by David Gentleman. The rich decorative feel is enhanced by the gold-stamping.

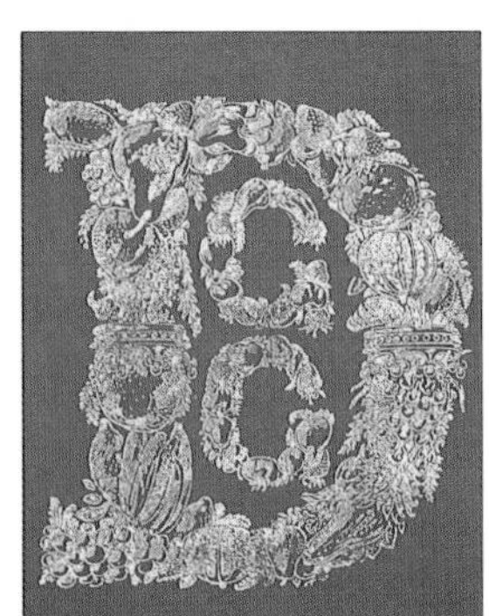

1

2

2 The decorative exuberance of the Victorian era is convincingly captured in this record cover design.

3 An example of how period styles can be interpreted to suit current tastes. In this design Trickett and Webb have successfully recreated the original mood of the product. Care must be exercised not to mix or use historical styles indiscriminately.

3

4

5

pace of life and rapid technological development. It has been pared down to the inventive use of shape, size, weight, color, and arrangement. Although we draw on our rich decorative heritage, current typographic decoration is more concerned with the interaction of elements than with the time-consuming, labor-intensive flourishes of the past.

DECORATIVE STYLES

The appearance, purpose, and appeal of any design are inevitably influenced by the period and place in which it is originated. Unique design styles have emerged from most of the major historical periods. Once rich and dense, now more open and geometric, they reflect the fashion and tastes of the times, with ornament changed accordingly. Not all styles survive the test of time, but those that have are evocatively mimicked or modified to fit the demands of today. Our rich ornamental heritage provides us with a wonderful source of decorative styles, material, and ideas.

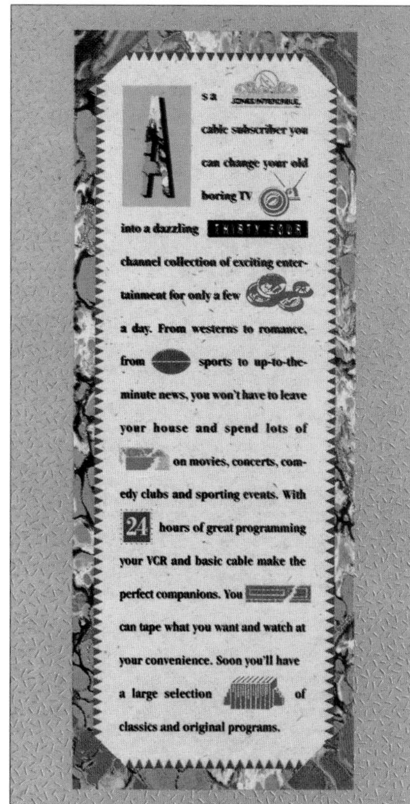

6

7

4 This logo recaptures the atmosphere of the 1920s and 30s in its borders and choice of type.

5 This range of packaging conveys the feeling of being pampered in its delicate yet effusive use of pictorial and typographic embellishment. Designed by Trickett and Webb.

6 Ornaments that are very much of today decoratively punctuate the text on this leaflet designed by Vaughn Weeden Creative Inc.

7 A tried and tested quality is communicated in this label. The color and typographic styles combine to give a feel that is both functional and decorative.

ne matutina pſalm⁹ Da-
uid. XXI.
Deus deus meus re-
ſpice i me/quare me
dereliquiſti/longe a ſalute mea verba delictorum
meorum.
Deus meus clamabo p
diem & non exaudies:&
nocte & non ad inſipien
tiam michi.
Tu autem in ſancto ha-
bitas:laus iſrael.
In te ſperauerunt patres
noſtri:ſperauerunt & li-
beraſti eos.
Ad te clamauerūt & ſal

one matutina pſalmus
Dauid. XXI.
Deus deus meus re-
ſpice i me/quare me
dereliquiſti/longe a ſalute mea verba delictorum
meorum.
Deus meus clamabo p
diem nec exaudies:& no
cte & non ad inſipientiā
michi.
Tu autem in ſancto ha-
bitas:laus iſrael.
In te ſperauerunt patres
noſtri:ſperauerunt & li-
beraſti eos.
Ad te clamauerūt & ſal-

tutino canticum Dauid.
XXII.
Deus meus / de⁹ me-
us/quare dereliqui-
ſti me? lōge a ſalute mea
verba rugitus mei.
Deus meus clamabo p
diem & non exaudies:&
nocte nec eſt ſilentiū michi.
Et tu ſancte habitator
laus iſrael/in te confiſi ſūt
patres noſtri:confiſi ſunt
et ſaluaſti eos.
Ad te clamauerūt & ſal-

1

1 The beautiful textural quality of this text is paced with decorative rules that visually extend both the line length and number of lines, creating an aesthetically pleasing and uninterrupted whole. This delightful form of typographic embellishment is rarely seen today, though it has a lot of potential.

2 Both the illustration and lettering are incorporated into the same woodcut in this title page. This results in the character of the lettering that forms part of the border blending with the tone and line of the image.

THE LEGACY OF BOOKS

Medieval books were richly ornamented, their pages decorated with painted borders, stylized illustrations, coats-of-arms, and illuminated letters. Contrasts of size, weight, color, and shape were already used to animate the page and provide visual enjoyment. A host of exquisite and sometimes ingenious typographic ornaments, borders, and rules made their appearance in the printed books of later years. Title pages set the tone of a book, combining typographic devices with figurative woodcuts or calligraphic flourishes. Chapters were introduced with a simple decorative numeral or initial letter and often closed with an ornament.

Within the text, stylized flourishes or decorative rules extended short lines. Paragraphs were introduced by an ornament still in use today. This form of pictorial punctuation provided relief for the eye and set the reading pace. It complemented the text and in no way detracted from it. A book could be enjoyed for the decoration itself. The legacy of books is an inspirational source of typographic ornaments.

2

3

3 The beautiful spatial proportions of this design for a catalogue cover are decoratively enhanced by the sensitive use of borders, rules, and color. The non-aligning numerals relieve the formality of the capital letters. Designed by Hans Shmoeller.

THE HERITAGE OF FASCIAS

4 & 5 This Penguin book cover (4 front and 5 back) illustrated by David Gentleman was the result of time spent drawing shopfronts, restaurants, and hotel kitchens in Italy. All the type is hand-drawn, giving it a very personal decorative quality.

During the Victorian era, display typefaces came into existence in response to the demands of the developing spheres of commerce and advertising. Shop and company fascias displayed the names of owners, manufacturers, and family firms in lively decorative styles. Early ornamented letters appeared in hand-painted, colorful shop fascias, tavern signs, and signboards. Gilded wooden letters and letters fashioned from wrought iron or cast in brass decorated the street. Commemorative headstones, carved wooden signs, etched glass, and panels all carried decorative examples of type and ornament. Some survive today. The originals are constantly revived and modified to suit changing fashions and tastes in materials and media.

Today, hoardings, newpapers, and magazines, television, posters, packaging, and labels all make use of decorative display type. In some cases the shape of the letter is retained and filled with tone, texture, pattern, or color. Elsewhere, the shape itself is decoratively modified to a particular style and enhanced with color. Very few rules apply to display type since its overriding purpose is to catch the eye and attract potential business.

4

5

7

8

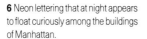

6 Neon lettering that at night appears to float curiously among the buildings of Manhattan.

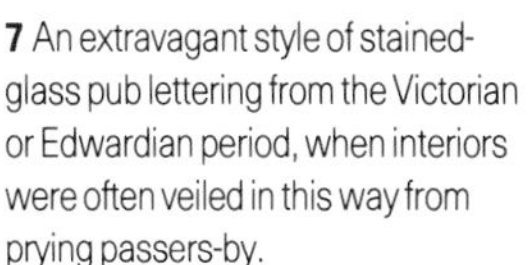

7 An extravagant style of stained-glass pub lettering from the Victorian or Edwardian period, when interiors were often veiled in this way from prying passers-by.

8 An intriguing three-dimensional sign for a bookshop.

6

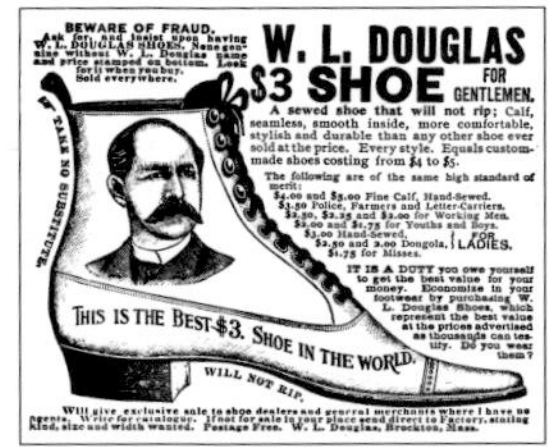

1

1 The wordiness itself of this early advertisement has an almost decorative feel.

2

THE VICTORIAN STYLE

The Victorians were concerned with decoration for its own sake, paying little attention to form or function. Theirs was an era of prolific exuberance, when ornamental eccentricities and embellishments abounded. Anything that could be ornamented was ornamented to the full. Ornament symbolized value. The Victorians drew on the whole of western heritage as well as on oriental cultures for their unprecedented mix of styles. Posters, playbills, tickets, packaging, and letterheads displayed an extraordinary exploitation of the shape, size, and weight of letterforms.

Engraving encouraged even greater freedom and a succession of new ornaments, and there emerged the elaborately decorated typefaces associated with this period. Decoration became so prolific that it began to disguise the original form. Victorians indulged in naturalistic themes, which they interpreted through intricately detailed motifs of foliage and flowers. Decoration often had a narrative content, depicting cameos of everyday life with fancy flourishes. These pictorial devices lent mood to printed display. Only book design, in keeping with the traditions of reading and handwriting, escaped the decorative fantasies of the times.

3

2 Here Banks's and Hanson's real ale poster deliberately uses ceramic tiles and Victorian-style letterforms to convey a traditional quality.

3 An ornamental mock-Victorian gold foil-stamped alphabet in paper strategically joined by delicate rules and ornaments. Letters might be used for individual decoration.

4 This authentic masthead of a daily newspaper is a typical example of the ornate style of its time.

4

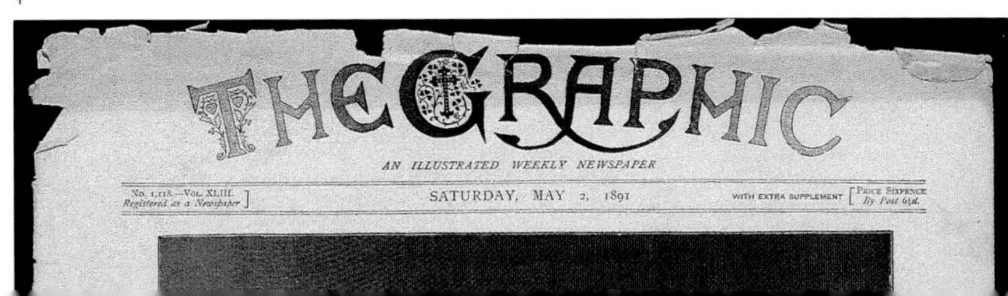
THE GRAPHIC

AN ILLUSTRATED WEEKLY NEWSPAPER

No. 1,118.—Vol. XLIII. Registered as a Newspaper | SATURDAY, MAY 2, 1891 | WITH EXTRA SUPPLEMENT | PRICE SIXPENCE By Post 6½d.

THE ARTS AND CRAFTS MOVEMENT

In the latter half of the nineteenth century there emerged the Arts and Crafts movement and, towards the end of the century, Art Nouveau. Although based on very different principles, they co-existed for a time. The Arts and Crafts movement despised the gratuitous decoration proliferated by the machine age of the Victorians. It sought to return to the simplicity of the Middle Ages, when art was craft and there was an honest enjoyment in creative work. Decoration enhanced rather than disguised designs. Naturalistic themes were modified and stylistically used in superb surface decorations. The result was a reformed, more flowing simplicity of ornament based on the purity of form. The decorative style of this school assumed a sense of beauty and calm in color and design that was prompted by the desire to be true to nature and materials. In contrast to Victorian frivolity, ornament and form were satisfyingly matched.

The Arts and Crafts movement reappraised traditional book design. Calligraphically derived text typefaces were closely spaced, producing a dark textural quality in contrast to the soft, gray tones of the Victorian page. Pages were heavily embellished with medieval-style borders and extensive ornamental woodcuts. Ornamental paragraph marks were used within the text to avoid any visual interruption. The result was flowing pattern and texture, where text ornament and border were evenly balanced and a delight to look at. Although significant, the Arts and Crafts movement remained small, appealing in the main to collectors and connoisseurs.

5

5 Ornament and typography evocative of this period create a sophisticated mood through both style and color in this music program cover designed by Cope Woolcombe and Partners. Note the decorative arrangement of the lettering in "and" and "the."

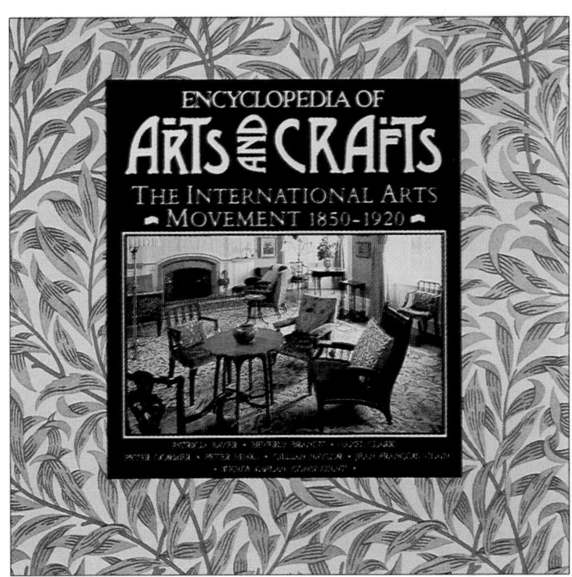

6

6 The overall background pattern of this book jacket designed by Quarto derives from a flowing, naturalistic theme typical of the Arts and Crafts Movement, renowned for its rich surface decoration. The lettering in the main title has the hand-drawn, calligraphic flavor typical of typefaces of that period.

ART NOUVEAU

This is a name given to a particular style of decoration that evolved in the last decade of the nineteenth century. Although its roots lie in the Arts and Crafts movement, it was internationally popular, spreading throughout Europe and the US. From today's viewpoint, there appear to be a great many similarities between Art Nouveau and the Arts and Crafts movement. But an important difference is that Art Nouveau was essentially a decorative movement based on art for art's sake. It had a strong, exotic appeal. Ornament was used in a very different way, and the decoration itself appeared to actually determine the form. Art Nouveau had a new, forward-looking style, inspired by sinuous natural forms.

Some of the designs for display type and the typography of this period reflect this idea in their oddly shaped forms, with their eccentric vitality. Flowing curves, sinuous lines, stylistic freedom, and a shift away from symmetry characterize Art Nouveau decoration. The contemporary interest in Japanese art was reflected in the fact that similar stylized lines and the use of space began to play a significant part in ornamentation. It was no longer necessary to fill every nook and cranny. Asymmetrical arrangements were decoratively used to enhance the sensual fluidity of the style. The gestural sweeps and turns typical of Art Nouveau lent themselves perfectly to the medium of wrought and cast ironwork. Wonderful examples of decorative lettering and ornamental oddities can be seen today in the wrought iron of the Paris Métro. Under the influence of Art Nouveau the poster first developed as a decorative art form.

2

2 Similar-styled lettering lent itself to wrought-iron work and can still be seen embellishing some of the entrances to the Paris Métro.

3

3 In contrast to the decorated letters in example 1, this plain, sinuous "S" emerges from an ornamental background which through its shape almost becomes part of the letterform.

1

1 The letters shown here are good examples of the controlled fluidity of line associated with the Art Nouveau period. They are in sharp contrast to the visual excesses of the Victorian period. This alphabet is the work of the French artist E. Mulier.

ART DECO

The highly stylized, fashionable decoration of the 1920s and 30s was in total contrast to the flamboyant embellishments of Art Nouveau. The pace of life had quickened. People were now more conscious of lifestyles and possessions. The bustling city, jazz, cinemas, and nightclubs symbolized modernity. New materials and technological advances encouraged experimentation in a variety of fields. Lettering in neon lighting and flashing signs appeared. Decoration no longer simply determined the form – it actually became the structure. Curving lines gave way to rectilinear forms and gridlike constructions. The new ornament and decoration made no reference to the natural environment. Simple, clean, abstract shapes were now used as part of the whole. Straight and zigzag lines, sun rays, and pyramidal stepped shapes, influenced by Cubism, were typical of the period. Display typeface designs showed a new vigor in their geometric simplicity of form. In some letterforms, dramatic contrasts were achieved with extremes of thick and thin stresses, while others possessed a geometric purity with even strokes. Balance and symmetry typified the age. Sharp, clean graphics carried a new stamp of modernity. Art Deco was associated with the modern quest for elegance, glamour, and luxury, a mood highlighted in the sophisticated use of gold and silver dusting, graduated tones, and bright colors.

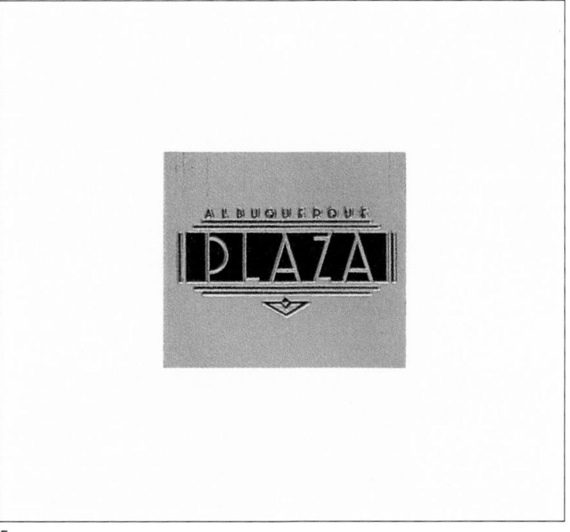

5

5 The geometric simplicity of this Art Deco-style logotype symbolizes the modernity of the period. Gold and burgundy hint at the glamour, luxury, and extravagance associated with that era.

6

6 Among the geometric influences of the period, floral designs also flourished. This display card uses bright, stylized blossoms on a typical black and gold background to advertise the floral perfumes of a French firm.

4

4 This wonderfully eccentric typeface, Bifur, was designed by Cassandre, the eminent poster artist of the period. He stripped the letters down to the bare essentials, concentrating on modularity and function. The letters assume a stark, decorative individuality.

2 Bold use of type, heavy rules, and strong color typify the constructivist art forms that made an appearance in the Soviet Union around this time. The diagonal layout of this broadsheet/ calendar designed by Dave King suggests the revolutionary spirit of the period.

3 A design in the De Stijl manner, taking as its theme the famous Gerrit Rietveld chair. It reflects the move away from naturalism to pure, logical forms.

4 This 1921 classic poster by Alexander Rodchenko combines strong geometry, bright colors, and bold lettering that reflect the shape of the sound. All three elements fuse into a dynamic pattern.

4

THE AVANT-GARDE MOVEMENT

In the experiments of the Constructivists, Futurists, and the Bauhaus, the twentieth century saw dramatic changes in typography and decoration. After the First World War these movements brought a new vitality to typography. In the wake of social upheaval new ground was broken and all the rules were disregarded. A radical new way of thinking reflected technological and cultural advances. Designs assumed a futuristic look full of optimism. New decorative techniques in the form of heavy typographic rules, photographic imagery, bold color, dynamic layout, impressive scale, and exciting use of space took the place of traditional ornament. The interplay between forms in space typified this period. Diagonal and vertical directions in layout reinforced the vigor and ideals of the time.

Heavy sans-serif letterforms, strong and clean, were the order of the day. Serifs were rejected, along with other conventional ornament. The Bauhaus even rejected capital letters in its quest for unity. It was a style of precision and modern energy, with no frills. Decoration was dramatically stark. Avant-garde typography made a powerful visual impact in its bold simplicity and had far-reaching effects on the nature and use of typographic ornament.

2

1 The linear nature of Tatlin's tower is mirrored in the style of the type, which fuses with the line in places to lend a subtle decorative quality to the design. Space and line were important characteristics of the Avant-Garde period.

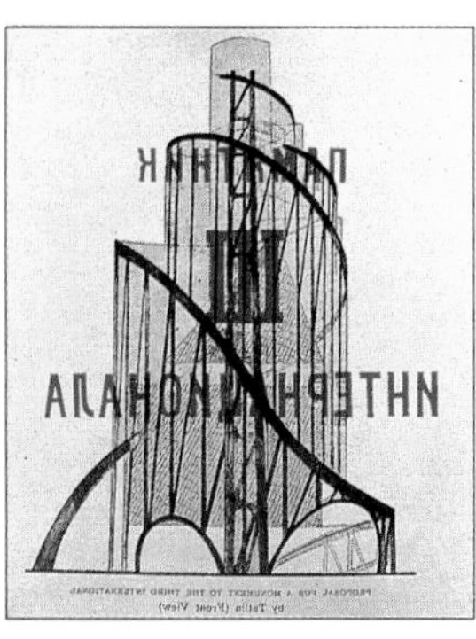

1

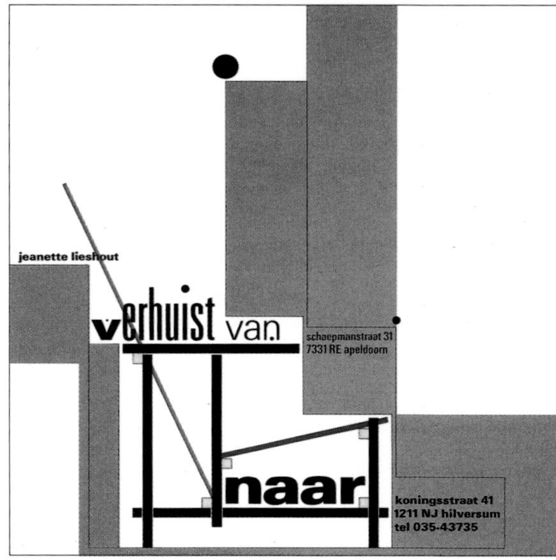

3

6 A three-dimensional typographic novelty typical of 1960s wit. This disposable child's chair in folded paperboard was designed by Peter Murdoch.

7 The 1950s enjoyed a popular interest in pattern and color. Abstract shapes, jigsawlike in character, and sans-serif typefaces were often playfully combined, as in this poster.

5

7

9

5, 8 & 9 No single style characterized the 1960s. Ephemerality and thematic variations made it an eclectic time. Form and color were used both expressively and decoratively, as in examples 5 and 9. The poster in example 8 is a visual extravaganza revealing the almost arbitrary use of modified styles.

THE 1950s AND 60s

This period saw a more playful approach to type and its decorative use. Form was frequently modified and reduced to strong, graphic imagery. Abstract, organic shapes and lines began to enhance the surface. Asymmetrically arranged bars and rectangles of color were decoratively overprinted with type or had letters reversed out of them. Typefaces of the day were mainly sans-serif, although several of the decorative Victorian faces enjoyed a revival. Decorative drawing, typography, and graphic shapes were whimsically combined in abstract configurations. Typography was functionally decorative.

The light-hearted trend in the typography of the 1950s continued and developed into the next decade. Letters, no longer strait jacketed, were interpreted figuratively. Decoration centered on the letterforms and their arrangement. Wit and humor crept in. Photographic images and type were innovatively manipulated and combined. There emerged powerful typographic images that informed and entertained simultaneously. Experiments with contrasts of size, weight, tone, and direction produced dramatic results. There was in design a new clarity and lively order, with an emphasis on symbolic elements.

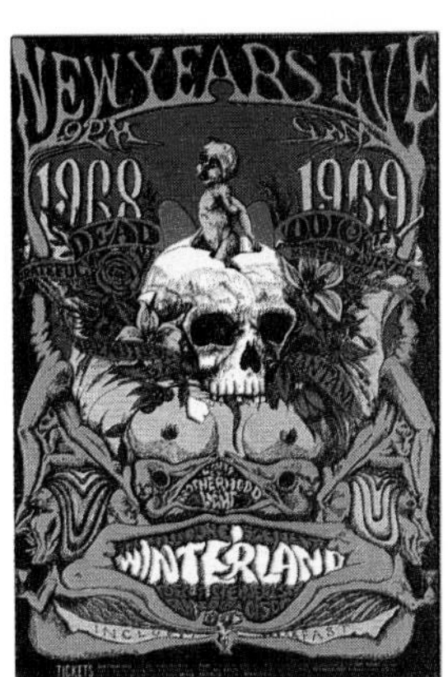

8

6

Rules and borders

3 Frans Lieshout's intriguing visual play with a recipe to be specially made in a Mondrian frying pan. Bold diagonal rules frame the central area, and lightweight rules form a framework for the decorative text, and at the same time capture the flavor of Mondrian's paintings.

4 Heavy typographic rules are inventively used to suggest arms or sleeves in this decorative poster.

Typographic rules and borders have been in use for many centuries. Like ornament, they echo the different styles functionally and decoratively in the way they are used. For example, unusually heavy, almost blocklike rules and borders are typical of avant-garde typography. An intricately ornate feel is more Victorian. A heavier, patterned quality echoes the Arts and Crafts movement. Art Deco promoted the use of geometric borders and rules contrasting in weight, while Art Nouveau generated curving borders and rules that wound their way around text and images.

1 This strikingly simple design makes dynamic use of rules to direct the eye to the text.

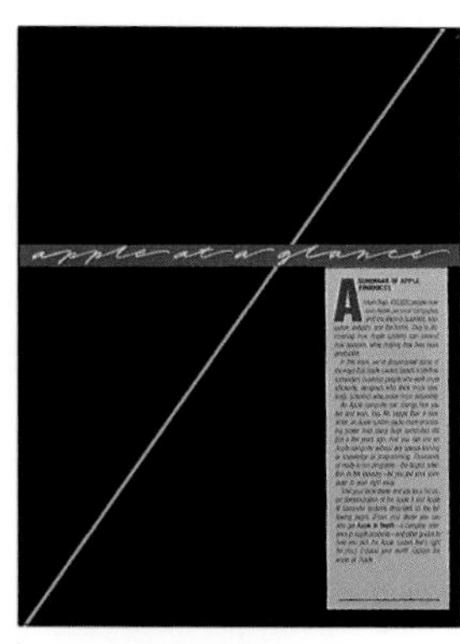

1

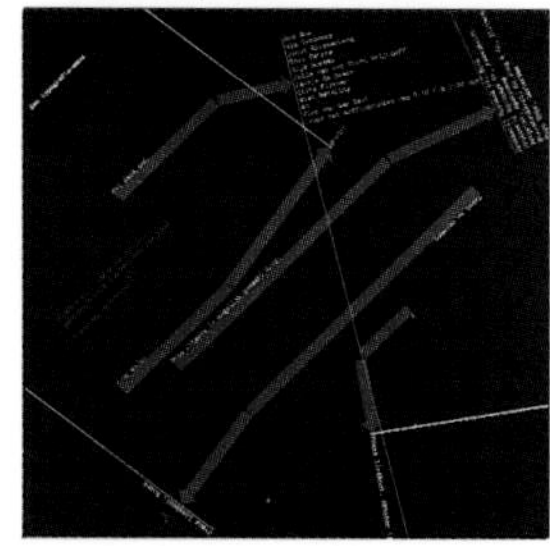

2

2 The innovative use of contrasting rules in this design by Total Design breaks up the surface, emphasizes the text, and lends an overall animated quality.

RULES

We tend to underline letters or words to draw attention to them. Printed rules are available in a range of weights and styles. Positioned underneath a word, either close to or a short distance away, they serve to emphasize. Placing light or bold rules above, to one side, diagonally adjacent to, or on both sides of letters and words is a dramatic way of highlighting. Rules can also be used in twos or threes and the space between them increased or decreased to give a variety of visual effects. Graduating the weight of several rules used together creates the illusion of perspective.

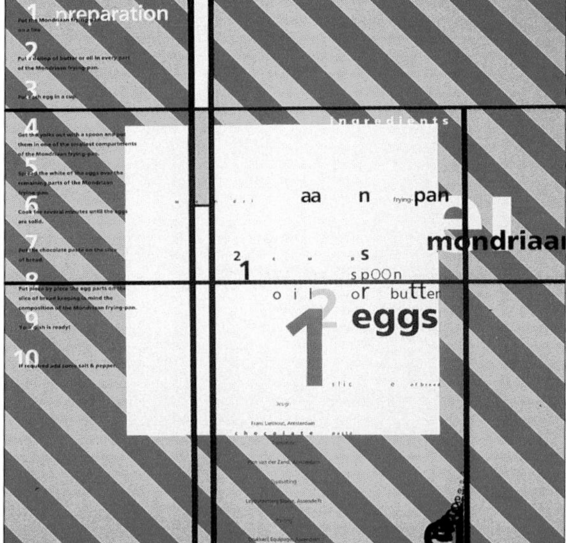

3

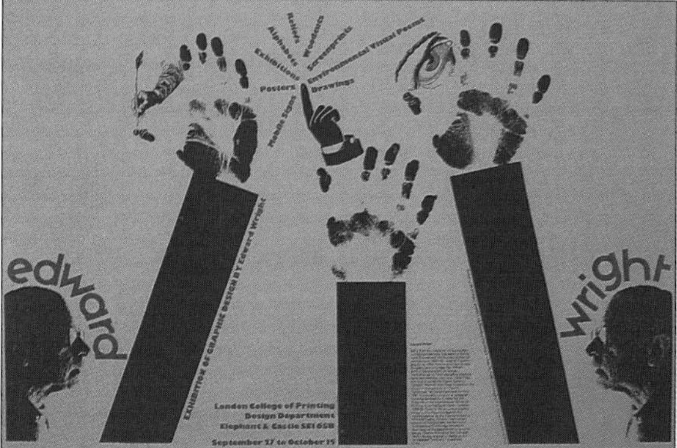

4

5

5-12 A collection of examples showing the decorative potential of rules and borders in both light-hearted and serious contexts. You can design your own borders from almost any texture, including type, color, symbols, pictorial imagery, or photographs. Almost anything can be used, whether hand-drawn, photocopied, or printed. Borders are most effective when they contrast with the rest of the design.

12

6

7

9

8

10

11

Tabular matter or information in columns can be divided up with vertical rules. Printed in a different color, they will add a decorative quality and make the information easier to read. Numbers and words can be linked with rules, while lines of text can be separated with horizontal rules. Names or words can be framed with a box rule. Magazines, company reports, labels, stationery, or any design where emphasis, division, or highlighting is needed, make use of rules. Fat or thin, black, white or colored, solid or tinted, rules are an effective way of functionally embellishing type. They might be roughly drawn, carefully printed, spontaneously painted, or torn or cut from paper. A whole area filled with rules could provide a soft typographic background texture for overprinting.

BORDERS

A more decorative form of rule, borders are ornamental by nature. They are often inspired by period themes and styles, taking the form of a modified motif repeated to form a linear pattern. Occasionally, a single motif will serve as an ornament on its own. Borders can be used at the head and foot of a page, as a decorative interval between sections of text or as a complete frame. Special corner pieces were sometimes designed to add ornament to a border used as a frame. Today decorative devices are often employed to evoke a particular period.

Pictorial devices

1

The origin of our graphic art dates from the pictorial representations of the Egyptians. Pictorial devices and ornaments tend to reflect the changing characteristics and styles of type design. Heavy, old-style letterforms generate a solid, rustic-looking ornament. Lighter and more elegant faces give rise to more delicate open images, banners, scrolls, and flourishes. Pictorial devices also depict real objects in well-designed woodcuts and engravings. Sold as accessories to type, they were used in early advertisements for millinery, clothing, footwear, and transport in seasonal ephemera, journals, almanacs, and calendars. Numerous trade cards were embellished with appropriately designed pictorial devices, flourishes, and borders. With these "instant images" words and letters could be illustrated, adding visual interest. Designs ranged from the frivolous to the serious, and subjects included animals, birds, flowers, fruit, transport, architecture, musical instruments, and food and drink. Motifs denoting rank, such as crowns, crests, or shields, were also available. Instructions and other information were highlighted decoratively with fists, scissors, telephones, and other symbols. You can enjoy drawing freely on our heritage of graphic art, adapting established

1 These charming little pictorial devices were used to enliven and illustrate text matter. A few, such as the Father Christmas, were suitable for two-color printing.

2 Here pictorial ornament is decoratively combined with type to form an embellished logotype.

2

3 A wide variety of delightful typographic ornaments was once held by printers. Today, dry-transfer systems offer an enormous, readily available range.

4 In this label design by Lewis Moberly decorative borders, ornaments, and illustrations are used to evoke a feeling of quality and tradition associated with the product.

5 Borders can be used inventively as a form of abstract imagery. This design by Lewis Moberly shows how effective this technique can be.

3

5

4

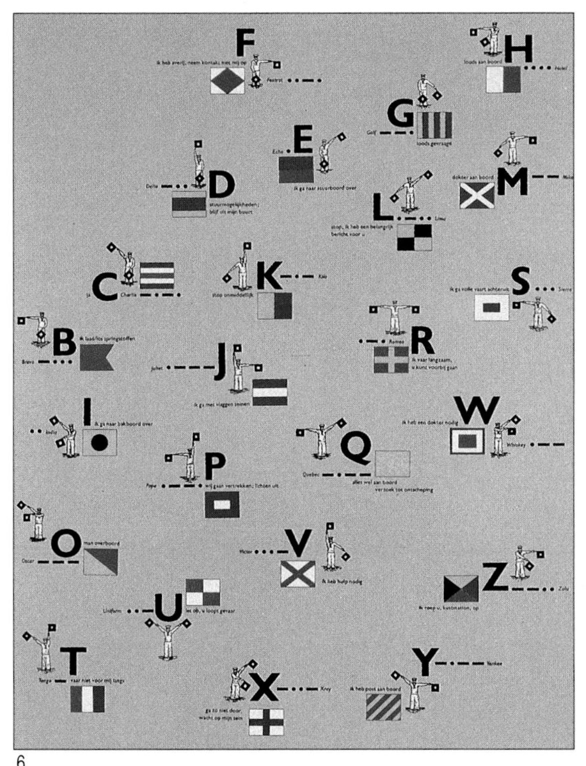

6

designs to modern contexts, or try originating your own ornamental devices.

Today book decoration is relatively sparse. The judicious use of tiny "bleeps" of color and shape can give visual relief. Magazine design offers exciting potential for the use of pictorial or symbolic ornament. It can be effectively used to enhance text, evoke a particular mood, to enliven headings, or soften the printed page. Bank notes, checks, and credit cards are embellished with decorative imagery. At the present time many traditional kinds of pictorial ornamentation are available and can be set alongside text type.

6 Letters and words can be encoded, and specific messages symbolized, by the functional yet decorative design of special flags.

7 Maps are a form of graphic imagery that lends itself to decorative use in this label and package design by Lewis Moberly.

8 The theme of this poster is intriguingly symbolized by a collection of early pictorial devices.

9 & 10 Bank notes make particular use of a whole range of typographic ornament and pictorial devices. Unusually, 10 is woven in silk. Both notes are of German origin.

7

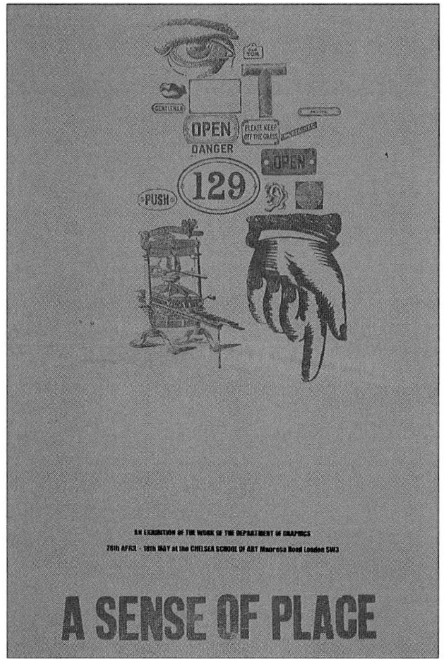

8

9

10

Punctuation and numerals as decoration

1 A collection of wood-type punctuation which, apart from its functional nature, has a decorative quality in itself.

2 A print taken from one of the above pieces. The "defects" lend an decorative texture to the surface.

1

2

The conventional use of punctuation in text serves to clarify meaning and control the reading pace. Essential as it is, it is visually almost unnoticed. By contrast, punctuation used at an unexpectedly large scale can act as a design element and provide decorative focal points. Used inventively, it can imply a variety of ideas, simply and directly. Quotation marks suggest personal communication, question marks invite a response, exclamation marks imply surprise, danger, or humor, periods visually conclude, colons, commas, and dashes offer visual pauses, and parentheses provide visual asides.

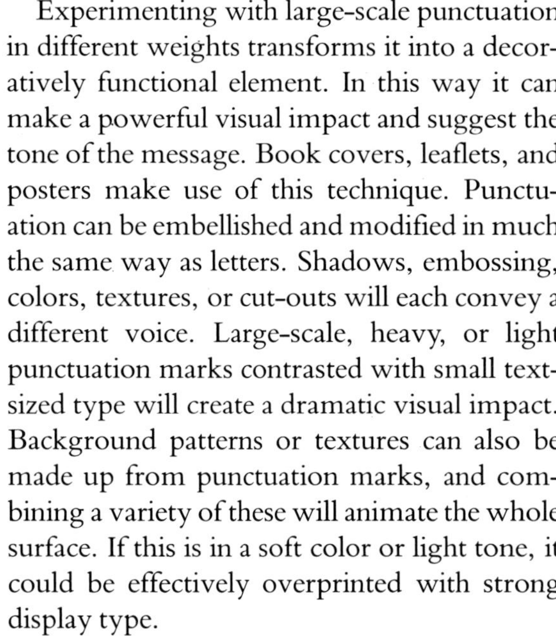

Experimenting with large-scale punctuation in different weights transforms it into a decoratively functional element. In this way it can make a powerful visual impact and suggest the tone of the message. Book covers, leaflets, and posters make use of this technique. Punctuation can be embellished and modified in much the same way as letters. Shadows, embossing, colors, textures, or cut-outs will each convey a different voice. Large-scale, heavy, or light punctuation marks contrasted with small text-sized type will create a dramatic visual impact. Background patterns or textures can also be made up from punctuation marks, and combining a variety of these will animate the whole surface. If this is in a soft color or light tone, it could be effectively overprinted with strong display type.

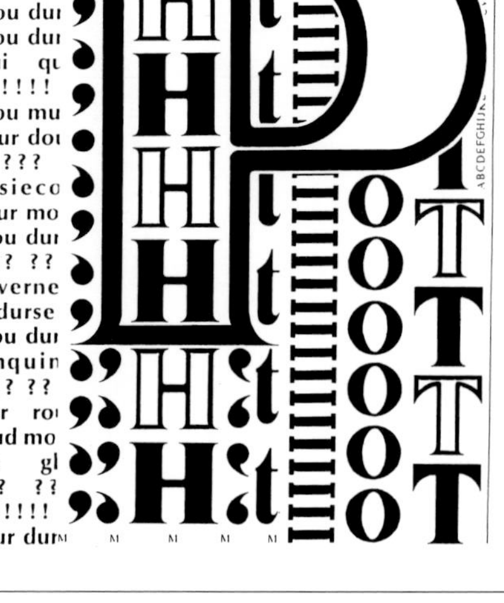

3

4

3 An experiment that explores the proportional relationship of punctuation and type, suggesting inner patterns and textures.

4 A most appropriate and witty yet decorative use of punctuation is this letterhead design by Dodd and Dodd.

5

5 A celebration of 50 years, each of which is symbolized by a decorative numeral.

6

6 A collection of clocks that make interesting use of numerals, designed and made by Paul Clark.

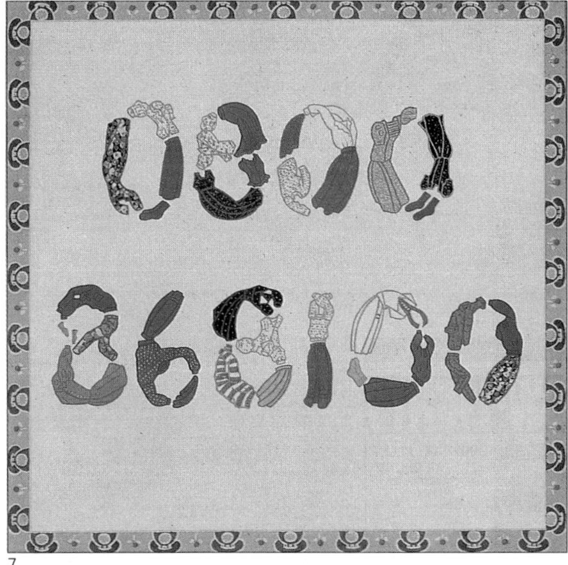

7

7 Decorative numerals illustrate the main copy line in this intriguing Laura Ashley advertisement.

8

8 An oversized three-dimensional birthday card.

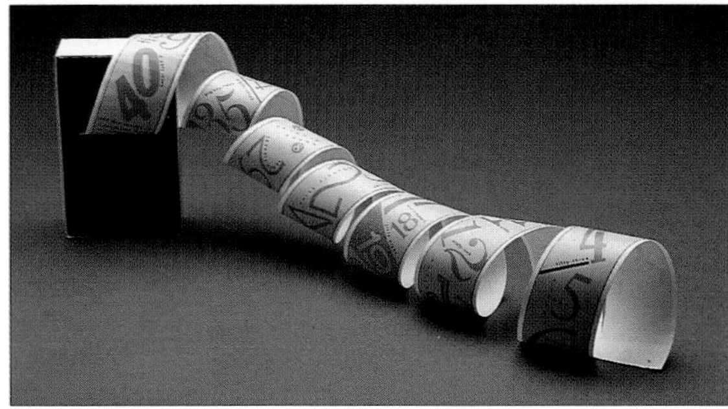

9

9 Another ingenious three-dimensional birthday card in which the years unfurl in a small decorative banner.

1234567890

10

10 Non-aligning italic numerals have a rhythm and decorative irregularity apart from their mathematical character.

In much the same way as large-scale punctuation, numerals can provide unusual decorative elements. Clockface typography offers good examples, from Roman numerals to digital figures. Watch and clockface designs change with fashion. In recent years, texture, pattern, and even pictorial images have decorated the background of watch faces. Numerals have been inventively used in a variety of scales, and in different styles and colors. They have sometimes been eliminated altogether or replaced with typographic ornament. Experiment with different forms of decorative numerals and typographic elements, remembering that the time is most easily read from the position of the hands. Different periods or styles can be evoked through choice of numerals and ornament.

House numbers are often embellished. Handpainted, shadowed, enamelled, carved, or cast, they reflect the style of the house or the taste of the owner. Certain types of numerals lend themselves to particular treatment: Roman numerals are handsome when carved, seriffed figures respond to painting, casting, forging, or enamelling. Sans-serif numerals can be fashioned from plastic, tubular metal, or neon tubes. Some typefaces carry old-style, or non-aligning, numerals, which possess a decorative charm in themselves. They have a visual rhythm similar to that of letters in words. Smaller than aligning numerals, they vary in size and have ascenders and descenders.

Numerals in books offer potential for decorative use. Chapter numerals can vary in style, be large or small, simple or elaborately embellished. Folios (page numbers) can be decoratively enhanced with rules, blocks, or bars of color or texture.

How to combine type and ornament

Integrating ornament into typography offers the designer great scope for the creative use of style, layout, and decoration. The context and the spirit of the subject should decide the style of ornamentation. Some contexts require coolness and reserve, others a more assertive or whimsical approach. Dipping into the "styles of ornament" section on pages 66-71 will give you the flavor of a particular period and suggest some ideas. You could indulge in generous decoration to evoke an opulent, leisurely air or create a more dynamic impact with simple geometric forms.

Ornament needs the same careful selection as typefaces if you are to enhance rather than confuse a design. The basic elements of composition – shape, size, weight, direction, and color – have to be considered and creatively orchestrated to produce a lively visual unity. How the typographic and decorative elements relate to each other within the overall design is important. These design components can be equally effective whether integrated or contrasted, once you have established the degree of legibility required. A grid provides a useful framework on which to hang apparently disparate elements. Flexible grids are used to coordinate magazine spreads and other areas

1

2

3

1 & 2 Label design and packaging often combine type with a variety of rules, borders, ornaments, and pictorial devices to suggest the essence of the product. The visual "tone" is set in this way. The visual interpretation in this design by Lewis Moberly conveys the idea of tradition.

3 A Christmas card that captures the festive atmosphere by the subtle use of type and ornament. The ornaments are kept in scale with the letters so as not to interrrupt the reading flow.

4 Type and image are sympathetically combined in this range of nostalgic packaging designed by Trickett and Webb.

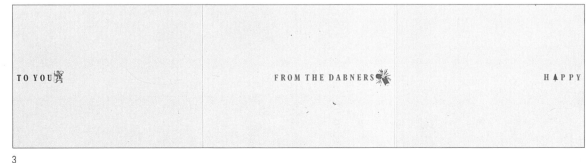

containing a variety of visual ingredients. Newsletters and magazine spreads can be decoratively enlivened with ornament, rules, borders, and pictorial devices. Large areas of text can be broken up into palatable pieces with typographic ornament. Within text, simple ornament can direct the eye or create decorative visual pauses, depending on the style of ornament used. Large lower-case or capital letters and numerals in Roman or italic style provide vigorous emphasis.

Ornamentation of many kinds can be created from dry-transfer materials. A wide range of ready-made borders, vignettes, colored tapes, pictorial devices, ornaments, and symbols are available. Your own designs could be cut from colored film or adhesive papers. Photo-montage, in which images from magazines or photographic prints are used in their entirety or cut up, can be used as an exciting decorative technique.

Today, many pictorial and typographic source books, free of copyright, are readily available to the aspiring designer. A great variety of instant decorative ephemera is also currently available. Individual typographic characters can be cut up and reassembled in inventive decorative forms. Color can be introduced to convey a mood or message.

PIN board
EQUIPMENT UPDATE
MAKE IT EASY
PERFECT PANSIES
STILL GOING STRONG
ASK KAFFE
QUILTS GALORE
25P OFF
PINS VOUCHER
LOVELY LACE
Living Crafts 89
4th 5th 6th 7th May
£1 off
LIVING CRAFTS
FLOWER POWER
FREE PATTERN
QUICK IDEA
TRULY GIFTED
PINBOARD 5

5

5 Magazine design makes exciting use of type and ornament in order to attract the reader's attention.

6 Ornament can be successfully incorporated into the type itself if the scale is large enough.

7 This elegant wine label design by Lewis Moberly shows how the restrained use of type and ornament can also convey a sense of great distinction.

4

6

7

Moving type ◆ Photography

In decorative typography, the camera and enlarger become inventive visual tools, departing from realistic representation. The lens provides a wonderful medium for creativity. In earlier sections tools and equipment have been simple, but photography requires certain technical, although still accessible, items of equipment. These include a camera and the use of a darkroom. With a working knowledge of photography's basic possibilities you will be able to exercise considerable control over your results. Experiment with the creative potential of this medium in order to manipulate type and image decoratively.

1 Time and space are effectively hinted at through color and the photographic manipulation of type, which gives added feeling to the message.

1

2

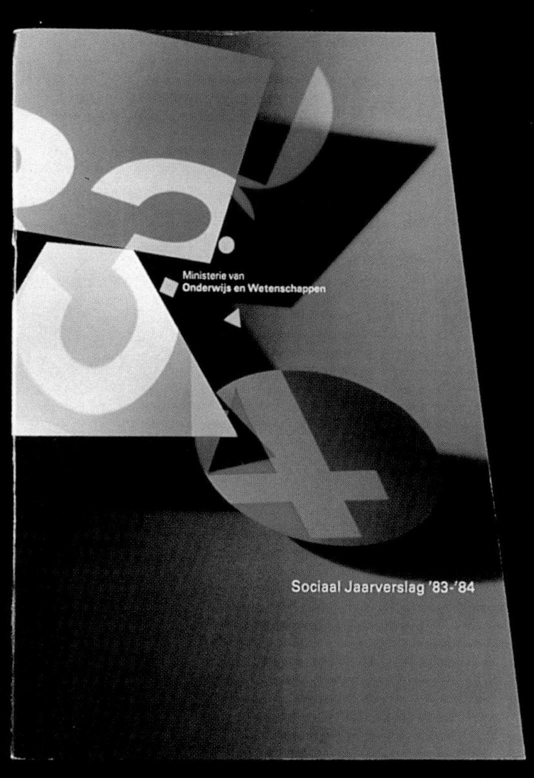

Ministerie van
Onderwijs en Wetenschappen
Sociaal Jaarverslag '83-'84

3

An easy and enjoyable way to familiarize yourself with photographic techniques is to experiment with making photograms. This requires only the use of a light-safe darkroom, an enlarger, light-sensitive photographic paper, and processing facilities. Start by cutting some shapes and letterforms from ordinary paper. Working in safe-light conditions in the darkroom, arrange your design on a sheet of photographic paper under the enlarger. Briefly expose it to white light. Then remove the letters and shapes and process the photographic paper. The result will be a white image reversed out of a black background. Using a paper stencil as an image will produce a black image on a white background. Gently moving the shapes during exposure will result in diffused edges. Double or triple exposures will suggest movement within a static image. Softly graduated or stepped tones can also be achieved by changing the length of exposure.

Paper masks can be used to create a variety of shadows on the paper while you are exposing it. If you curve the photographic paper when

2 Different layers of vibrant colors are visually reinforced by means of the cast shadows which are photographically captured in this work. Contrasting shapes of letterforms also help to visually separate the planes.

3 Abstract shapes, photographically projected type, and cast shadows combine in this unusual Ministry of Education and Science magazine cover designed by Frans Lieshout. Photographically projecting typographic images can produce exciting and unpredictable results.

4 & 6 This poster for the London College of Printing's degree show was designed by Sandy MacMillan, who creates layers in space through a combination of video, photographic, and graphic techniques. The text assumes an almost decorative quality in that it becomes distorted, wrong-reading, and shadowed. A dynamic sense of movement is created in the background. The three-dimensional model (6) was made and photographed for the poster.

printing from a negative, distorted shapes will occur. Double exposures of shifted images can be made, or one image can be superimposed on top of another to give intriguing effects. A mask of letterforms can be cut and placed on the paper before exposing the negative, resulting in highly decorative letters. An endless permutation of simple ideas can be explored. Playing with the enlarger in this way produces results that can be inventively incorporated into your designs.

The camera can be used to record carefully set-up three-dimensional designs and ideas. For example, letters might be floated in a tank of water and photographed to suggest movement, or shadows can be thrown across type to imply a third dimension. Used in conjunction with sound and animation film on television, the finished design sequence bears surprisingly little resemblance to the initial photographic image. Creative manipulation and mixing media can produce surprising results.

There is a wide variety of filters for the camera that generate highly decorative effects. The prism filter produces a blurred effect, the multi-facet filter lots of identical little images, the starburst several rays from a single point, and the diffraction filter vivid bands or streaks of light. All of these effects can be used to embellish type and ornament. Type can also be modified to dramatic effect by photographing it through different-textured or shattered glass.

4

5

6

5 An amazing range of shadows can be simply created and photographically recorded, through the controlled use of lighting and three-dimensional letters cut or torn from card. The end result could be combined with other techniques or used in its own right.

7–9 Michael Graham-Smith's opening title sequence to a BBC drama serial. Thematic images flow into each other. The typography was shot through a tank of water in still and agitated states. Colors and shadows were electronically added and the type and background digitally combined.

7

8

9

Phototypesetting and creative copying

1

It is perfectly feasible to achieve special effects with type by using commercial typesetting. Some knowledge of the various systems' capabilities is useful in order to be able to instruct the typesetter. Phototypesetting equipment allows you to select from a range of typefaces and create small or large areas of text, as well as originate display type. It is possible to specify expanded, condensed, backwards- and forwards-slanting, mirror-image, or reversal (white on a black background) type, either individually, in combination, or with conventional text setting. The results are highly accurate and pin-sharp.

1 Security printing set and manipulated by phototypesetting fuses function and decoration into a typographic texture.

2 An interesting new shape is formed when reversed, modified typesetting recedes into space and disappears downward.

3 This example shows how elements can be tipped backward during typesetting to create an illusion of perspective. Rule or border thicknesses are also adjusted.

6

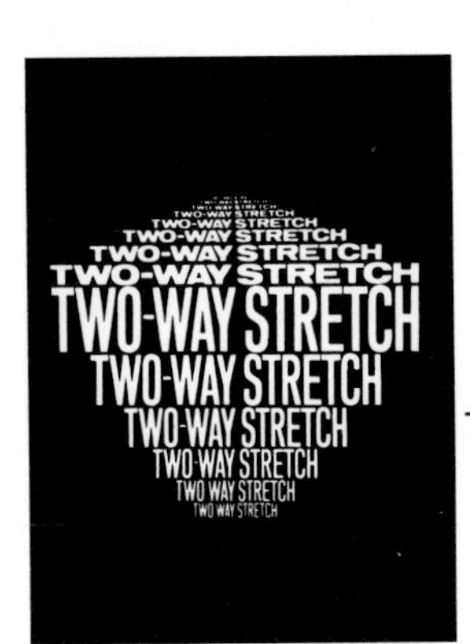

2

Water Quality International

4 A new journal for water pollution control professionals

3

4 Both uniform and totally free typographic images can be created by bending or distorting the original text.

5 Computer typesetters can condense type by almost any specified percentage, but care must be exercised when legibility is important.

6 A powerful illusion of depth or perspective can be electronically generated by the typesetter.

5

PHOTOCOPIERS: CREATIVE POSSIBILITIES

Black and white (monochromatic) and color (panchromatic) photocopiers fall into two main categories: those that use traditional optics and those based on laser technology. In the hands of the innovative designer both have great decorative potential. Unexpected and dynamic results can be achieved by placing images or letters on the platen and moving them during copying, to generate a curious sense of speed. In this way, copiers using traditional optics will produce a soft, blurred image, whereas laser technology will produce razor-sharp distortions. Designs can be built up by copying onto previous copies, turning, or moving the image around. Interesting graphic textures and patterns can be produced in several ways. For example, you might screw up printed paper, make a copy from it, then enlarge that several times over and perhaps re-copy it onto colored paper, tracing paper, or acetate. Mirror images can easily be made from flipped acetate photocopies. Decorative collages and montages can be designed directly onto the platen, then modified, added to, or subtracted from.

Both black-and-white and color laser copiers extend the creative and decorative possibilities. Many features are available at the touch of a button. You can control independently the width and depth of an image or letter. Letters can become extraordinarily tall and thin, wide and fat, or slanted at various angles. Whole alphabets can be creatively modified in this way. Most laser copiers will reduce type and image four times down and four times up, producing, for example, an image 5ft (1.5m) high from an A3 original. They also reproduce photographic images very well.

7

7 & 8 Two examples that show the versatility of color copiers. Wonderful ranges of subtle tones can be produced. Colors can be individually heightened or softened to produce decorative effects. Simple colors can be selected and colorways changed. Laser technology's generous depth of field allows the use of a variety of media, including cut-out papers, relief and textured surfaces, fabrics and film overlays, all of which offer broad decorative scope.

8

Typography in film and television

The concept of type in motion presents an irresistible challenge. Static photography gradually evolved into the moving images of the cinema, opening up a whole new dimension to the designer/typographer. Typography in motion means seeing and using letters as active rather than static components. In the early days of the cinema, decorative typographic skills supplied the captions that punctuated the moving pictures; rules, borders, and ornaments fashionable at the time embellished the narrative. The invention of the synchronized soundtrack provided a catalyst for experimentation with sound, movement, and animation.

Working with letters and words in this field means thinking three-dimensionally and progressively in time and space in order to exploit its full potential. The moving interaction of shape, size, weight, direction, and color calls for a keen sense of timing. Today, countless techniques are available to the designer. Combined with imagination, wit, and humor, letters and images can be subjected to amazing contortions. Extraordinary visual metamorphoses can be engineered in which abstract lines or shapes can be transformed electronically into letters and words. Typographic patterns can be animated and manipulated into messages. Symphonies of words can be decoratively orchestrated by the inventive designer.

1-6 The outstanding student film "Amore Baciami," directed, designed and animated by Oliver Harrison, was inspired by an Italian record found in a London junk shop. It is a synthesis of typography, music, and film. The graphic symphony animates the words of the song using evocative typefaces of the 1920s and 30s and sixteenth-century calligraphic styles.

1

2

3

4

5

6

7

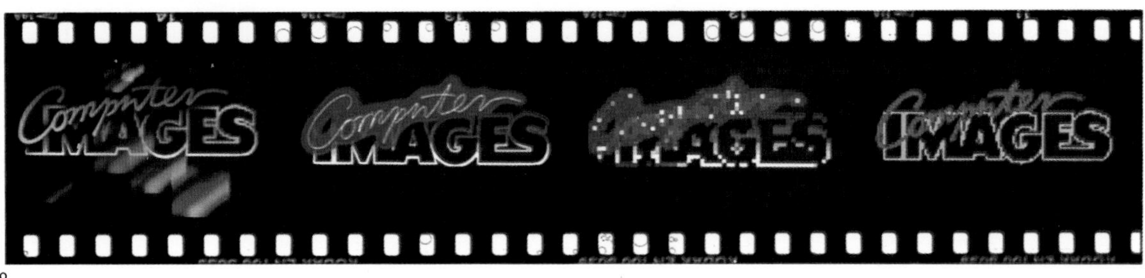

8

7 & 8 An exciting range of variations on a theme generated electronically by Graham Young. The almost endless possibilities and speed of the medium are only hinted at in these wonderfully decorative images. Hand-originated equivalents would be extremely labor-intensive, though not impossible.

The computer has revolutionized the world of moving type and image in film and television. An essential part of today's visually orientated society, computers provide the designer with a versatile labor- and time-saving workhorse with huge storage and rapid retrieval facilities. This ever-evolving technology demands an open-minded and inventive approach. No matter how sophisticated the system, it can never dress up a poor idea.

Most designers today use some form of electronic media, but this should never become an end in itself. To get the most out of it, you need at least a basic understanding of what a computer can and cannot do. Then, almost limitless horizons open up. Typefaces, textures, images, shapes, the illusion of a third dimension, and rich color palettes are instantly accessible through a keyboard, electronic tablet, and stylus. This comprehensive range of automated facilities makes for individuality of design and experimentation, lending freshness and vitality to decorative typography. The imagination sets the only real limits. Film titles, television graphics, and advertising, children's films, and advance publicity of programs all make extensive use of computer animation.

In the last decade, audiences the world over have been exposed to an innovative presentation of words and images on the screen. Surreal and dreamlike images are created. Textured letters that radiate, glitter, and reflect soar through time and space. Shapes, images, and letters zoom towards the viewer, apparently from nowhere, twisting, turning, fusing together, dispersing, and reassembling into new forms. These dazzling decorative forms and effects, in an incredible array of colors and textures, rush across the screen in seconds, designed to make a memorable impression, both informing and entertaining the audience.

Highly sophisticated equipment is needed to achieve such effects and is best approached with an idea of what you want from it. Different techniques are sometimes combined into a variety of persuasive styles. You can add decorative finishes to type, such as embossing,

1-3 Examples of the kind of stimulating thematic variations that can be achieved with electronic media. Freed from the conventional, static printed page, the potential of type can be re-evaluated from a new standpoint. It can be modelled in space, moved and rotated, and subjected to an amazing range of graphic effects. Computers, film, and television add a totally new dimension to the use of letters as decorative, dynamic shapes.

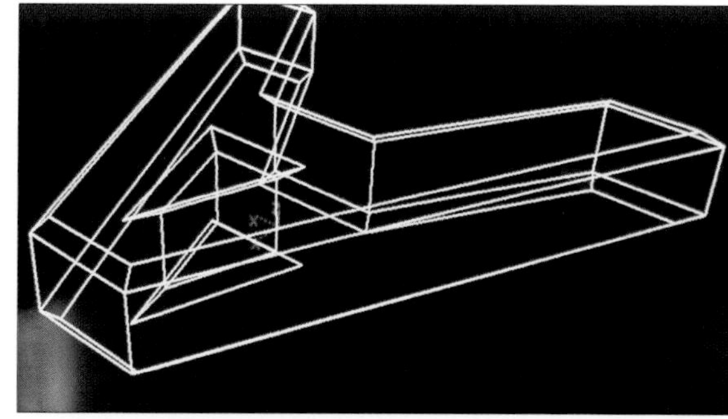

1

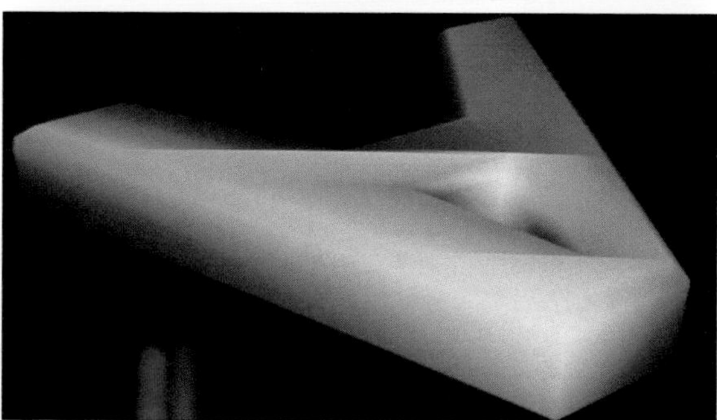

2

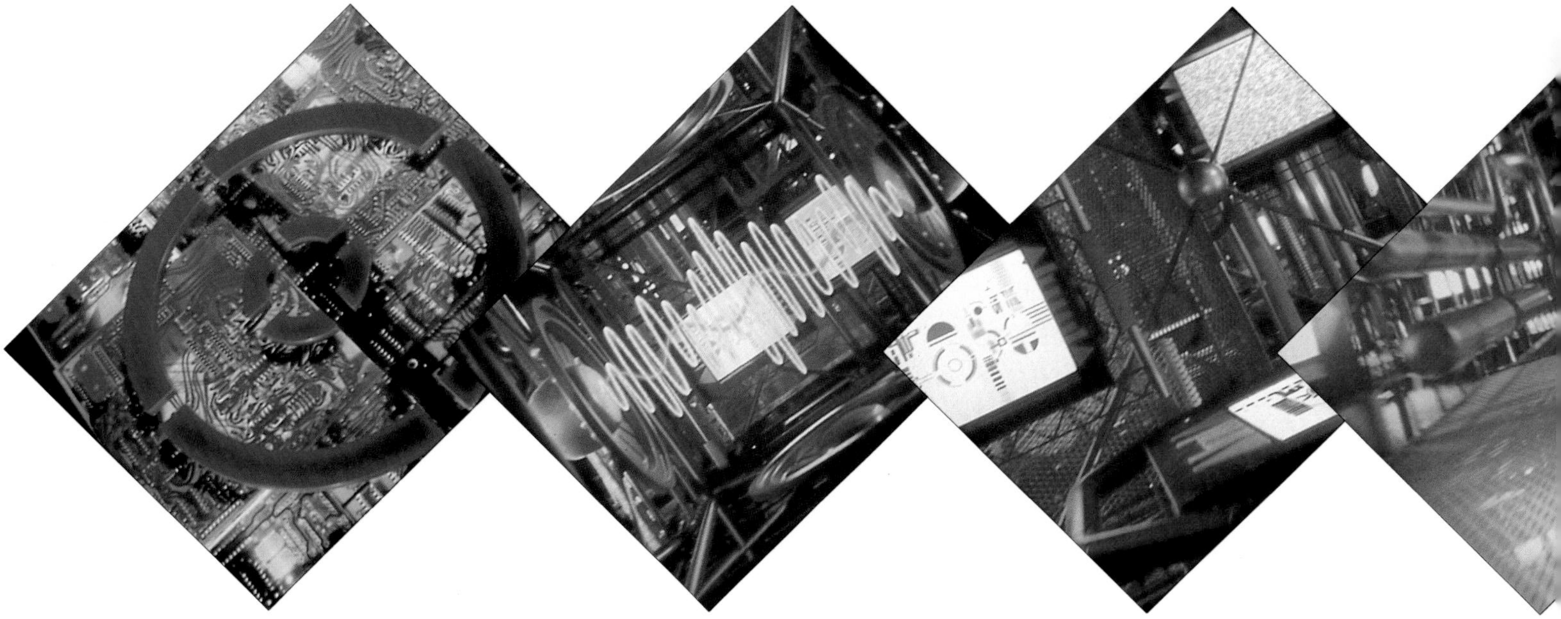

4

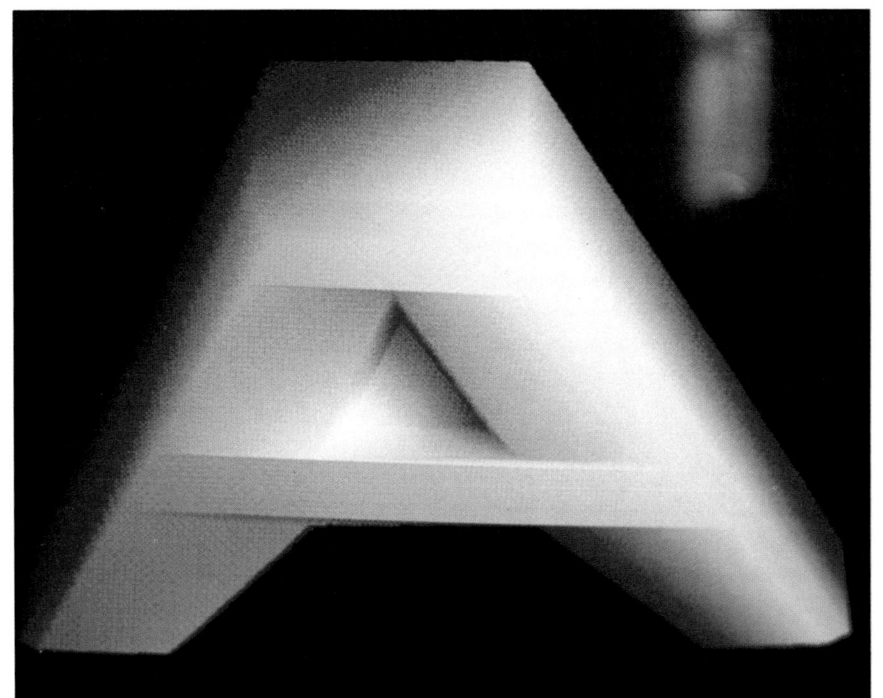

3

graduated color, shadows, and highlights. Images and type, graphic displays, live images, photographs, drawings, colors, textures, perspective, light, movement, sequences, and sound can be generated. You can select and mix these to create the required visual impact and mood. Designs must be strong enough to communicate ideas and at the same time be intriguing enough to hold the viewer's attention.

4 This BBC title sequence was designed by Margaret Horrocks to celebrate the 25th anniversary of "Top of the Pops." The sequence was shot using a snorkel lens on the motion-control camera. The lens was pointed down inside an elaborate model of corridors and mazes surrounded by front-silvered mirrors to create the illusion of continuity in all directions. The cyclical movement of the logo was animated by hand. The final logo was a model which used typically vivid computer-generated colors. The typographic theme of the titles was reflected in the inventively decorative variations on the "O" throughout the sequence and in the final model.

First, the ideas are discussed and an outline storyboard produced. Two- or three-dimensional ideas might be considered and tried out by the designer and animator. Action might be traced off photographs frame by frame (in a process known as rotoscoping) and re-filmed in an animated sequence. Hundreds of individually shot cells are used to create the final effect. For special effects, props and software are sometimes used in preference to more conventional artwork. Convincing historical contexts can be created by the computer, light, shadows, and textures added and elements made to move through space.

The television news, current affairs, educational programs, and the weather forecasts make innovative use of computer graphics and animation. Images and text are mixed or graphic displays superimposed. Decoratively informative charts combine animated graphic shapes with type, texture, and color. Meteorological symbols embellish the weather maps. Opening title sequences serve as visual appetizers, setting the mood of the program. Such topical programs demand high-speed preparation and have to be pre-planned. Long-life images such as television company logos and regular program titles offer more opportunity for experimentation. Today's world of film and television allows an endless permutation of simple ideas. Setting type in motion liberates the letter, merging graphics and typography.

1 & 2 Part of a rough storyboard and workings for the title sequence for BBC2's "The Late Show," designed by Oliver Harrison. The sequence is based on the idea of a definitive book of culture which, when opened, releases a Pandora's Box of contradictory definitions of the word – typographically embellished.

3-6 are stills from the finished sequence.

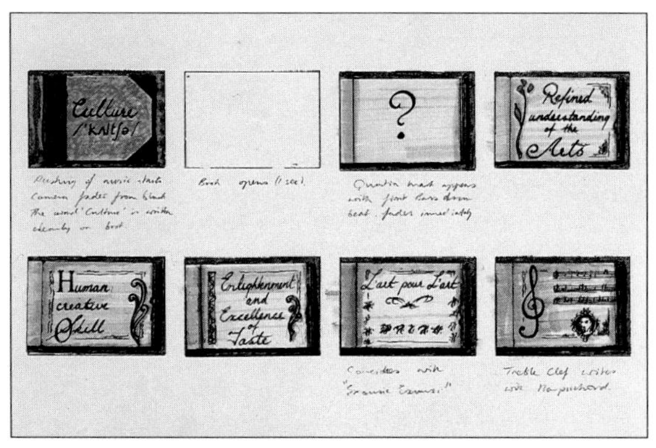

1

2

3

4

5

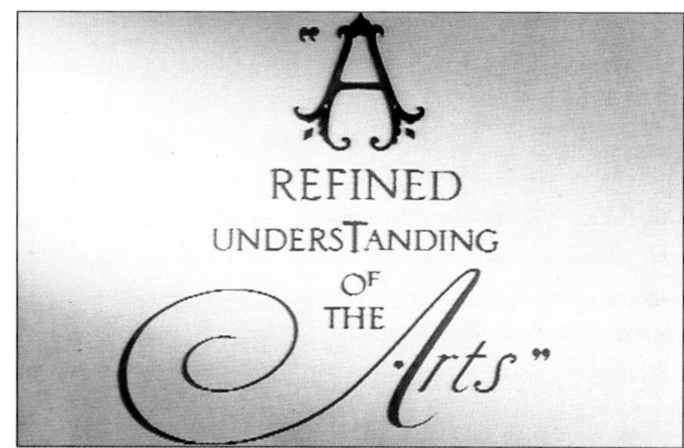

6

7

8

9

7-9 An amazing visual metamorphosis is effected in this BBC title sequence for "Chronicle" designed by Liz Friedman. An unusually large model was specially built and shot with a camera mounted on a motion-control rig in order to capture the mood and scale of the architectural "environment." This feeling is carried through to the highly relevant yet decorative interpretation of the concluding title (7).

11 A sample of the initial storyboard for the film. The alphabetical theme allows a typographic narrative to unfold decoratively in which the letters "perform" to the words, capturing the mood of the music and lyrics of "A – You're Adorable". Paper cut-outs were used for the final artwork for ease and speed of execution and their brilliant, opaque colors.

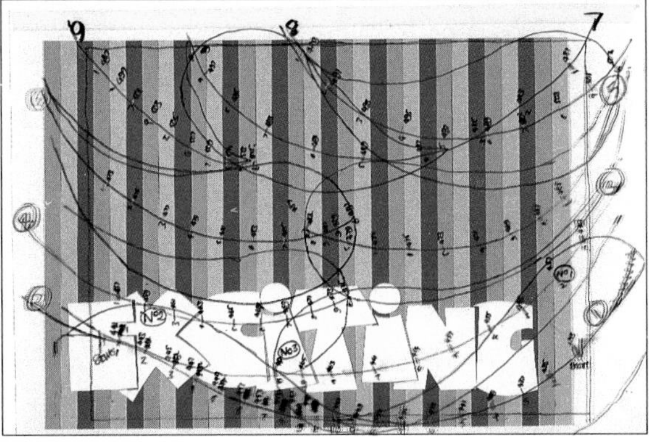

10

10 A cell overlay taken from an animated film designed and produced by Christine Büttner.

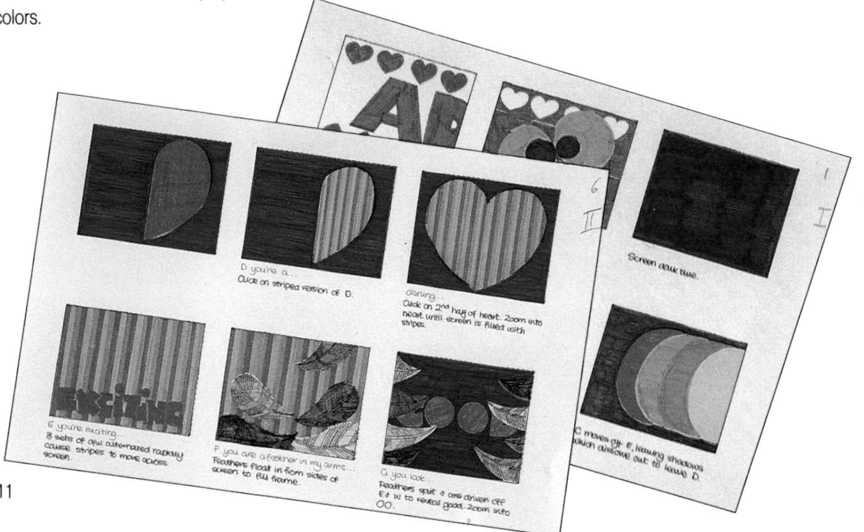

11

Desktop publishing

Decorative typography can be very effectively exploited with electronic media. Many designs produced on a computer tend to have a similar look, and the results can be dull if you work completely within the constraints of the software. As a creative designer you need not stick to off-the-peg graphics – be adventurous and create your own. You can throw letters into a three-dimensional format, create the illusion of perspective, slant characters backward or forward, stretch, compress, rotate, mirror, or flip them. You can design your own decorative typeface, editing the letters pixel by pixel, without spending hours redrawing. Normally very time-consuming typographic textures and patterns can be designed, modified, or overlaid. The freedom and potential offered to decorative typography by electronic systems are enormous. Experimenting with your software's capabilities and learning to evaluate the potential of "mistakes" rather than automatically discarding them will avoid the already familiar stamp of desktop publishing.

A system will include a personal computer,

1 & 2 Two exciting typographic experiments generated on a computer that give an idea of the versatility of this tool. However, try not to get caught up in a whirlwind of enthusiasm for the electronic medium. A keen visual judgement can in itself insure good design and visual impact.

3 This progressive modification of an alphabet electronically plays with the viewpoint, creating strangely decorative perspectives.

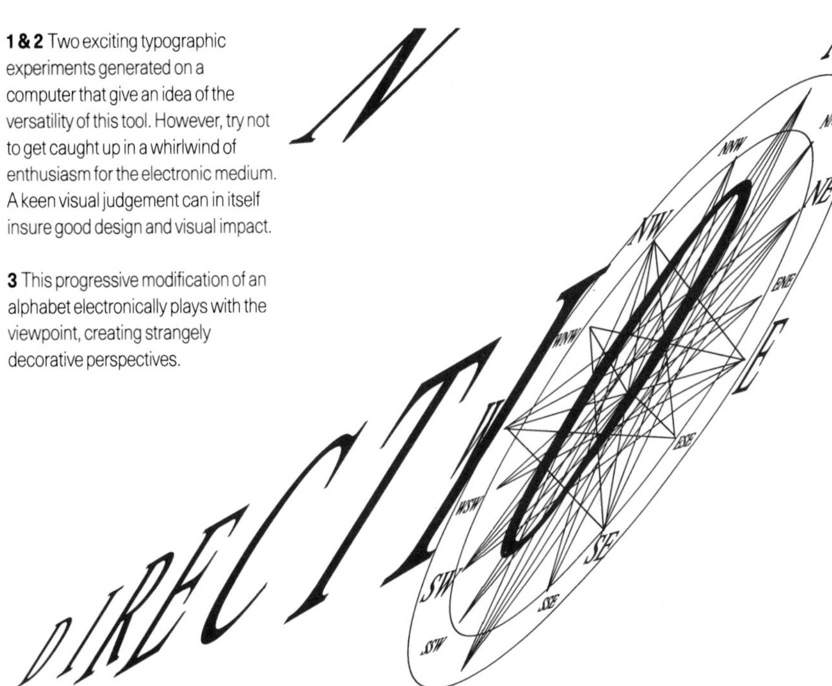

1

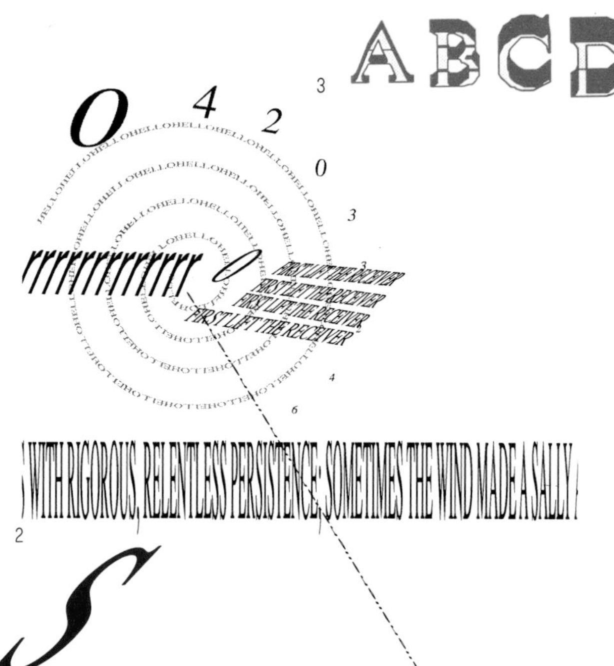

3

2

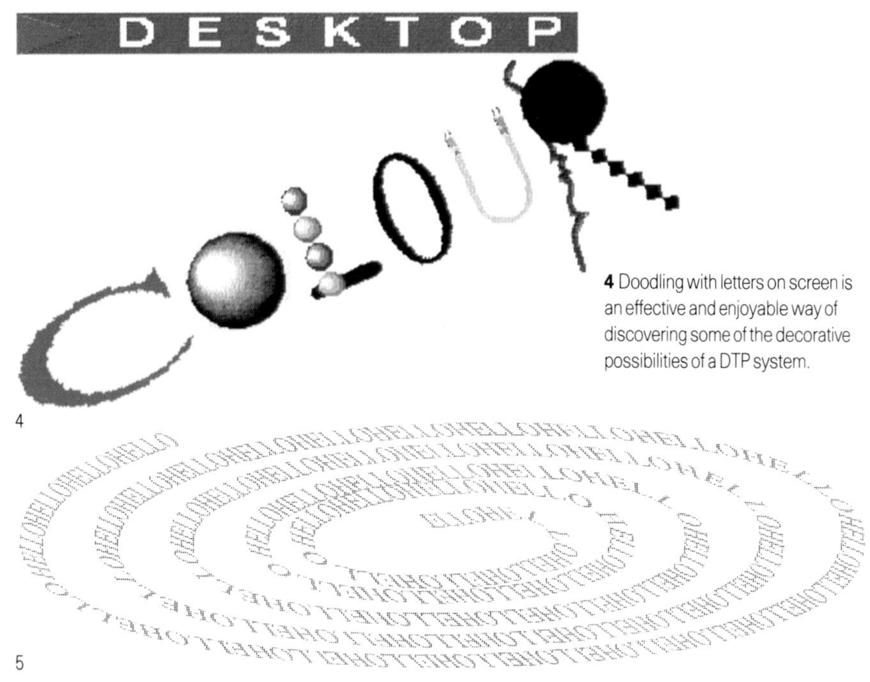

4 Doodling with letters on screen is an effective and enjoyable way of discovering some of the decorative possibilities of a DTP system.

4

5

software, and usually some form of output. The computer will have a black and white or color monitor, a keyboard, and an electronic "mouse." DTP software includes word processing, page layout, and graphics packages that provide a range of facilities for creating text and headings, drawings, diagrams, charts, and a wide variety of graphic effects. Output modes vary from a dot-matrix printer to a high-resolution laser printer, which gives a crisp, professional quality close to that of conventional printing. If the design is to be printed by conventional means such as offset litho, the printer can be linked directly to phototypesetting equipment. A scanner is an optional extra that allows you to introduce into your design other visual material such as photographs, found images, lettering from other sources, pre-planned diagrams, or charts and drawings.

5 An extraordinary sense of space and movement is created in this innovative piece.

6 Computers can generate the kind of vibrant, decorative effects used in this poster, which takes Energy as its theme. Textures can be overlaid, shadows added, colors changed, and letters almost endlessly modified quickly and efficiently. Designed by Rodammer Morris Associates.

6

Working with a DTP system gives you enormous flexibility and saves a lot of time and effort. You are not restricted to working at any one scale since you can resize your work very simply. One of the most useful features is that you can "copy" and "save" your design while you work on some other aspect, then recall the original design and add in the new element. Electronic media is forgiving with mistakes, which can be automatically deleted or relocated, erased, or airbrushed away. The electronic airbrush is much cleaner than the conventional type and there are no spatters or drips.

It is a good idea to experiment with all the basic drawing tools and the word-processing facility on your software before starting on a specific design project. Playing or doodling will help you gain the confidence to innovate type decoration ideas. Your personal computer has the power to produce hundreds of variations on any theme with the minimum of effort, but it can only do what you tell it to. Spending time familiarizing yourself with the standard facilities before attempting anything ambitious will minimize frustration. Whatever project you tackle, it will help if you rough out your ideas first. Disillusionment can set in when the system itself is expected to produce designs of its own accord. If necessary, your hand-drawn visuals can be electronically scanned into the system and then worked on. Design projects suitable for electronic publishing include invitations, greetings cards, small posters, stationery, timetables, forms, advertisements, cover designs, and newsletters. Starting with a simple task, consider the size it is to be, the kind of typeface you want, and any

1 The stepped nature of the pixels, combined with textures, gives to this greetings card a decorative feel evocative of hand-worked samplers. The example shows how even the characteristics of low resolution can be creatively exploited.

1

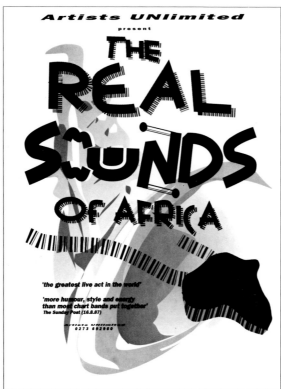

2

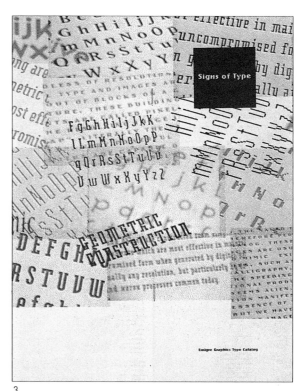

3

2 Rhythm, movement, sound, and cultural style are graphically represented in this lively poster produced entirely on a DTP system.

3 Zuzana Licke designed this highly decorative type catalogue for personal computers, which suggests that current technology is re-evaluating the traditions in which letterforms are still deeply rooted.

decorative elements or graphics you may wish to include. If the software does not carry exactly what you need, either create your own ornamentation or scan in other material.

A greetings card might require an elaborate initial letter, which you could "trace" onto the screen using a graphic tablet. You could produce your greeting message in an outline typeface and fill the letters with a variety of visual material such as images, textures, or patterns. Photographs, typefaces, drawings, and virtually any visual material can be introduced in this way. They can then be modified to fit your own design. The copying facility is an effortless way of creating exciting repeat patterns for wrapping-paper and card designs.

When you need to combine elements such as headings, text, photographs, drawings, and various typographic embellishments, electronic publishing comes into its own. Newsletters, journals, and magazines usually carry this kind of content. The tedious aspects of organizing pages and layout can all be electronically generated and saved in the computer's memory, leaving you free to experiment. Structuring type and images on a page is usually best done with the aid of a simple grid. The computer will allow you to move your different design elements freely around this basic framework until you achieve the desired effect. You can then lock them into position on the grid and save everything until the next stage. Any graphics, drawings, or roughs on paper can be automatically scanned in, cleaned up, or modified on screen before you integrate them into the final design. This ability to move from working to stored material is a tremendous asset. It allows you to gradually build up designs with almost total flexibility.

4

5

4 Here the idea of a grid has been decoratively interpreted by using names set in small type. The grid also serves to visually anchor the display lettering without overpowering it. The skewed type, size variations, and bleeps of typographic color subtly animate the whole structure.

5 Distortions such as those used in this letterhead design by David Collier can be achieved using paint and font-manipulation programs. Always start by evaluating the context of such effects, gradually building up your design. Text and pictorial elements can be added or rejigged, background tints and textures added at will.

When deciding on a typeface for copy, set a few sample lines in a variety of type designs and sizes to see what it will look like, how legible it is, what sort of texture it creates. Look at its tonal value in relationship to the overall design. Once you have selected the typeface and size, decide on a setting style. Most software offers flush left and right, justified and centered settings. Run a few lines out in the various modes to get the feel of the visual rhythm and reading pace. You can increase or decrease the legibility by varying the character, word, and line spacing, individually or in appropriate combinations. This automated visualizing is another facility that helps build a slick design.

Mastheads (the main heading or title style of regular publications) and logotypes can be originated in decorative or inventive forms by using the graphics software to modify existing letterforms. Headings and sub-headings can also be decoratively emphasized. Dropped or raised letters in capital or lower-case form could introduce opening paragraphs. Rules, boxes, circles, ovals, or free shapes can be used both decoratively and to direct the reader around the page. Pictorial devices, typographic illustration, punctuation, and numerals can all be used to animate the printed page. Tint panels and bands will highlight specific areas of print effectively. It is also possible to further

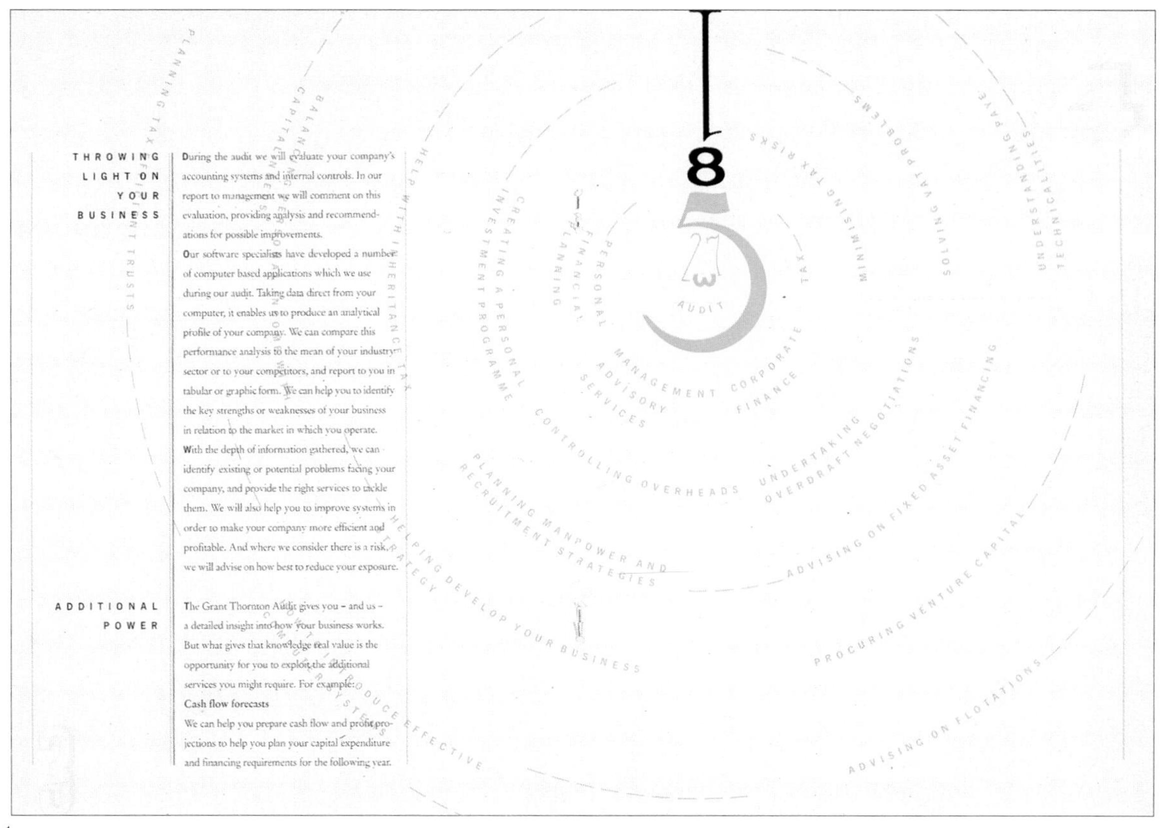

THROWING LIGHT ON YOUR BUSINESS

During the audit we will evaluate your company's accounting systems and internal controls. In our report to management we will comment on this evaluation, providing analysis and recommendations for possible improvements.

Our software specialists have developed a number of computer based applications which we use during our audit. Taking data direct from your computer, it enables us to produce an analytical profile of your company. We can compare this performance analysis to the mean of your industry sector or to your competitors, and report to you in tabular or graphic form. We can help you to identify the key strengths or weaknesses of your business in relation to the market in which you operate.

With the depth of information gathered, we can identify existing or potential problems facing your company, and provide the right services to tackle them. We will also help you to improve systems in order to make your company more efficient and profitable. And where we consider there is a risk, we will advise on how best to reduce your exposure.

ADDITIONAL POWER

The Grant Thornton Audit gives you – and us – a detailed insight into how your business works. But what gives that knowledge real value is the opportunity for you to exploit the additional services you might require. For example:

Cash flow forecasts

We can help you prepare cash flow and profit projections to help you plan your capital expenditure and financing requirements for the following year.

1

1 This delightfully decorative center spread, part of Grant Thornton's publicity by Addison Design, both informs and entertains. It shows how type can be electronically curved without distortion when legibility is essential. The "typographic light-bulb" is the kind of illustration that can be originated and scrupulously refined on screen with relative ease.

2 A newsletter cover for the book trade designed by David Collier. The masthead makes decorative use of size, as does the issue number. The information is clear and the typographic embellishment discreet. DTP design does not have to be visually "loud."

3 An alternative design to 2, in which weight variation and color are quietly decorative. Delicately ornamental rules separate the copy with their appropriately traditional book character.

PART TWO

Projects

This section shows you how to apply the principles of decorative typography explored in Part One. Each of the key areas is highlighted and related to individual projects. All five chapters provide background and source material. The projects are arranged so as to consolidate your skills as follows:

Project 1 A decorative alphabet.
2 Logotype design.
3 Typographic gift wrap and tags.
4 Menu design.
5 Label design.
6 Double-page magazine spread.
7 Newsletter cover design.

In this example from a sixteenth century initial letter design, an undistinguished letter form is enriched by the decorative border and the textured pattern applied to it. The curving flow of the letter "S" draws comparison with the organic shapes of stems and petals.

The first two projects are concerned with rediscovering letterforms as shapes and how they can be used decoratively. Project 3 investigates the rich potential of typographic pattern and texture. Projects 4, 5, and 6 show how and when hand-drawn letters, current calligraphy, decorative styles, and ornament can be inventively used for different purposes. Project 7 explains how to generate and apply decorative typography effectively using a desktop publishing system. Each project carries a summary followed by a synopsis of the overall project and how it might be resolved. Visuals are shown of ideas and how they might be further developed. Examples and analysis of unsuccessful solutions help to underline the success of others. The most appropriate design solution is then carried through to final presentation. Further examples show how a variety of designers have used the same principles in different contexts.

HOW TO TACKLE A PROJECT

This is one of many methods of getting started with virtually any project. It offers a sequence of activities that almost inevitably produces results, although several attempts may be necessary before you are satisfied with the end product. It is important to go through the complete sequence each time rather than start half-way through.

Identify the nature of the task. Is it a self-generated piece of work or is it in response to a specific set of criteria? Is it a one-of-a-kind piece or will it need multiple copies?

Determine its purpose. Is it to inform or entertain, or a combination of the two? Where will it be displayed or used?

Find an appropriate design vehicle. This might take the form of a card, poster, cover design, newsletter, label, advertisement, gift wrapping, or stationery. Consider the approximate shape, size, and proportions of the vehicle.

The message or copy. What is your punch line? Does it create the right impression or is it open to interpretation? Should it be serious or humorous? Should it be rewritten? Where text is involved, approximately how many words are needed? Does the information need ordering into a sequence? Is any editing needed? Could any unnecessary or repetitive text be discarded?

Themes and Ideas. Looking through Chapters 1 to 5 will start your ideas flowing. Once you have a few themes in mind, make a list of word and idea associations. Consider how certain colors, shapes, and textures might evoke a particular season, a decorative style might conjure up a particular occasion or mood, certain graphic elements could suggest thematic fun, movement, or intrigue. Working in this way allows you to make an informed judgement on the decorative potential of your ideas and themes. You will then need to gather relevant visual material for reference purposes in order to give your design credibility. Photographs, drawings, magazines, and books are useful sources. However much you intend modifying and experimenting with ideas, basing them on good reference will lend conviction to the end product. Working solely from imagination tends to give mundane results.

Work Method. Always work at a size that you find comfortable, making sure that it is roughly in proportion to your design's proposed finished shape and size. Working from your visual research, experiment with themes and ideas. It is important to think visually and freely at this stage and not worry about the finer details. Color should be intrinsic to your initial thinking and not merely applied at the end. Use colored markers, crayons, or paints from the start. When you have exhausted your ideas on paper, identify those you consider to be the most appropriate and evaluate how they could be further explored or refined. Focus on one of them and develop it further. Before bringing it to completion, explore all its aspects. Consider the shape, size, weight, color, pattern, texture, and overall arrangement. Even what seems like a mistake can sometimes provide exciting material with decorative possibilities. Finally, bring your design to a conclusion.

The first attempts are not always the most successful. If you are not entirely happy with the end product, work through the sequence a second or third time. Each time, start at the beginning in order to explore your various ideas in depth. Flitting from idea to idea can be frustrating and fruitless. No system is infallible, but this method of working will provide a good foundation. The presentation of your final artwork will depend on the nature of the design. If it is to be a one-of-a-kind piece, you could use a whole range of different media either singly or in combination. You could then photocopy the result in full color to give a professional look. When the job requires several copies, you will need to select a means of graphic reproduction from pages 140–141.

It is sometimes possible to combine different methods in simple projects. For example, a decorative initial or border cut in lino could be added to pre-printed text. A background color or texture could be screen-printed and images or type copied or printed onto it. More complex projects where photographs, text, ornament, and typographic embellishments are combined are better suited to offset-litho printing or an electronic publishing system.

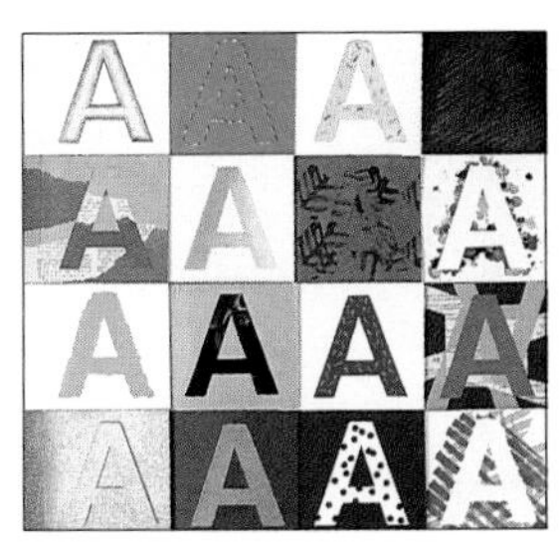

These three designs draw on our familiarity with Latin letterform. In each case the designer interfered, by graphic means, with parts of the letterforms, yet was careful not to jeopardize legibility. The border line between functional form and graphic treatment is fluid and needs objectivity.

PROJECT 1

A DECORATIVE ALPHABET

Design a thematically decorative alphabet suitable for display use.

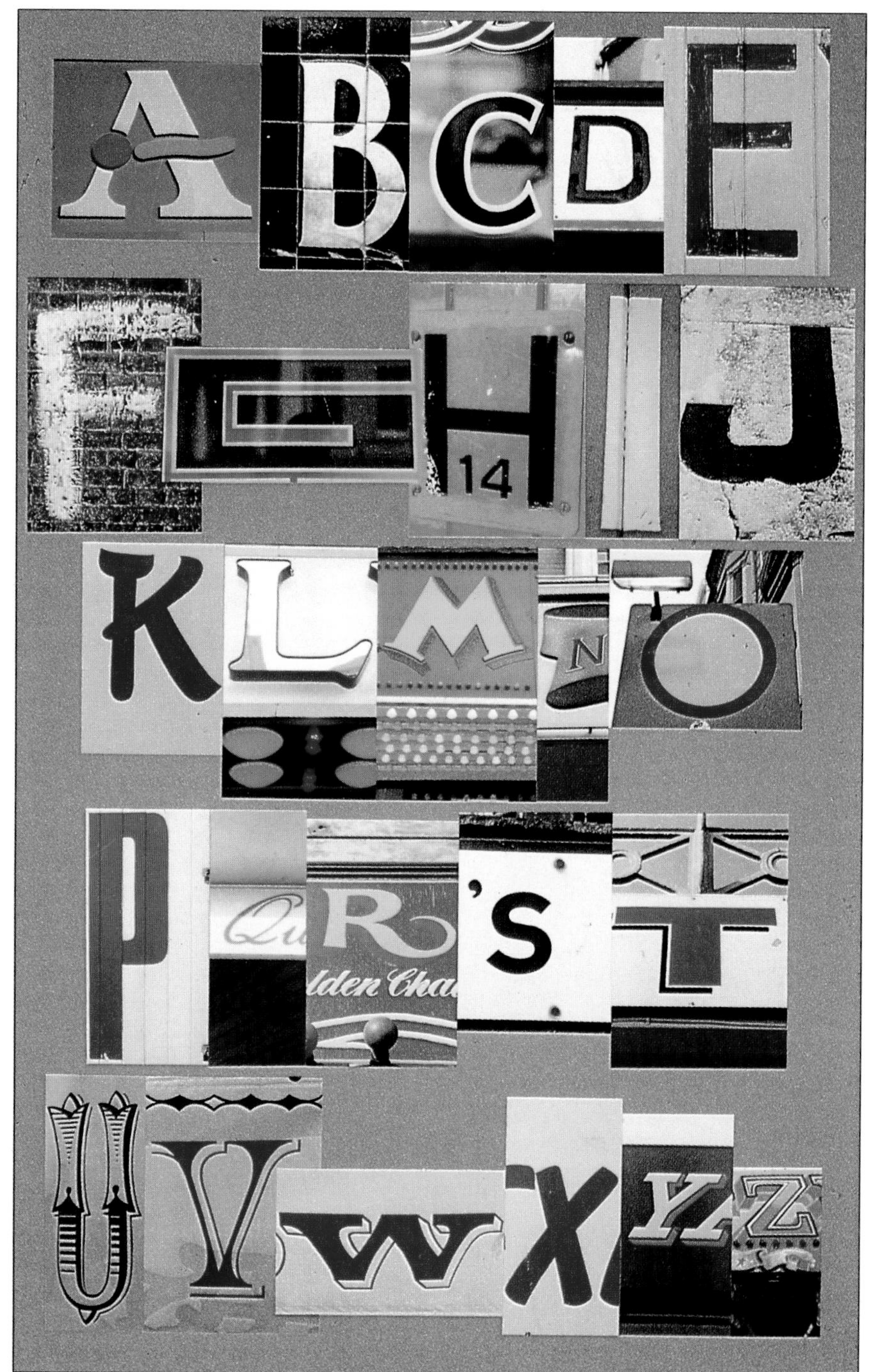

1

This project is linked to various topics discussed in Chapters 1 and 3, with particular reference to the section on alphabet design (see page 30). Using the method of working described in the introduction, try out a variety of themes. Start by listing themes that interest you: political, humorous, zoomorphic, anthropomorphic, environmental, color, fantasy, historical, celebratory, architectural, musical, and so on. Different media and techniques can also act as themes. For example, you could design an alphabet based on rubbings, collage, torn or cut paper, photography, drawing, or calligraphy. A particular medium might be matched to a theme in order to heighten its visual appeal.

Try out a variety of themes before discarding any. It is surprising how often the least likely themes can produce exciting ideas once you start thinking visually. Experiment with individual letters to see how they might be adapted in different ways to particular themes. Make a list of visual images relating to the theme. It is helpful to divide the letters of the alphabet into the following three basic "shape" groups. Wide letters: O, C, D, G, Q (all the basic rounded letters). Medium letters: H, A, N, M, T, U, V, W, X, Y, Z (all symmetrical letters). Narrow letters: E, B, F, L, P, R, S (all non-symmetrical letters). K, I and J are the obvious exceptions.

Once you have begun to generate a few ideas that have potential, select a typeface suitable for modification. (See Chapter 1, "How to create visual interest with different techniques.") Compare the shape of the letters with any pictorial material you have. Try to find a visual compatibility between the images and typeface. The size of both image and type will have

1 This lively High Street alphabet; made up of letters found and photographed in the urban environment, hints at the amazing variety of decorative type that is readily available as a source of inspiration.

2 Cutting letters from colored paper with a scalpel is an enjoyable way of creating a simple decorative alphabet and allows great freedom. The inherent irregularities of the letters lend an eccentric rhythm to the alphabet.

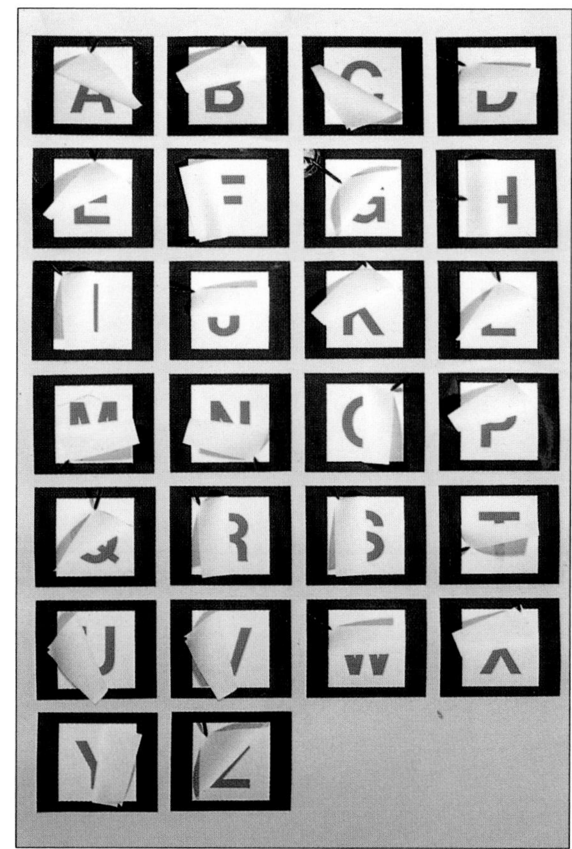

4

2

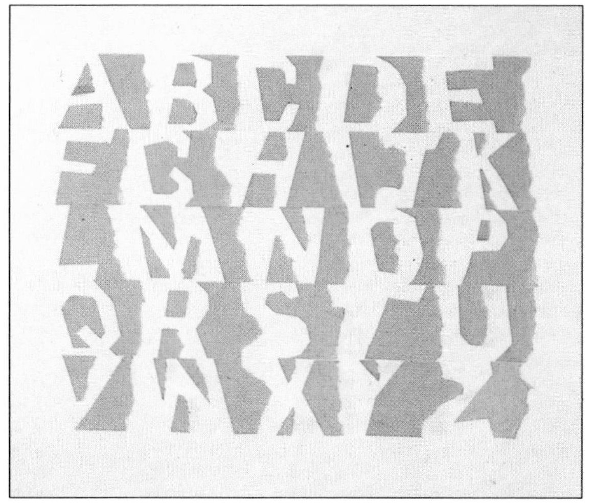

3

3 Counterforms and interletter spacing are creatively used to make a "negative" alphabet which is designed as a decorative entity rather than as individual letters. Cut and torn edges add a subtle contrast.

4 This intriguing alphabet was constructed three-dimensionally. It is based on the idea of revealing the printed image once it has been proofed. The design aptly captures the anticipatory mood of this process. Just enough of each letter is visible to make it recognizable.

1 This decoratively functional alphabet was created by Peter Gill for a furniture designer. It reflects the nature of the client's approach to furniture design.

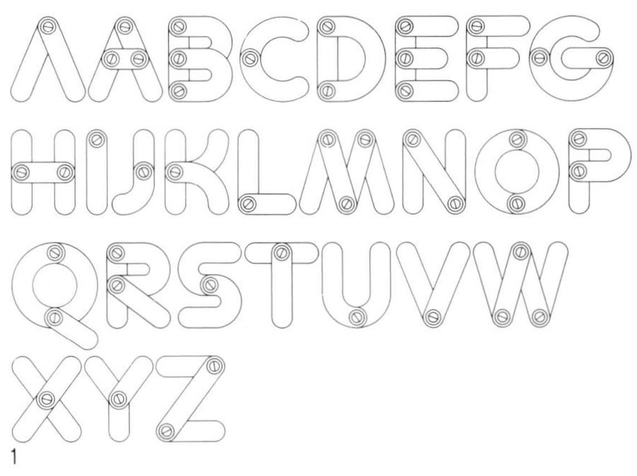

1

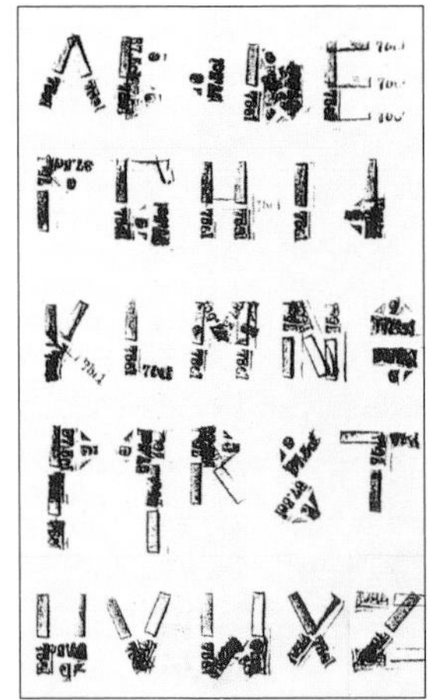

2

3

to be adapted to match up. This can easily be done with a photocopier with enlarging and reducing facilities. Make a tracing of one or two appropriate images and overlay them on different letters to test their suitability for modification. Never attempt to force an image or letter into an uncomfortable form. It is better to gradually adapt pictorial material, working on overlays.

Decorative alphabets can make inventive use of wit and humor or turn into typographic fantasies. Once you have successfully designed one or two animated letters, begin to build up a complete alphabet. At a later stage you could

2 Unusual decorative alphabets can be fun to originate from all sorts of unlikely media. An inventive, resourceful approach will prove fruitful, as this "rubber stamp" alphabet shows.

3 In this work by Pat Russell, scissors and colored tissue paper have been used to create this alphabet. The cut-paper technique clearly influences the design of the letters and throws up unexpected forms.

use them as initial letters or be more adventurous and make them up into a whole word comprising individual modified letters.

5 The hand-drawn quality of this end-paper design for example 4 sets up subtle movement, preventing the design from becoming mechanical. A gentle pattern with an overall texture is also created.

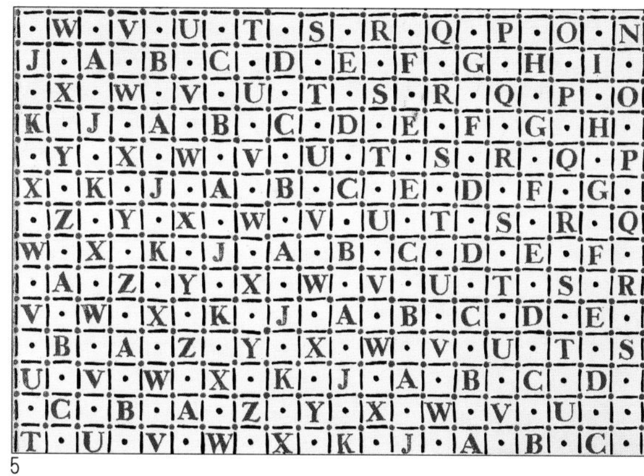

5

4

4 This beautiful book cover design by Christine Büttner reflects through the decorative title the delightful architectural styles and eccentricities of its contents.

6 The decorative character of pencil shavings has been put to creative use in this alphabet design. Relief and three-dimensional alphabets can be created from an endless variety of media.

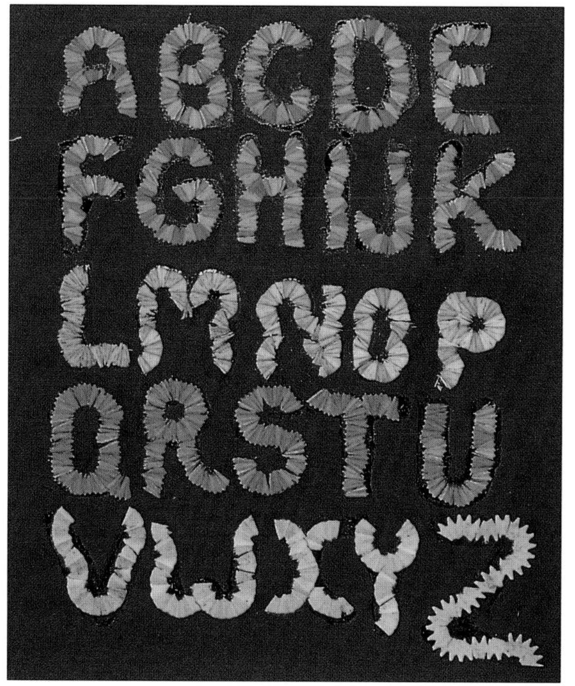

6

PROJECT 2

LOGOTYPE DESIGN

Design a logotype for Pentangle – an enterprise dealing in geometric puzzles, toys and games – and show how it might be applied to basic stationery.

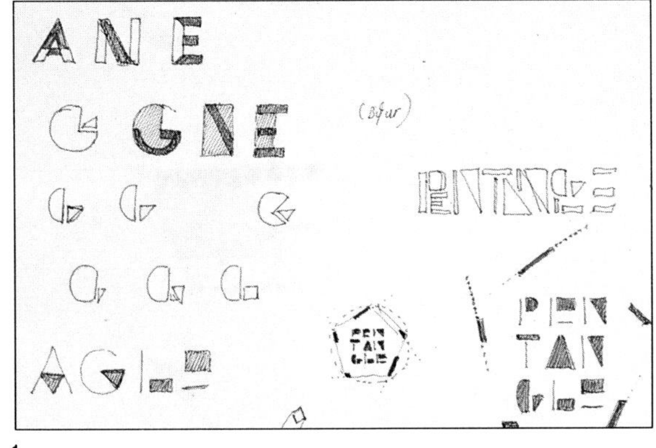

1

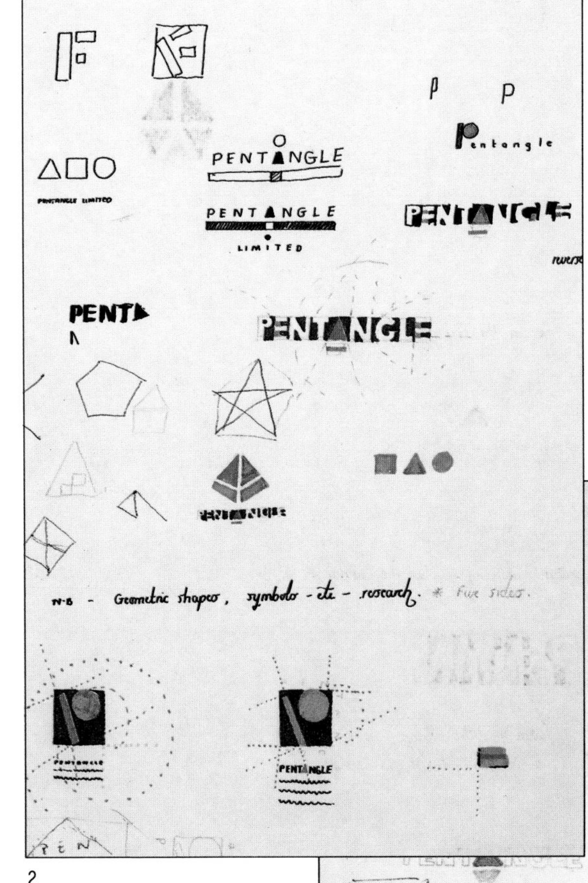

2

1 & 2 The letters that make up a logotype are a good starting point for decorative ideas. Analyzing their individual characteristics and then visually interpreting them can suggest a variety of approaches. Thinking about the meaning of the word or name and any possible associations is also useful in generating ideas.

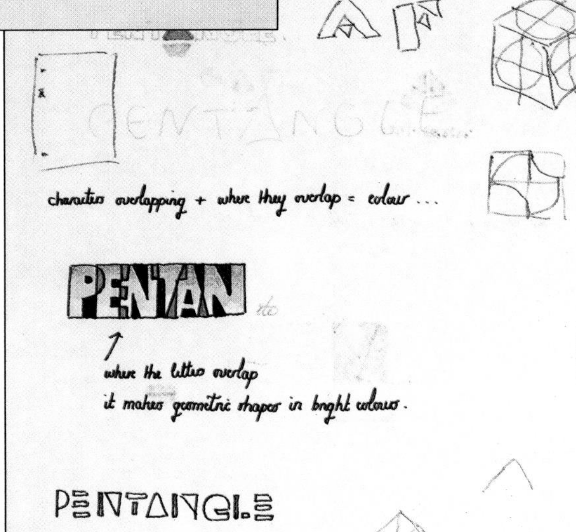

3

3 Color should come into play early on in the visual thinking process. So should a consideration of the shape of the typeface to be used, since this affects the way the logo is read. Color can be used to highlight shapes as well as add mood.

Chapters 1 and 3 provide useful reference points for this project. A logotype is basically a highly individual configuration of letters or words used to represent an organization, company, enterprise, or activity. It is a visual shorthand. A good logotype is often deceptively simple yet both decorative and functional. A clear understanding of the nature of the organization for which you are designing a logo can give clues to various approaches you might take. Whichever typographic devices you explore, they should echo the fundamental nature of the client. For example, a high-tech

4 Playing with and combining graphic shapes and type can provide relevant decorative solutions. However, to retain legibility, care must be taken when a logotype is fragmented into sections.

5

5 Two experiments that use the reversal technique to throw up a pentagon within the arrangement of letterforms. Although visually lively, the logotype is difficult to read.

4

6

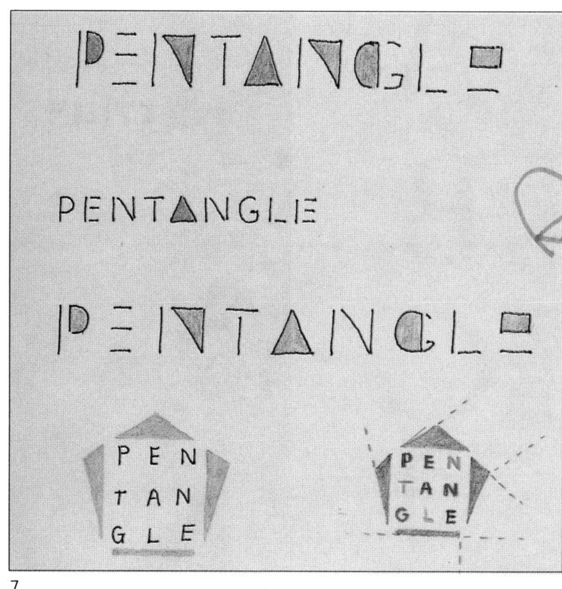

7

company could be represented by clean, geometric shapes and bright colors, whereas a horticultural enterprise might be better represented by more organic forms.

The very name Pentangle suggests a style of decorative typography that is clean, sharp, and based on geometric principles. Puzzles, toys, and games of this nature imply fun, intellectual challenge, involvement, and intrigue. Bright, lively colors combined with playful typographic shapes could reinforce this mood.

Once you have decided on your logotype design you need to consider how it will work in the context of basic stationery. Normally, a letterhead carries the logotype at the top or side, leaving enough space for the letter or message. Business cards and compliments slips should echo the style of the letterhead but not slavishly follow its layout. You can be decoratively creative with your logotype design by changing its position and scale and alternating the colorway within a range of stationery. The image or concept should remain intact, however, or it will not be instantly recognizable. Establish a sense of continuity rather than resorting to repetition.

6 Here the shape of a pentagon is suggested by graphically highlighting the angles. The name breaks down comfortably into groups of three letters.

7 A further investigation into how the "geometric" nature of the name can be visually reflected within the logotype or as a border.

1 Reducing letterforms to their absolute essence creates strong geometric shapes that are enhanced with color. The arrangement makes a crisp and decorative unit but reduces legibility.

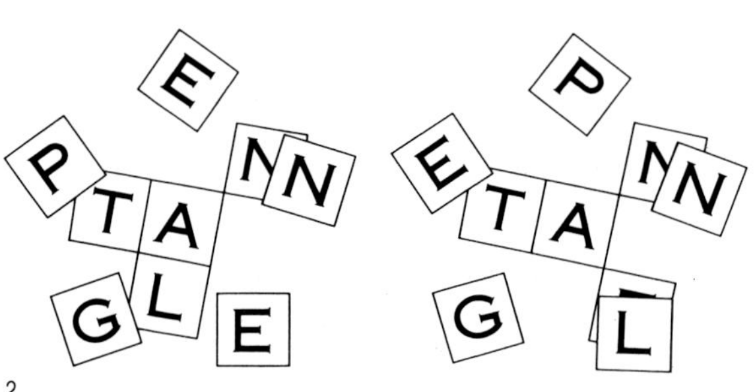

2

2 A sense of play and puzzlement is suggested in these decorative arrangements of "Pentangle," which invite the viewer to discover the name for himself. A good idea, but perhaps rather too complex to allow the company name to register reasonably quickly.

1

3 These graphically modified letterforms become totally legible when used in traditional linear form. Notice the difference that the fine outline makes to the way you "read" the shapes. It tends to weaken them.

3

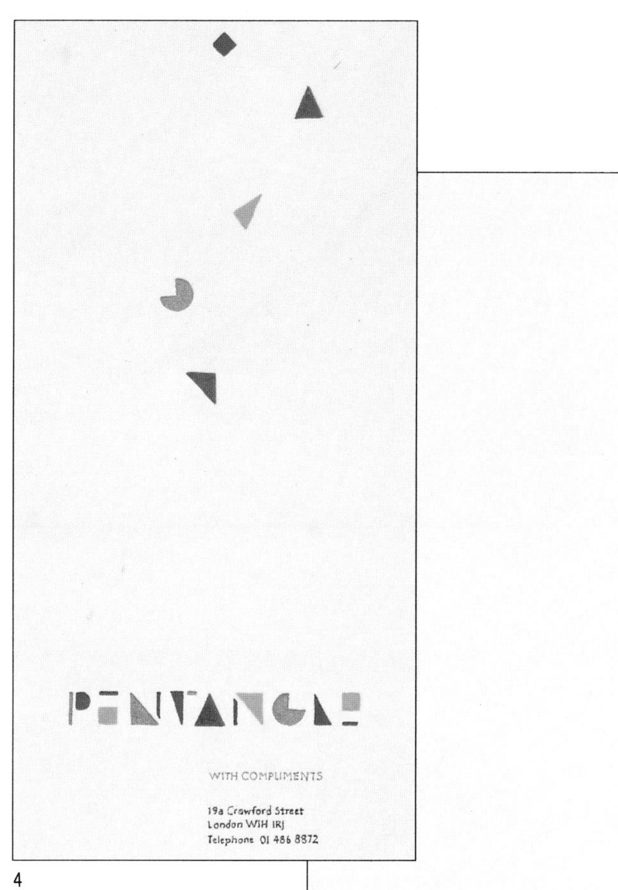

PENTANGLE
WITH COMPLIMENTS
19a Crawford Street
London WIH IRJ
Telephone 01 486 8872

4

Registered Office :
1 Bentinck Street
London WIH SRN
Registered Number :
1828075 England
Directors :
Kevin Collier
Richard Hanson
Elizabeth Webb
Julie Flood

PENTANGLE

19a Crawford Street
London WIH 1RJ
Telephone : 01 486 8872

5

4 & 5 The compliments slip and letterhead designs, respectively, show how the final logo would be used. A freeform aspect has been added in the decorative use of parts of the letter shapes that are scattered in the space. These also draw the eye down to the logo itself. The color scheme is decoratively extended into the small copy, giving a visually cohesive feel to the whole design. The final solution encapsulates the theme through shape and color.

3 Letters share the same stroke without harming the legibility of the logo for an American lighting products store. This technique forms a visual unit, but its success depends on the suitability of the letterforms.

3

1 This logotype decoratively yet informatively combines modified type with image. The natural curve of the whales effectively mirrors the relevant cross bars in the characters. This and the other examples on this page were designed by Tim Girvin Inc.

WHALEBACK

1

4

4 The Russian version of the "Un Bleu Choix" logo. The unfamiliar non-Latin script allows the enjoyment of the shapes for themselves. The heavy rules that contain the design are matched in weight to the main type and create a strong visual impact.

2 A logotype design that successfully creates visual interest through the individual character of the letterforms and through the additional minute ornament.

METROPOLIS

2

5 This embellished style of type has a period feel that lends a sense of tradition and quality. An engraving is decoratively incorporated and evocative colors further enhance the mood. The logotype works well asymmetrically or symmetrically.

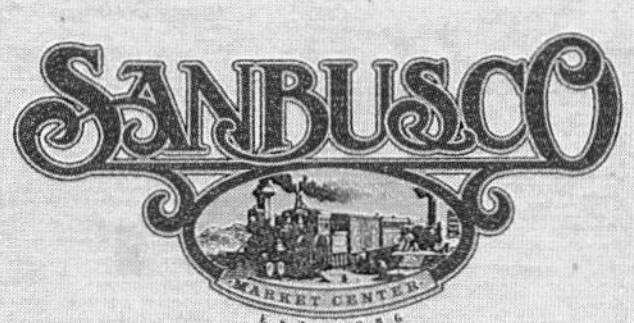

5

6 A contrast in styles is used to give a visual flourish that is almost musical to this logotype design. The soft tone, color, and movement of the script allow a background pattern that looks decorative but which does not affect the legibility of the logotype.

SYMPHONY 10K RUN

6

PROJECT 3

TYPOGRAPHIC GIFT WRAPPING AND TAG

Design typographic wrapping paper and a gift tag based on celebratory numbers such as 18, 21, 25, or punctuation.

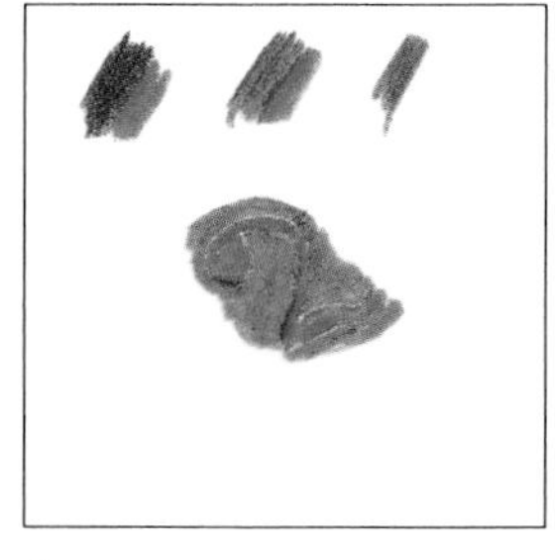

4

4 You can vary the value and intensity of a single color to create different effects. It is therefore essential to experiment thoroughly before deciding on any color combination.

5 Brush and ink lend a fluidity to this "21," which is quite different from the character generated by pen and ink. Exploring different media in relation to a project theme, as well as experimenting with the shape and nature of the type, can often suggest ideas.

1

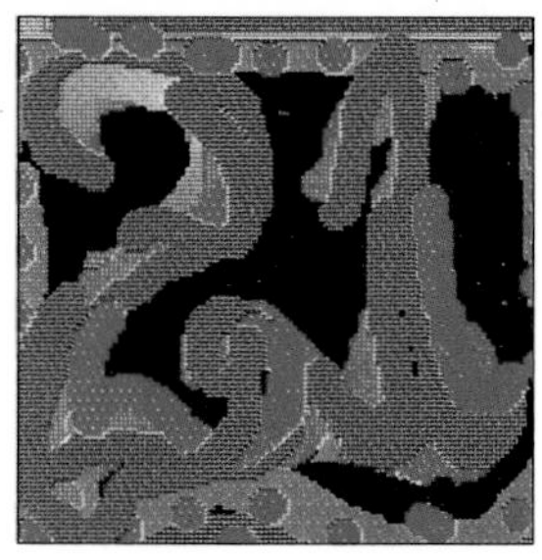

2

1 & 2 These two are details from example 4 on page 112, which shows a whole area of electronically generated patterns. Seen in isolation, they could make vibrantly decorative gift tags.

Chapters 2 and 3 provide the main points of reference here. Gift wrapping stimulates anticipation, enjoyment, surprise, and celebration. Try out a few different numerical themes using a variety of contrasting type styles, seeing what sort of patterns they make and how the numbers fit together. Look at Roman and digital numerals. Think about repeat patterns, mirror images, overprinting in transparent colors, positive and negative images. The shape, size, and weight of the numerals will suggest different qualities. For example, script figures convey a sense of formality. Hand-drawn numerals, calligraphy, and graffiti suggest a more intimate, spontaneous feel. Ornate numerals allude to traditional celebration, sans-serif examples give a more youthful feel.

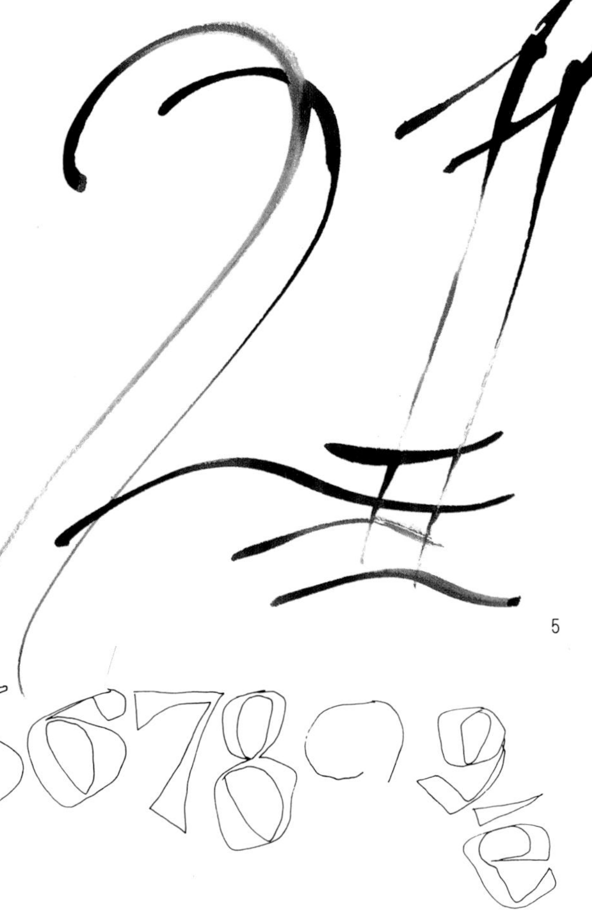

5

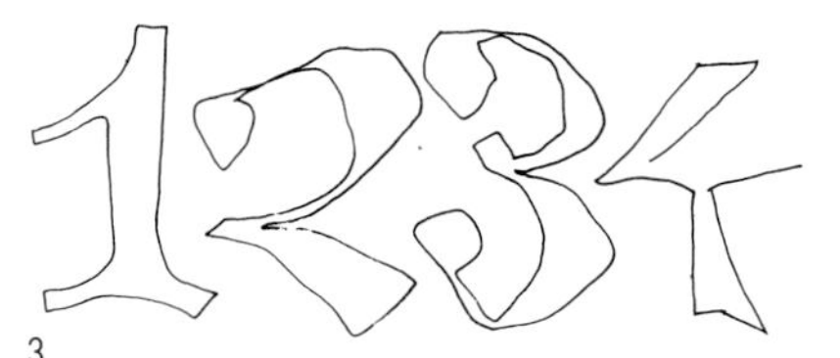

3

3 This rather eccentric set of numbers was originally freely cut from paper and then redrawn to give them a linear character that retained the spontaneity of the paper-cuts. The resulting figures exude a sense of fun.

6 The unusual architectural quality of this design is picked up in the dropped shadows and marblelike treatment of the surface. Together with the silver background, these suggest the significance of reaching 21.

7 An experiment that play by means of line and color with the rhythmic pattern potential of an ampersand.

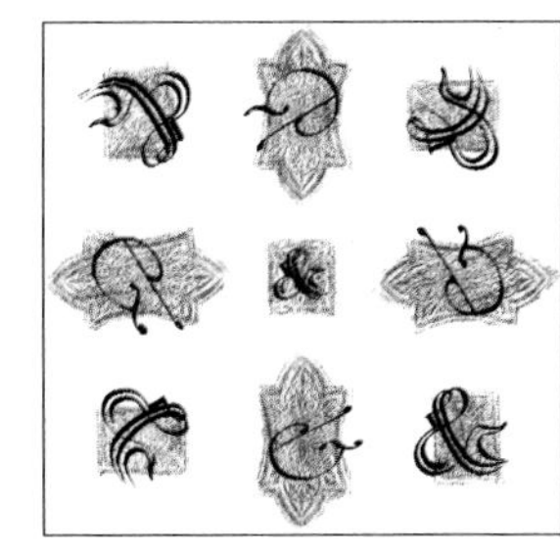

8

8 Evocative backgrounds can be used to enhance the character of letterforms.

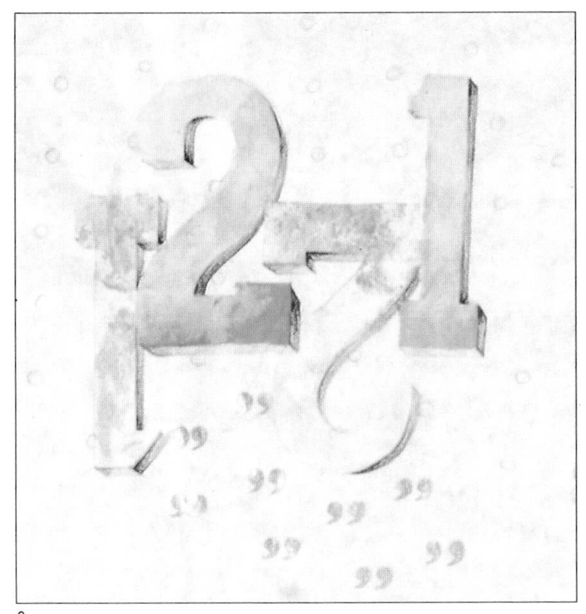

6

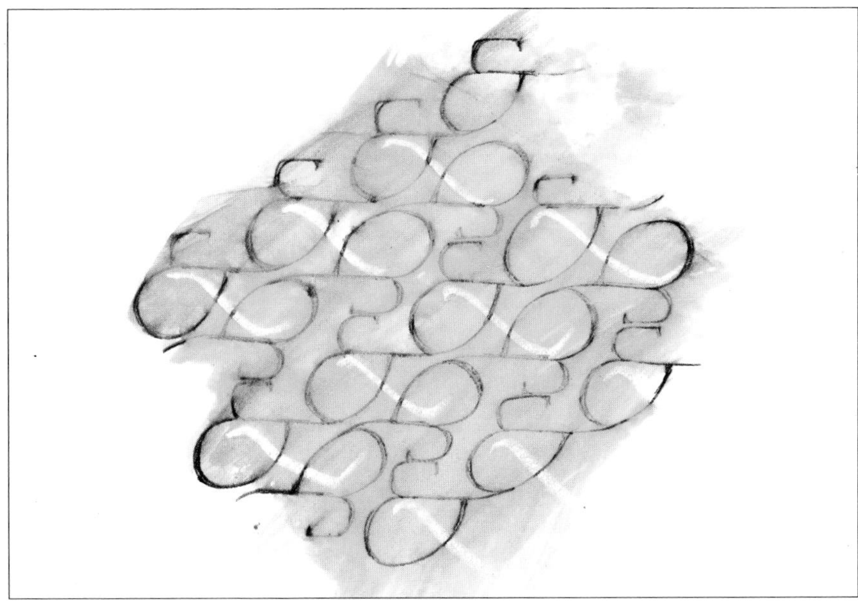

9

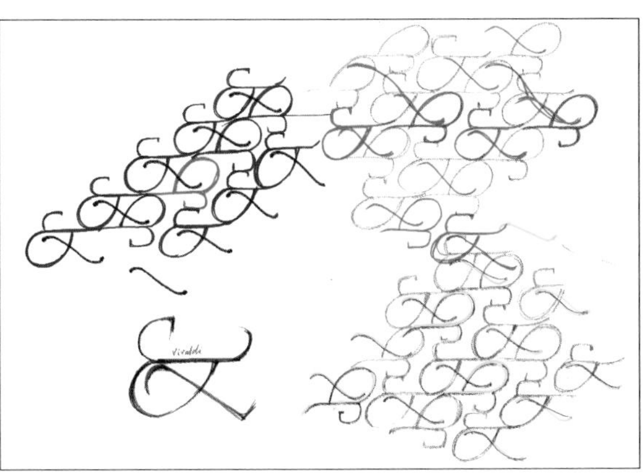

7

10

9 A development of 7 that explores textural and tonal possibilities, adding depth and subtlety.

10 Rubbings from embossed surfaces can be creatively manipulated to form rich, decorative textures that blend or contrast with type.

The addition of color to the type will set the mood of the occasion. Using a background color can lend further richness or vitality to the overall design. The numerals could equally well be used at a large or small scale. You could generate small numerals on a computer or typewriter. Cut and paste them into different patterns to create animated typographic textures. Numerals cut or torn from paper have a sense of immediacy and fun. Lino cuts or even simple typographic potato cuts can give wonderful textural qualities. Large areas can be printed in this way, and color changes can be made simply and effectively. You could cut a paper stencil from a numeric pattern and screen-print it, rotating the image as you print or superimposing one image on top of another, creating typographically based patterns and textures. Photocopiers also save time and effort when you want to generate areas of pattern.

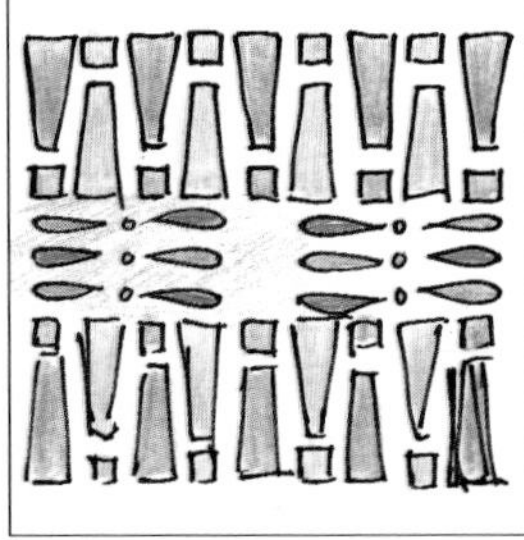

1

2

1 & 2 By its nature pattern covers an area. It is useful to look at different ways of arranging the type. Both ordered (1) and random (2) patterns can have equal visual impact. Color can be used to visually reinforce the rhythm and mood of the design. The exclamation marks hint at surprise and the unexpected, while the numerical patchwork suggests the bustle and enjoyment of celebrations.

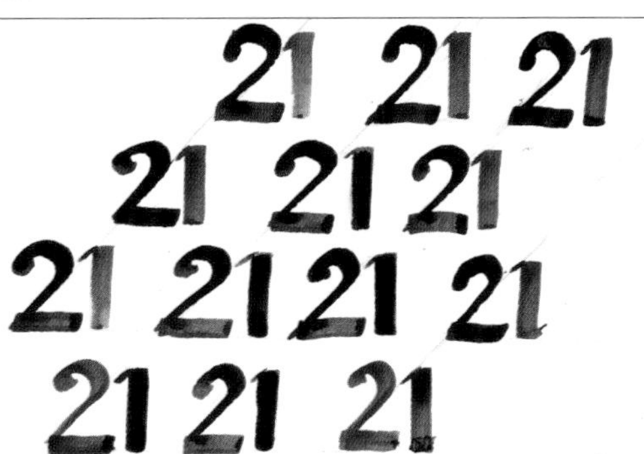

3

3 & 5 These visuals explore a more formal approach to the "21" theme. Rhythms such as the diagonal one in 3 can be created through the layout and structure of the numerals themselves. The decorative trellis on the surface of example 5 embellishes and is evocative of natural growth.

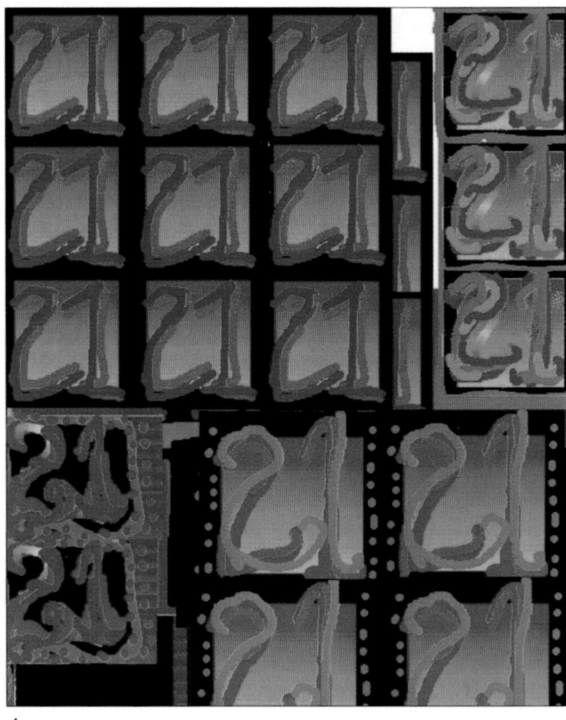

4

4 This highly decorative collection of computer-generated pattern experiments makes exciting use of the brilliant colors that can be created on screen. Working with this medium allows endless exploration of graphic techniques and is a quick and almost effortless way of manipulating designs. It gives a finished look even to doodling.

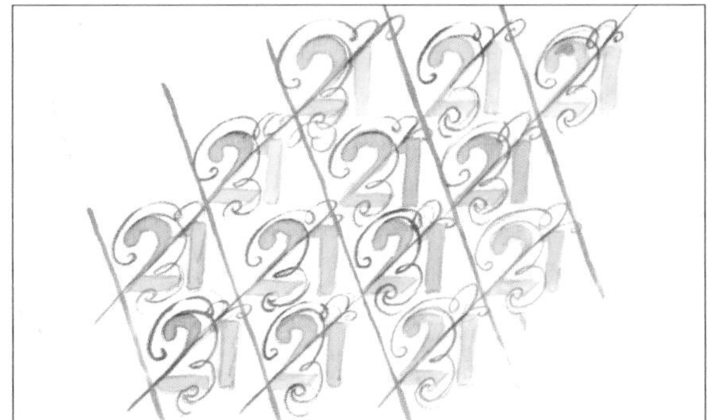

5

10 A further development of the ampersand theme in which is explored a way of combining the rubbing texture and pattern with the type. The background tone is rather heavy in parts, making the design solemn.

10

6

8

6 & 7 The rough-cut and subsequently redrawn numerals are decoratively strung together in Oriental fashion. Different interpretations are explored. This kind of experimentation is very worthwhile and helps develop your visual judgement.

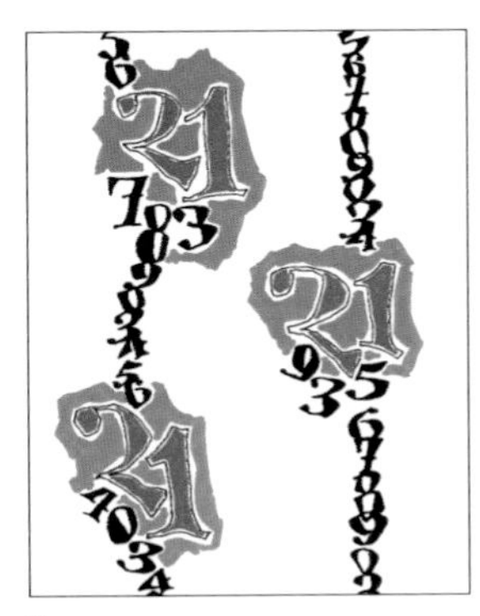

7

9

8 This numeric pattern is based on Bodoni Ultra Bold. "25" has been mirrored and reversed to form a textured pattern that in character and color is seasonally evocative. A simple but radical color change to silver and white would allow the same design to make a silver wedding wrapping paper. Cutting and pasting on screen or using a photocopier reduces the effort required by typographic pattern-making.

9 A black and white version of this visual would produce a dramatic result. In this example colors soften and control the overall visual impact. Try out several combinations in the first instance.

3 The text was hand-drawn onto this silk scarf, giving it a very uncontrived quality. Although decorative in essence, the typographic pattern is legible.

3

Using decorative punctuation can create unusual visual interest. When you think about exclamation marks, for example, ideas such as fun, surprise, amazement, even caution or danger, spring to mind. Question marks are associated with curiosity, intrigue, and the unknown. Quotation marks might imply personal conversation, a whispered aside, or something of particular significance, depending on their style, size, and weight. The surface treatment of large-scale punctuation and numerals provides much scope for the use of texture and pattern. The section on "Textured Letters" in Chapter 2 offers many ideas. You could make intriguing abstract typographic patterns by using only parts of numerals or punctuation, or the countershapes. When you have arrived at the pattern for the wrapping paper, be inventive about how it could be adapted to a gift tag. Avoid simply repeating the design. Try enlarging, reducing, or isolating part of it and see what impact it creates at this much smaller scale. Be as creatively decorative as possible, experimenting with a wide range of media.

1

1 A gift tag designed to complement the wrapping paper shown in example 2. The different colorways will draw attention to it and give variation to the theme. Subtle changes in the theme, rather than repetition, retain a sense of continuity while preventing "corporate" designs from becoming visually dull.

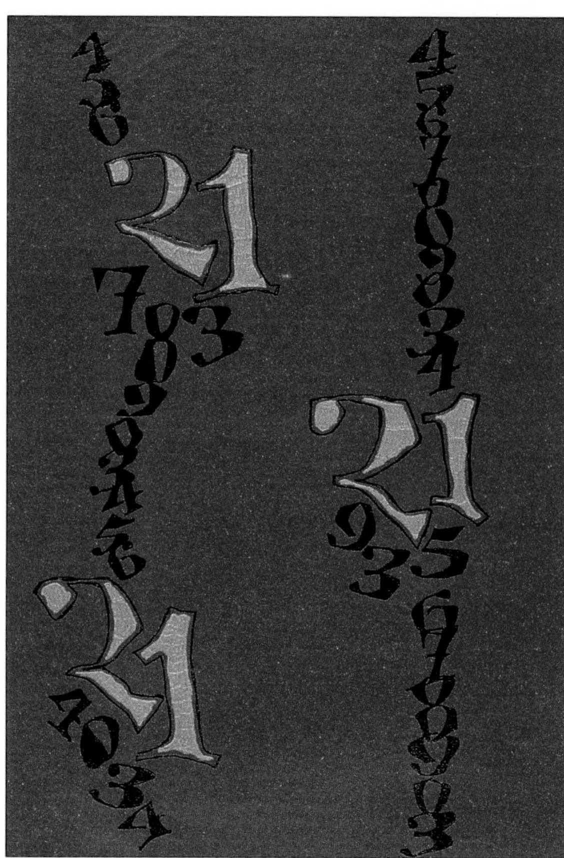

2

2 The use of colors to give sophistication to the final hand-drawn design for this 21st birthday wrapping paper is an excellent example of the important role color plays. Compare this design with examples 6 and 7 on the previous page.

5 Exclamation marks are treated in inventive ways and combined with fluorescent color to create dramatic anticipation. Both structured and random patterns have been successfully incorporated. Notice how the shape of the gift tag reflects the exclamation mark theme.

6 18s drawn freely with a pen and bleach onto colored tissue paper make up this gently decorative wrapping paper for a special birthday. The meandering linear quality is picked up in the gift tie.

4

5

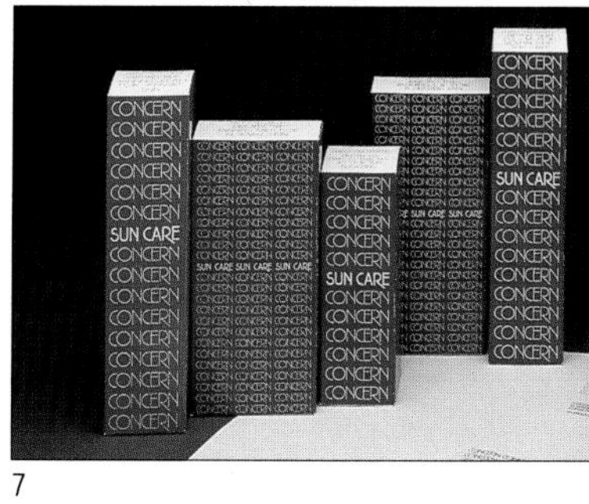

7

7 This range of skin-care products makes use of formal typographic pattern in its packaging design to communicate the notion of quality with an appeal across a wide age range.

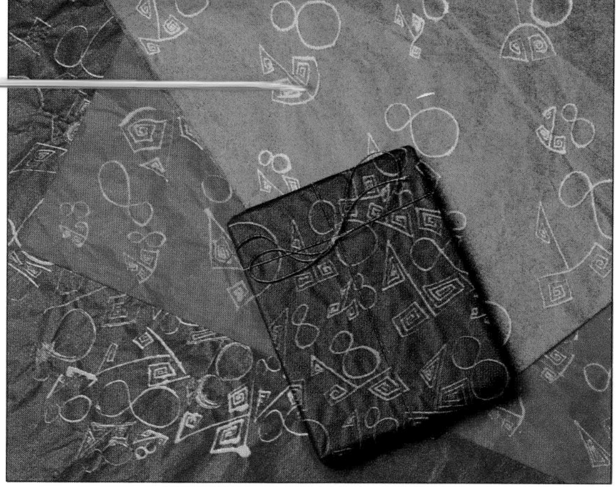

6

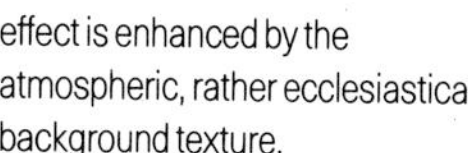

4 The final design for a wedding gift wrap. The background has been tonally softened and a decorative variety of ampersands has been used to add to the sense of occasion. The calligraphic ampersands celebrate the theme in their flourish, and their effect is enhanced by the atmospheric, rather ecclesiastical background texture.

PROJECT

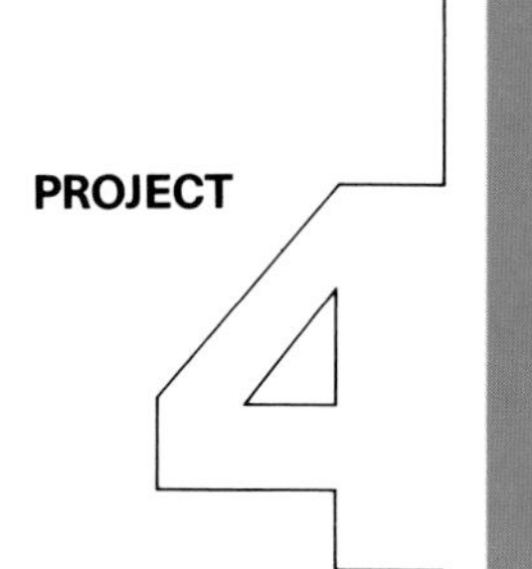

MENU DESIGN

Design a menu and associated material for one of the following restaurants, using a name of your choice:

An Italian restaurant
An ice-cream parlor
A Japanese restaurant.

1

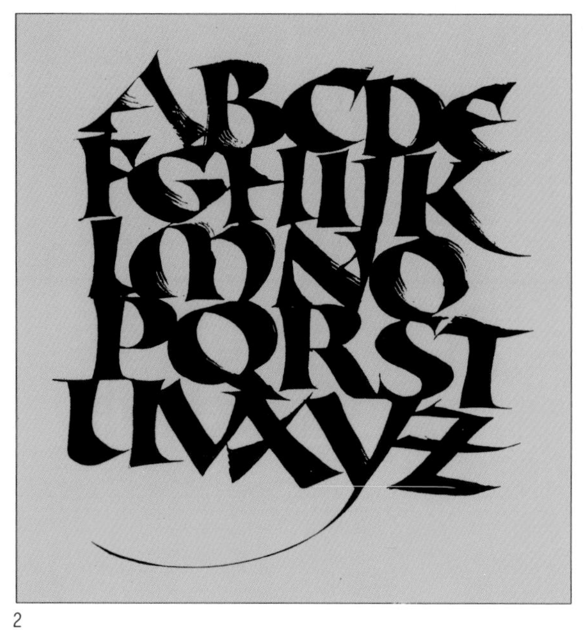

2

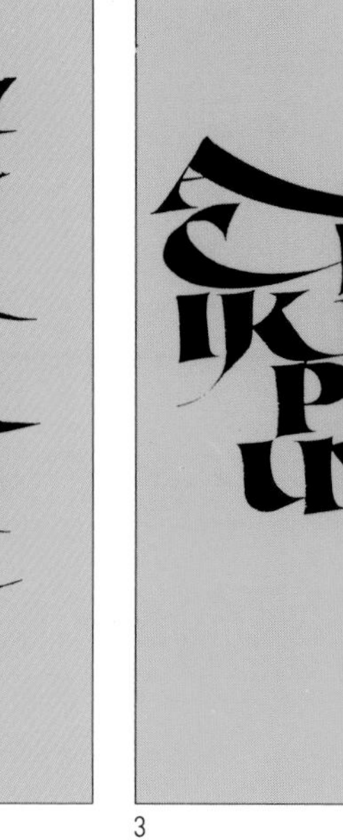

3

1–3 Experimenting with the calligraphic flow of letters helps to establish a sense of shape, pattern, and rhythm that could form the basis of a visual idea. The potential of these characteristics can then be evaluated within the framework of the project.

Chapters 3 and 4 should provide inspiration and background material relevant to this project. Each of the restaurants offers a specialist cuisine. It is worth spending time considering the decorative potential of each. You will need to create a visual identity for whichever one you choose, so careful selection is important. Familiarizing yourself with the various types of dishes, presentation, textures, colors, and even ways of eating is useful initial research.

Following the suggested work method, explore as many associations as possible. What sort of visual identity might reflect the feel and style of a particular cuisine or culture? Consider ways of making the design inviting and unusual. Color, typographic pattern, and style of ornament need special consideration. Also, the choice of typeface and how you might appropriately modify the letterforms (see Chapter 1) need careful evaluation. Alternatively, hand-drawn letters or a calligraphic rendering of the restaurant name could give it a personal and more intimate quality. The overall menu design should echo the visual identity. It could imply freshness, personal attention, and service, the idea of wholesome food, or could emphasize an intimate or formal atmosphere. Different styles of handwriting, hand-drawn letters, calligraphy, or typefaces could be used to symbolize the food or culture. Whichever style you use, it can be decorative but must be legible. Typeset text can be combined, with equal success, with appropriate borders, patterns, rules, and typographic ornaments. The embellishments could be hand-drawn to create a lively contrast with the typography.

Color is particularly important when used in the context of food. Experiment with different combinations – those associated with food will be close to the natural colors of

4 Doodling with restaurant names, looking at the shapes they make and the decorative possibilities that these might offer, helps to start ideas flowing.

4

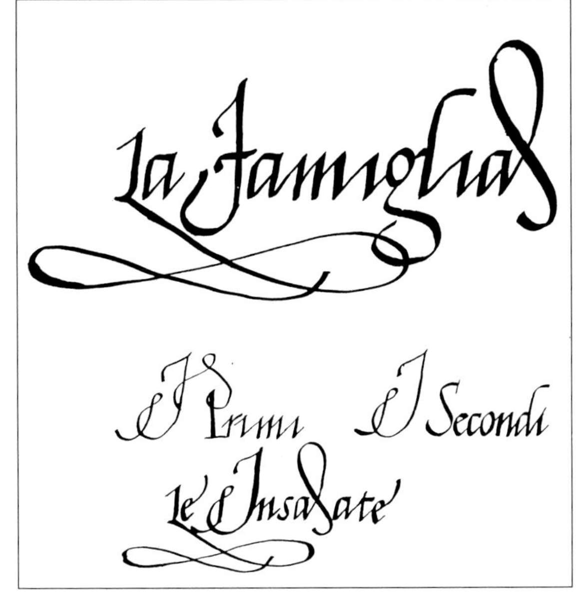

6

5

5 The Oriental characteristics of this visual are decoratively enhanced by photocopying the original artwork on to hand-made Japanese paper.

6 Calligraphic flourishes and handwriting can suggest a personal quality. At this early stage of a project a wide variety of approaches should be freely explored, and color incorporated where appropriate.

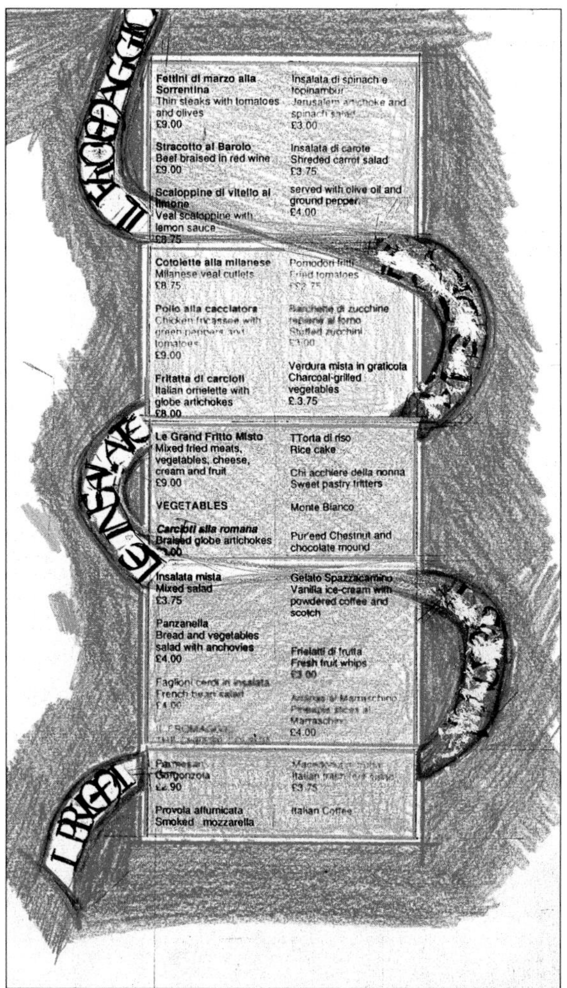

1

2

1 This idea for a menu design suggests a festive mood in the way that the ribbon winds itself decoratively around the display area. The use of a national color reinforces the theme of the visual.

2 Conventional, legible type is decoratively contrasted with, and integrated into, the calligraphic flourishes of this logotype concept which, with a touch of gentle humor, also hints at traditional Italian food.

food, while those associated with its preparation should have a fresh, healthy, and clean feel. Another source of inspiration for colors and patterns could be the different countries and cultures themselves. The visual identity of the menu could be adapted to that of associated promotional material such as matches, napkins, the bill, a business card, or wine label. Such visual links should be varied and lively. Avoid straight repetition.

3 Evocative shapes can be another way of exploring thematic associations. In this example the Oriental mood is graphically emphasized by means of the background fan shape.

3

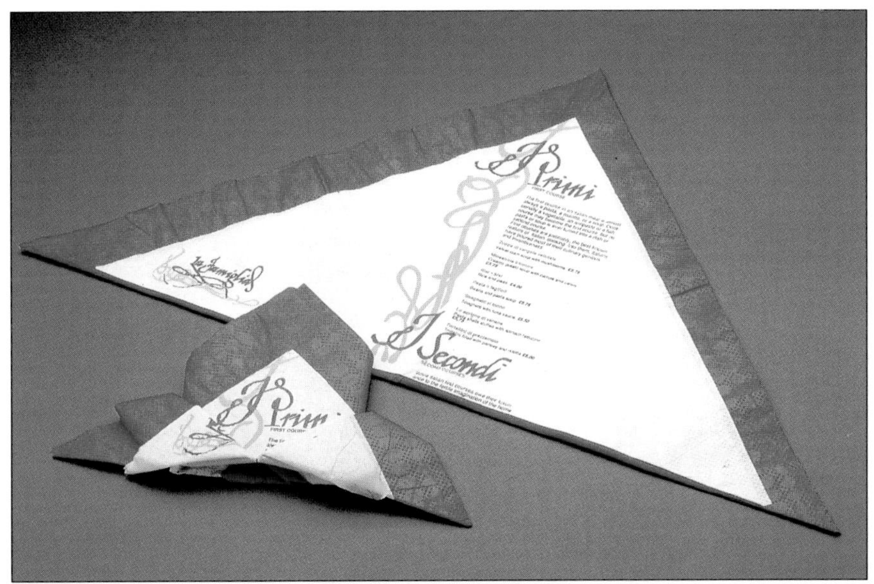

4

7

5

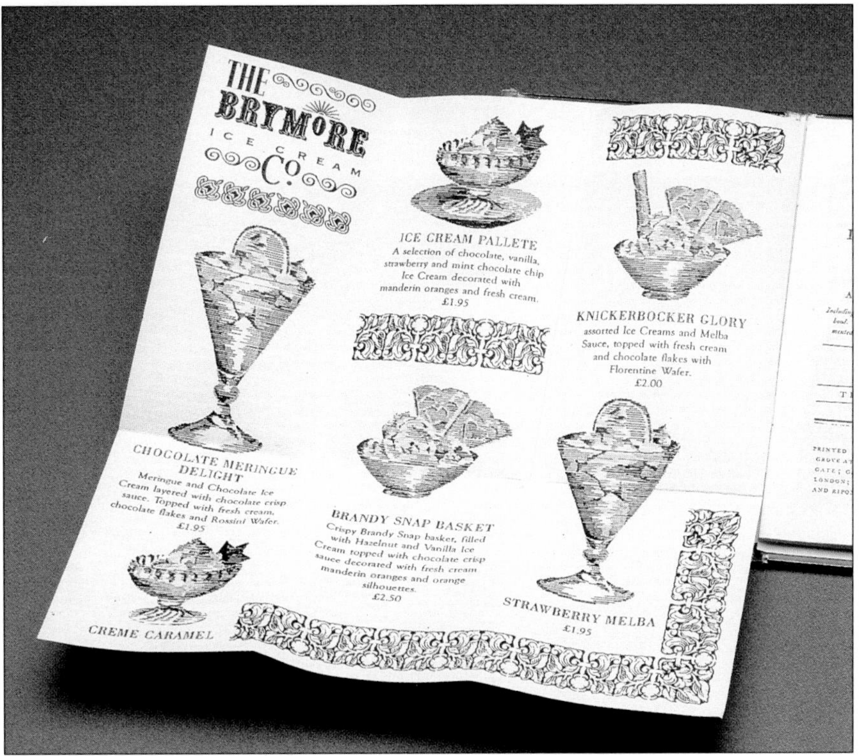

6

4 This versatile menu design is printed onto disposable napkins for lunchtime use. These can be decoratively folded to fit around a glass, and could be adapted for other uses such as being heat-sealed to make place mats.

5 & 6 This decorative booklet creatively promotes tourism and an ice-cream parlor in Harrogate. It is evocative of the Victorian era, when leisure was beginning to play an important part in life. The menu is tipped into the front cover and unfolds to display a pastiche of engravings embellished with decorative rules and borders.

7 A printed version of example 4 was designed for use at dinner, adding elegance to the table setting.

3 The use of hand-made Japanese paper in this solution is carried through to the labels for the house wine. The bottles themselves are decoratively colored to correspond with the wine. The red used is entirely appropriate to the Japanese theme, but less so to the wine. The white bottle suffers from the same problem.

1

3

4

1 This discreetly decorative design for an upscale Japanese restaurant successfully combines minimal imagery with an individual calligraphic logotype and conventional type. The package illustrated, to be offered to each guest on arrival, contains the menu, chopsticks, a complimentary gift, and a book of matches, all designed in the same vein.

2

2 & 4 This elegantly decorative fan is both menu and unusual souvenir. The closed version shown in example 4 would ornament each place setting. Exploring word or object associations at the start of a project encourages a "lateral" approach to discovering solutions.

5

5 Decorative headings of this kind were often used by printers to enliven commercial material such as menus and wine lists, among other things.

6 Handwriting and hand-drawn letters combine in this menu design to convey the intimate atmosphere and individuality of the restaurant. The freshly prepared, home-made food that is served is also reflected in the directness of the chosen medium, which lends a delightful decorative quality to the whole menu.

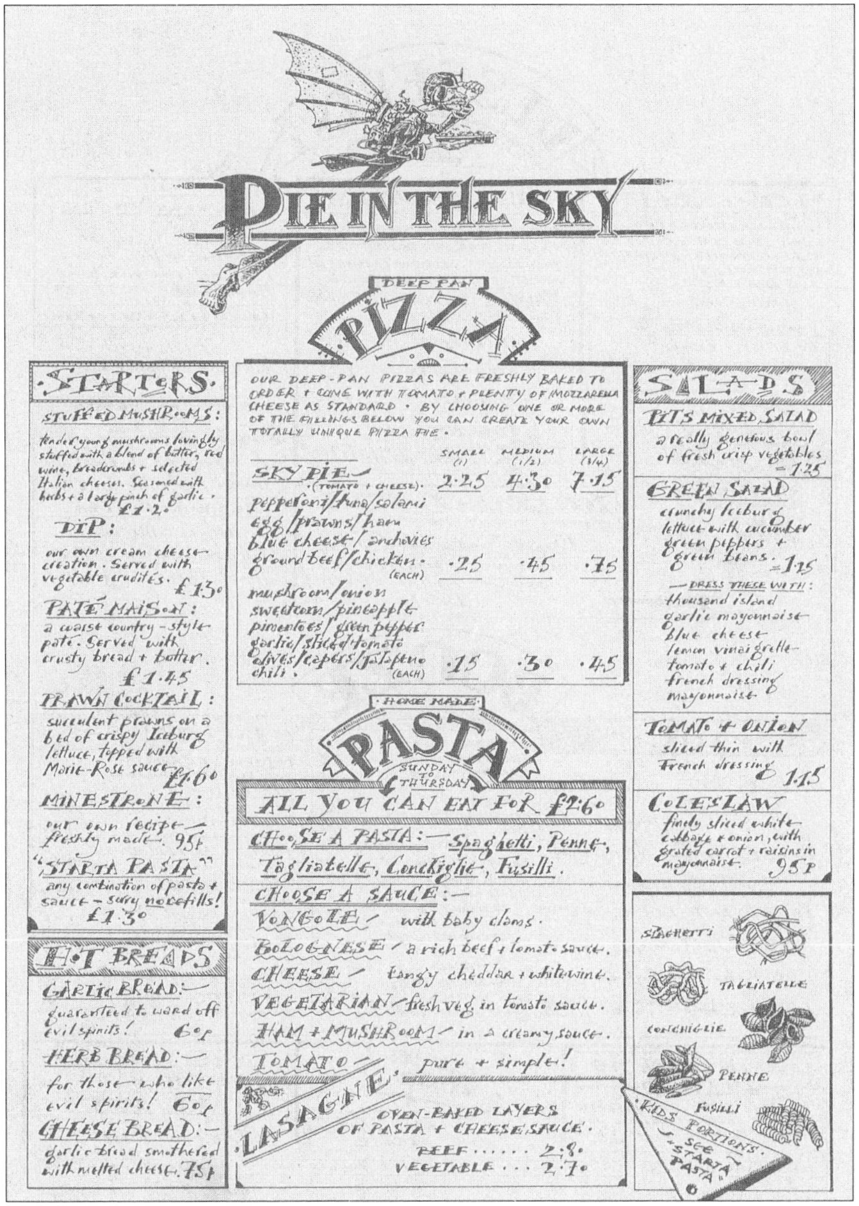

PIE IN THE SKY

DEEP PAN
PIZZA

OUR DEEP-PAN PIZZAS ARE FRESHLY BAKED TO ORDER + COME WITH TOMATO + PLENTY OF MOZZARELLA CHEESE AS STANDARD. BY CHOOSING ONE OR MORE OF THE FILLINGS BELOW YOU CAN CREATE YOUR OWN TOTALLY UNIQUE PIZZA PIE.

	SMALL (1)	MEDIUM (1/2)	LARGE (3/4)
SKY PIE (TOMATO + CHEESE)	2·25	4·30	7·15
pepperoni/tuna/salami, egg/prawns/ham, blue cheese/anchovies, ground beef/chicken (EACH)	·25	·45	·75
mushroom/onion, sweetcorn/pineapple, pimentoes/green pepper, garlic/sliced tomato, olives/capers/jalapeno chili (EACH)	·15	·30	·45

STARTERS

STUFFED MUSHROOMS: tender young mushrooms lovingly stuffed with a blend of butter, red wine, breadcrumbs + selected Italian cheeses. Seasoned with herbs + a large pinch of garlic. £1·20

DIP: our own cream cheese creation. Served with vegetable crudités. £1·30

PATÉ MAISON: a coarse country-style paté. Served with crusty bread + butter. £1·45

PRAWN COCKTAIL: succulent prawns on a bed of crispy Iceburg lettuce, topped with Marie-Rose sauce. £1·60

MINESTRONE: our own recipe — freshly made. 95p

"STARTA PASTA": any combination of pasta + sauce — sorry no refills! £1·30

HOT BREADS

GARLIC BREAD: — guaranteed to ward off evil spirits! 60p

HERB BREAD: — for those who like evil spirits! 60p

CHEESE BREAD: — garlic bread smothered with melted cheese. 75p

HOME MADE
PASTA
SUNDAY TO THURSDAY

ALL YOU CAN EAT FOR £2·60

CHOOSE A PASTA: — Spaghetti, Penne, Tagliatelle, Conchiglie, Fusilli.

CHOOSE A SAUCE: —
VONGOLE — with baby clams.
BOLOGNESE — a rich beef + tomato sauce.
CHEESE — tangy cheddar + white wine.
VEGETARIAN — fresh veg. in tomato sauce.
HAM + MUSHROOM — in a creamy sauce.
TOMATO — pure + simple!

LASAGNE: OVEN-BAKED LAYERS OF PASTA + CHEESE SAUCE.
BEEF ...... 2·80
VEGETABLE ... 2·70

SALADS

PIT'S MIXED SALAD: a really generous bowl of fresh crisp vegetables — 1·25

GREEN SALAD: crunchy Iceburg lettuce with cucumber green peppers + green beans. — 1·15

— DRESS THESE WITH: thousand island, garlic mayonnaise, blue cheese, lemon vinaigrette, tomato + chili, french dressing, mayonnaise

TOMATO + ONION: sliced thin with French dressing. 1·15

COLESLAW: finely sliced white cabbage + onion, with grated carrot + raisins in mayonnaise. 95p

SPAGHETTI
TAGLIATELLE
CONCHIGLIE
PENNE
FUSILLI

KIDS PORTIONS — SEE "STARTA PASTA"

6

PROJECT

LABEL DESIGN

Design a label for Roots and Shoots, a garden center, including any additional copy you may require.

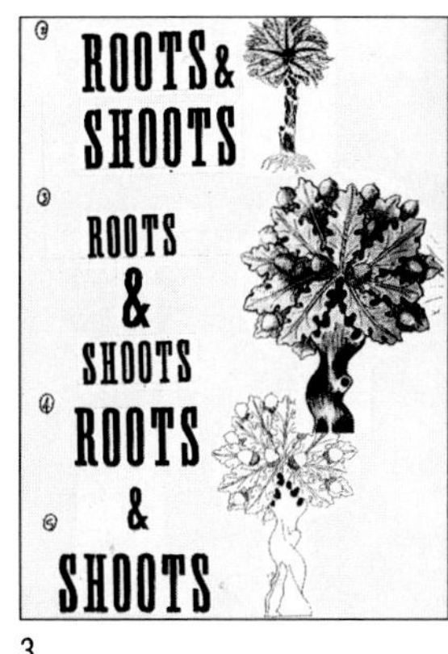

3

2 & 4 The tree top breaking through a typographic border conveys an unmistakable sense of growth. Exploring different label shapes can be a way of interpreting the "feel" of gardens. The serif typeface in 2 has an empathy with the subject matter.

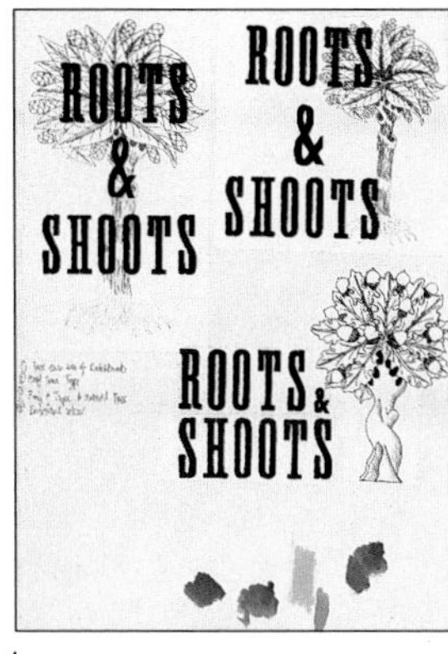

1

2

4

1 & 3 Combining display type and an image is not always as easy as it looks. The arrangement of the type itself is as important as the choice of the image. Working the two elements together so that they form a decorative yet legible unit calls for a lot of experimentation. The verticality and size of the type used in these visuals tend to visually dwarf the tree.

The main points of reference are covered in Chapter 3, and Chapter 4 is also useful. Labels are a means of identification and a small-scale form of advertising. They both inform and entertain. A variety of visual elements is often combined in both simple and embellished label designs. Images, rules, borders, ornament, and information must be selected with care. They should be interrelated so that the whole design acts as an appetizer, the visual identity of the label conveying the nature of the product itself: elegant or brash, fashionable or traditional. Labels should be visually alluring, despite their miniaturized style, in order to suggest the product's highly desirable qualities.

Consider all the visual options offered by the brief rather than seizing on a single one at the outset. This is a useful exercise even if it serves only to reinforce your initial inclination. What associations do the products have? A seed packet suggests home-grown produce or a garden embellished with flowers and plants. It conjures up the enjoyment of planting, growth, and expectancy. Some of these associations could be visually explored through images, the choice of type, and the way it is rendered. Color will lend a lively, decorative feel.

5 Often the subject matter suggests ideas that can be visually interpreted. These doodles play with the possibilities of a monogram that both modifies and amalgamates the "R" and the "S" decoratively.

6 Sometimes it is worth drawing up a slightly more accurate version of a rough in order to refine and evaluate it. These curving lines display an inherent growth.

7 Visual thinking is essential to the sequential development of ideas. It also helps to generate ideas: one doodle leads to another, often in unexpected ways.

8 The natural tendency of gardens to embellish is thematically explored through pictorial ornamentation, style, and arrangement of type.

7

5

6

8

9

9 The two different elements are sensitively combined into a label format. The design conjures up a feeling of splendid, mature gardens.

2 & 5 A more traditional approach to label design. The varying styles of type, decorative borders, and formats suggest in their refined way a sense of quality and achievement.

3

3 Designs can be creatively adapted to work in different contexts without losing their essence. This wrapping paper design belongs visually to the same family as in example 2.

4 Adding color to designs brings them to life and can be used to visually reinforce the theme.

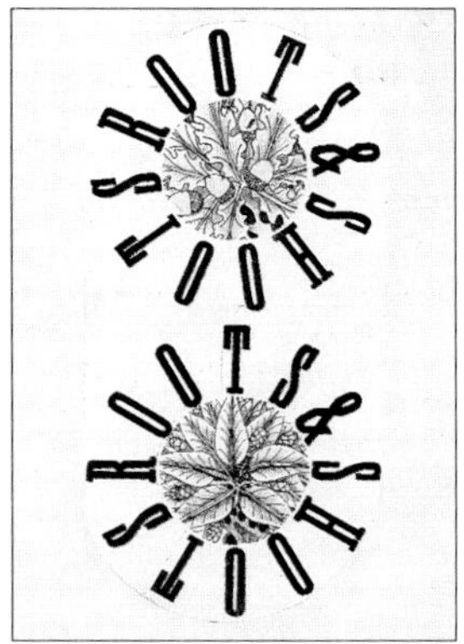

1

2

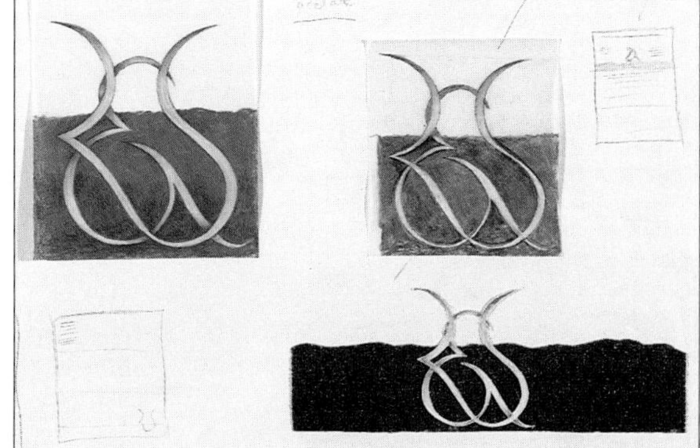

4

1 Reducing the image to a circular format and surrounding it with type overcomes the slight visual conflict in the previous attempts. The way in which the type radiates from the image relates much better to the idea of growth.

5

6 This solution has captured the fullness of a flourishing garden. The wonderfully decorative yet totally functional character of the ampersand combined with ornament conjures up a period feel.

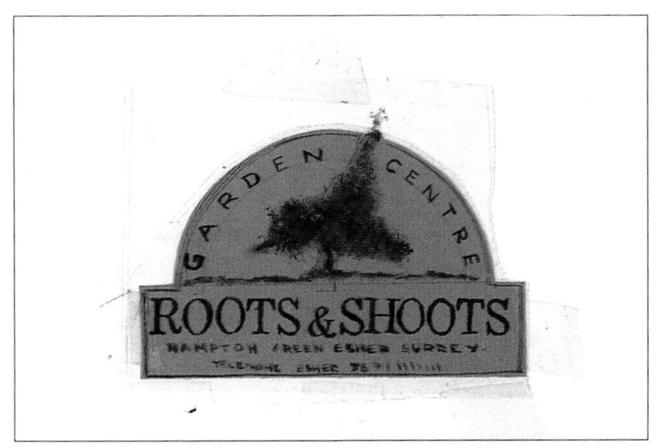

7

7 & 8 Always try out a range of evocative colorways before you make your final choice. Notice the difference in legibility between the labels, which is affected by the color. Color can be used to play down elements just as effectively as it can emphasize them. It is important to establish a hierarchy of information, so that it can be appropriately handled.

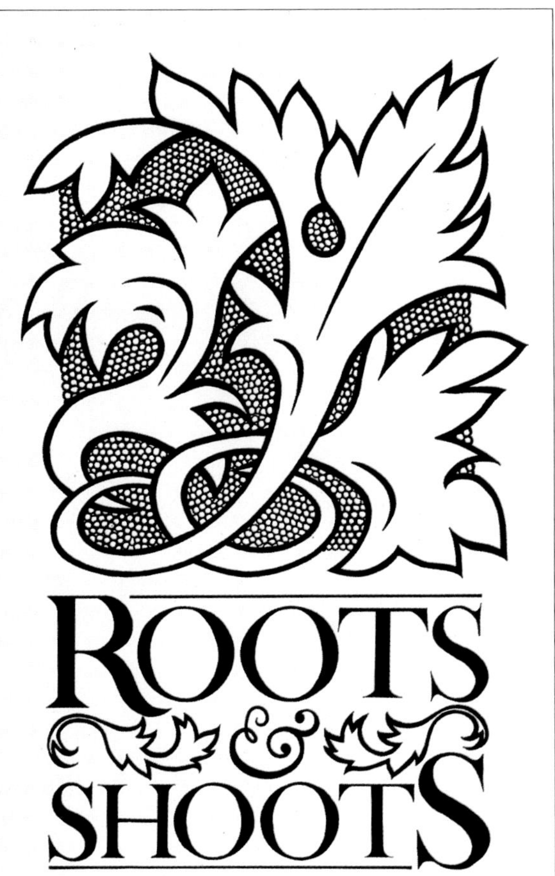

6

8

1

2

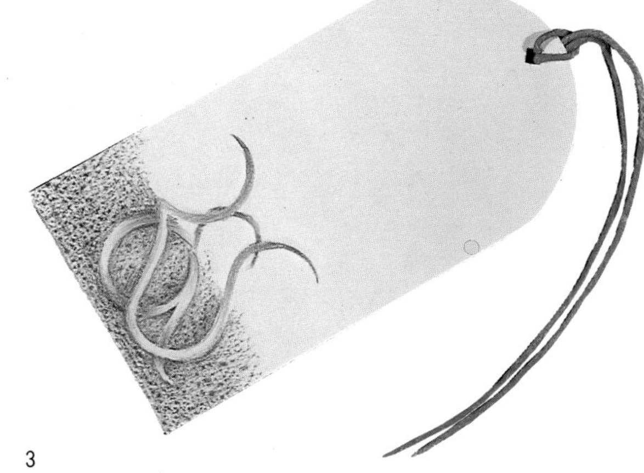

3

4

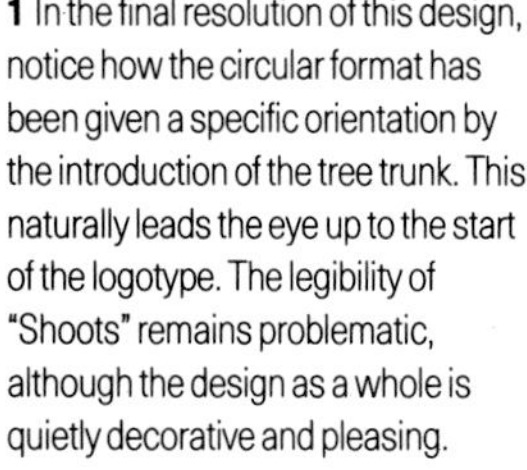

1 In the final resolution of this design, notice how the circular format has been given a specific orientation by the introduction of the tree trunk. This naturally leads the eye up to the start of the logotype. The legibility of "Shoots" remains problematic, although the design as a whole is quietly decorative and pleasing.

2 The "reversal" of this label design adds to its ornamental quality. It is extremely versatile in that it works in color, monochrome, and in reverse.

3 Organic form, color and textures are successfully combined in this swing ticket. Notice how the color theme is carried through into the string. The decorative shape of the ticket subtly evokes garden cloches and conservatories.

4 Subtle textures contrast decoratively with the graphic imagery in this solution. Expressive typography mimics the import of the name.

5

6

7

5 A simple, elegant wine label designed by Lewis Moberly that exudes quality in its use of space and subtle decorative imagery and in its minimal color.

6 Decorative self-adhesive labels are used by "Salute," a men's wear boutique, to seal customers' carrier bags once purchases have been made. Designed by Chris Bigg.

7 A label-style pack design that decoratively echoes an herb garden through ornamented and script typefaces, rules, and flourishes.

8

9

8 This design uses the characteristics of a label to emphasize the main heading. A very simple but effective technique.

9 Trickett and Webb designed this richly ornamental "label" to celebrate the centenary of Marks and Spencer. The book spine is also decoratively color co-ordinated.

PROJECT

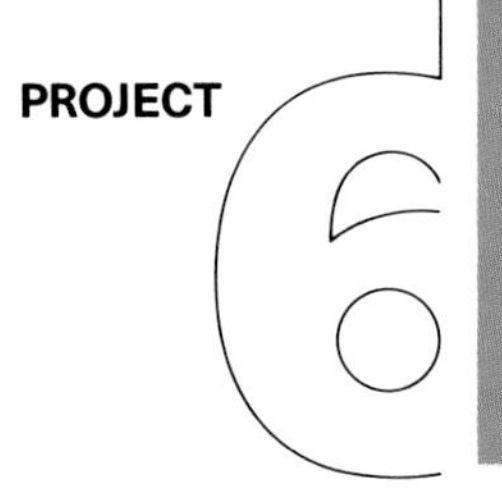

DOUBLE-PAGE MAGAZINE SPREAD

Design a double-page spread for an A4 magazine promoting typefaces. Your spread should feature one typeface and include a small amount of text.

Chapters 1 and 4 provide decorative inspiration for this project. Since magazines are made up of a variety of contents we tend to pick them up and put them down, rarely reading from start to finish. Decorative typography plays an important role in this context, providing focal points and signposting the reader through the often busy design. The graphic treatment of the different topics needs to be visually strong in order to arrest the reader's attention. Articles are often highlighted with a typographic embellishment such as a striking heading, initial letter, or border. When an article covers more than one page these can also form a visual link from one spread to the next.

The text in popular magazines is designed to provide informative leisure reading. It can be set into different shapes, run around images, or be emphasized with color, rules, or borders. Larger areas of text might be visually punctuated and broken down into palatable sections with typographic decoration. A grid is nearly always used in magazine design to help combine the formal and informal elements such as text, photographs, drawings, and headings into a satisfactory whole. A balance and vitality in the interaction of the individual components needs to be established. Free images and typographic decoration can break out of the grid, creating a dynamic feel. A well-designed

1 It is a good idea to draw your working area to full size so that subsequent thumbnail visuals can be kept more or less in proportion.

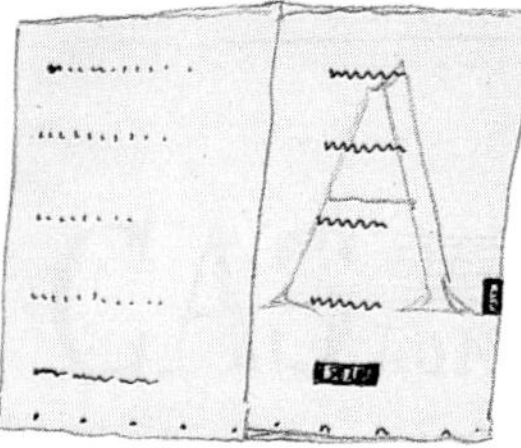

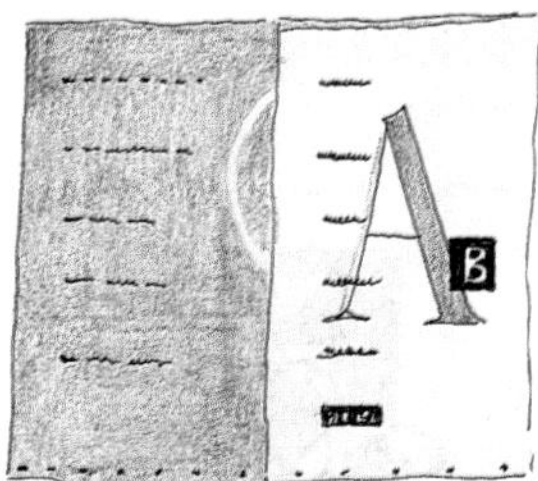

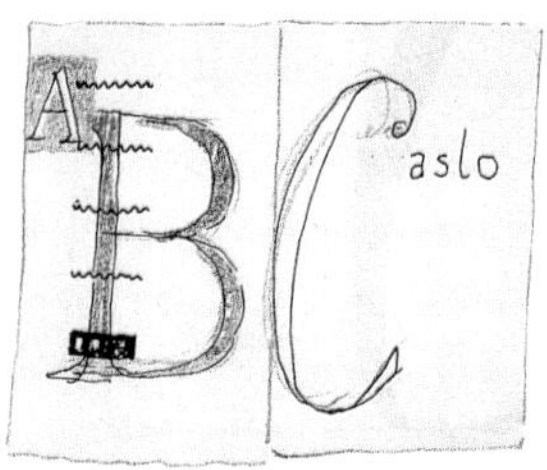

1

2 Dividing up the working area by means of a simple grid will give you a framework within which to work. However, the grid can be ignored from time to time, to prevent the layout becoming too rigid.

3 It is important to visually interpret the atmosphere of the subject matter. The typeface Gill Sans is evocatively displayed here.

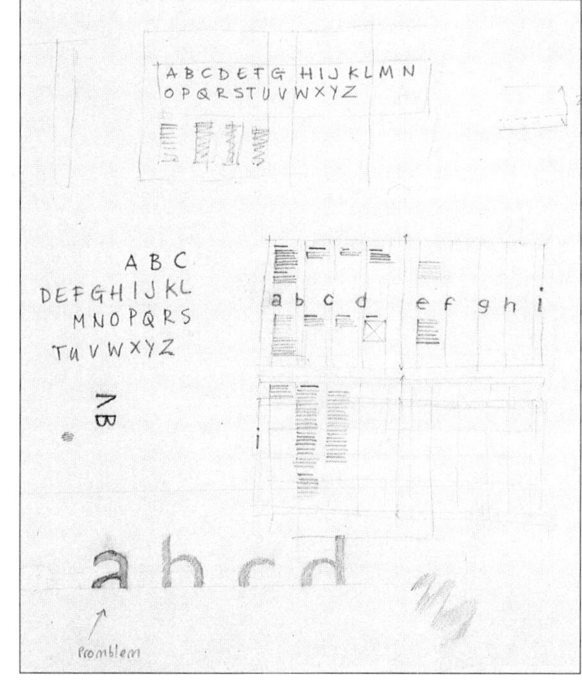

2

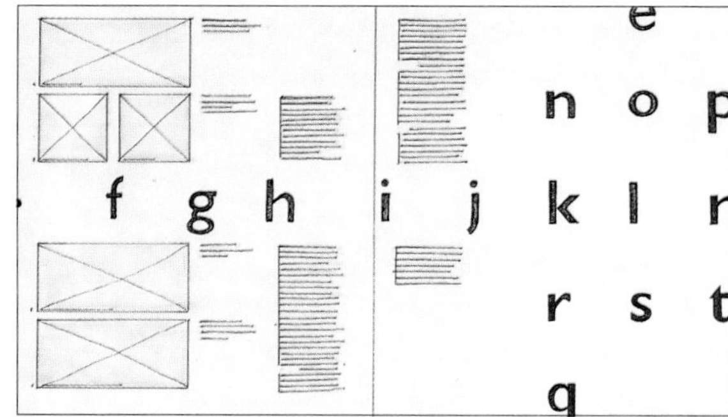

3

magazine spread creates a feast for the eye.

In this project for a magazine you could introduce some of these devices. You have only a small amount of copy to deal with, which gives you great freedom to experiment visually. First, consider the format of the double-page spread, bearing in mind that you can create a wide variety of other shapes within it. When you have looked at a range of different typefaces, select one that has a strong visual appeal for you. Analyze its character and any distinguishing features (see Chapter 1). Try experimenting with various letters at different sizes and in different weights. Look at the related forms of the typeface, such as italics and small capital letters or swash characters, con-

4

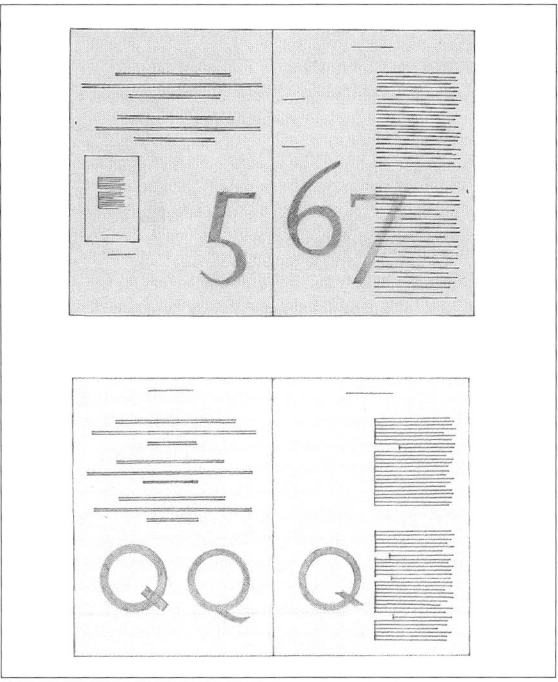

5

4 Using letters, numerals, or punctuation at a large scale can provide decorative focal points. In this instance it also creates an awareness of the characteristics of the individual letters.

5 Changes in scale within a design can enliven the page layout. Different styles of text setting can also complement each other but need careful handling so as to avoid visual confusion.

6

6 At this scale the countershapes of the lower-case "a" almost become graphic shapes in themselves. Notice how the double-page spread is visually linked by the careful placing of the caption in the center.

sidering how they might be used as ornamental devices. Explore the rhythmic qualities of the typeface.

Once you have developed a feel for the letterforms, think about the spread design. Use thumbnail sketches to try out alternative ideas for the overall layout until you capture the typeface's essence. Be flexible in your visualization of the spread layout. Too often, predictable designs result from a rigid, preconceived approach. The theme of this project encourages you to use letters as decorative imagery and to think about strong contrasts of size, weight, and style. Introducing color, a variation of tones and even textures will give an added dimension. Space should be used to lend clarity and direction to your overall design.

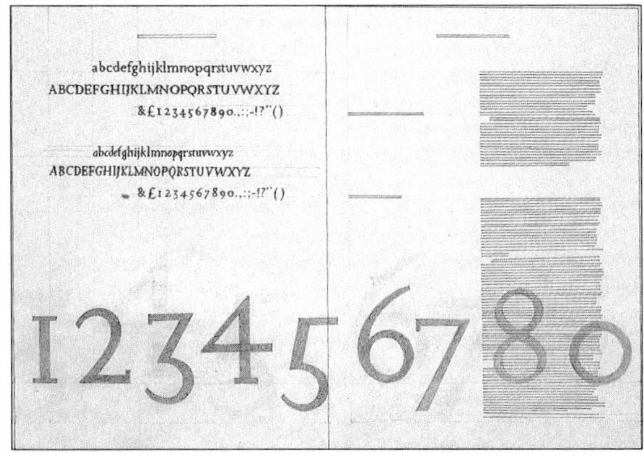

1

1 A further-refined visual which takes account of the typeface and its characteristics. The letters and numerals have been given plenty of "breathing space" in order to enhance their shape and rhythm. Space is one of the most valuable elements in good design. So often it is filled to capacity, resulting in a visual jumble.

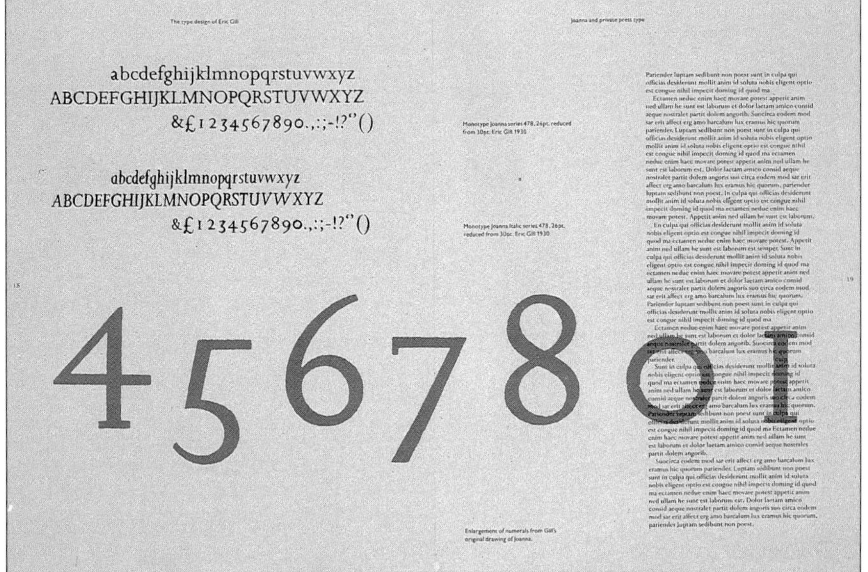

2

2 The rather musical quality of these non-aligning numerals tends to visually counteract their mathematical nature. Their use right across a magazine spread gives them a decorative quality normally associated with letters.

3

3 Reorientating words can add to their visual appeal and still retain legibility. The soft gray of "Gill" optically plays down the size aspect so that the tone and color of the text are not overpowered visually.

4

4 The crossbar of the "G" is used to structure this spread, drawing attention to its handsome form. The widely spaced text allows visual movement across the whole area. Dramatic cropping of letterforms creates decorative, abstract typographic shapes.

5 This typographic "frieze" makes decorative use of the space offered by a double-page spread in the way that it unwinds across the surface with playful elegance.

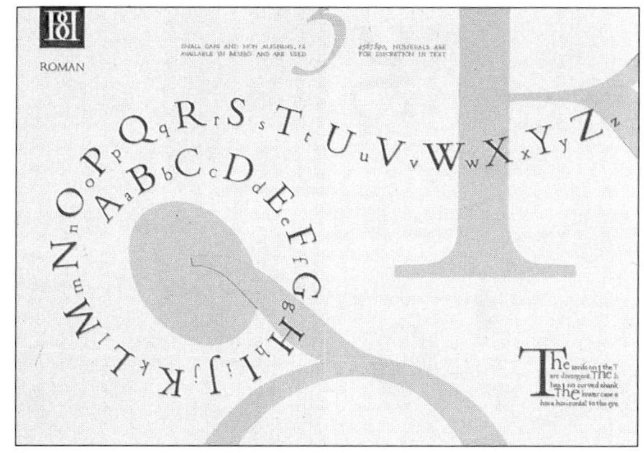

5

6

6 The geometric characteristics of Futura, the typeface promoted in this spread design, is reinforced in the strong visual impact made by the architectural feel of the layout. The clean shapes of the letters are enhanced by the crisp, decorative line and "reversing out."

7 This magazine spread decoratively exploits the exuberant nature of a Caslon italic ampersand. Once again size is used, then played down through tone, to allow the eye to enjoy the lyrical curves of this typographic masterpiece. Ornament in a border and rule form discreetly embellishes the whole of the design.

7

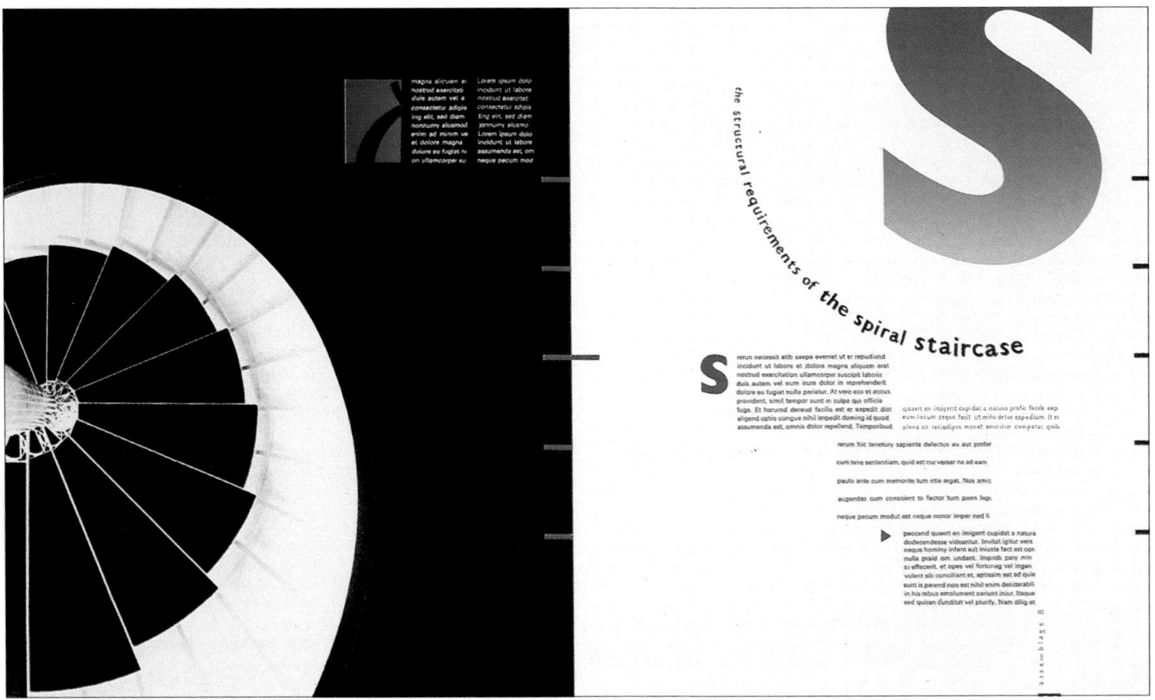

1

1 The structural and ornamental essence of a spiral staircase is creatively echoed in both the typography and spatial organization of this spread design.

2 Grids should be an aid to magazine design rather than an end in themselves. This example shows how a rather mechanical quality can be decoratively relieved through the creative use of size, weight, tone, and texture.

2

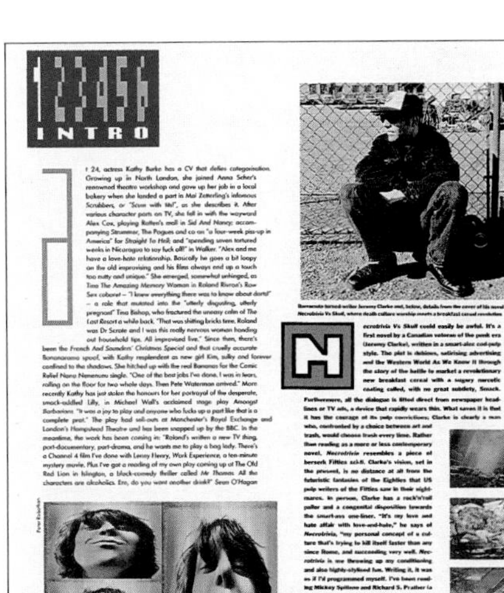

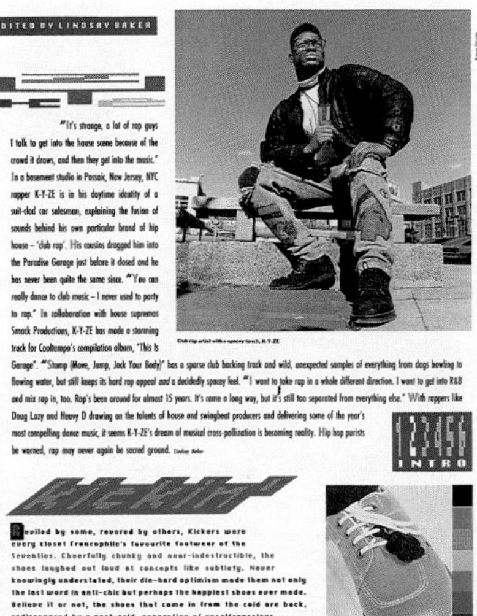

EDITED BY LINDSAY BAKER

"It's strange, a lot of rap guys I talk to get into the house scene because of the crowd it draws, and then they get into the music." In a basement studio in Passaic, New Jersey, NYC rapper K-Y-ZE is in his daytime identity of a suit-clad car salesman, explaining the fusion of sounds behind his own particular brand of hip house – 'club rap'. His cousins dragged him into the Paradise Garage just before it closed and he has never been quite the same since. "You can really dance to club music – I never used to party to rap." In collaboration with house supremos Smack Productions, K-Y-ZE has made a storming track for Cooltempo's compilation album, "This Is Garage". "Stomp (Move, Jump, Jack Your Body)" has a sparse club backing track and wild, unexpected samples of everything from dogs howling to flowing water, but still keeps its hard rap appeal and a decidedly spacey feel. "I want to take rap in a whole different direction. I want to get into R&B and mix rap in, too. Rap's been around for almost 15 years. It's come a long way, but it's still too separated from everything else." With rappers like Doug Lazy and Heavy D drawing on the talents of house and swingbeat producers and delivering some of the year's most compelling dance music, it seems K-Y-ZE's dream of musical cross-pollination is becoming reality. Hip hop purists be warned, rap may never again be sacred ground. *Lindsay Baker*

Reviled by some, revered by others, Kickers were every closet Francophile's favourite footwear of the Seventies. Cheerfully chunky and near-indestructible, the shoes laughed out loud at concepts like subtlety. Never knowingly understated, their die-hard optimism made them not only the last word in anti-chic but perhaps the happiest shoes ever made. Believe it or not, the shoes that came in from the cold are back, rediscovered by a post-acid generation of unselfconscious casuals. Kickers are widely available in the original colours, with orange, purple and green to come. Who said the French don't have a sense of humour? *Ekow Eshun*

3

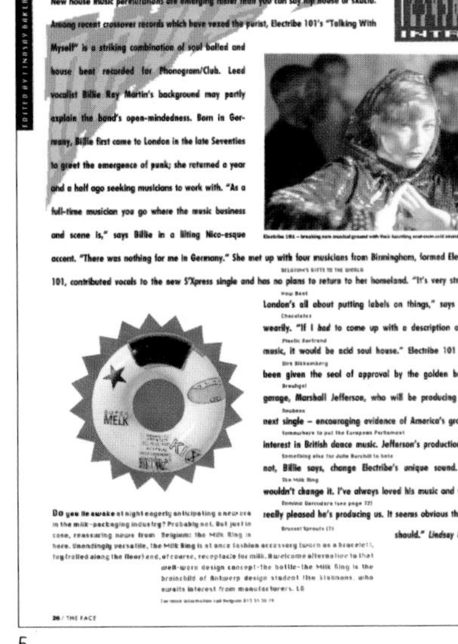

EDITED BY LINDSAY BAKER

New house music permutations are emerging faster than you can say hip house or skacid. Among recent crossover records which have vexed the purist, Electribe 101's "Talking With Myself" is a striking combination of soul ballad and house beat recorded for Phonogram/Club. Lead vocalist Billie Ray Martin's background may partly explain the band's open-mindedness. Born in Germany, Billie first came to London in the late Seventies to greet the emergence of punk; she returned a year and a half ago seeking musicians to work with. "As a full-time musician you go where the music business and scene is," says Billie in a lilting Nico-esque accent. "There was nothing for me in Germany." She met up with four musicians from Birmingham, formed Electribe 101, contributed vocals to the new S'Xpress single and has no plans to return to her homeland. "It's very strange, London's all about putting labels on things," says Billie wearily. "If I had to come up with a description of our music, it would be acid soul house." Electribe 101 have been given the seal of approval by the golden boy of garage, Marshall Jefferson, who will be producing their next single – encouraging evidence of America's growing interest in British dance music. Jefferson's production will not, Billie says, change Electribe's unique sound. "He wouldn't change it. I've always loved his music and we're really pleased he's producing us. It seems obvious that he should." *Lindsay Baker*

5

3 A variety of decorative focal points lend a sense of fun and immediacy to this spread from *The Face* magazine, giving it great visual pace.

4 Type is decoratively used to echo the space theme. The textured "W" becomes an image in its own right. The colored typographic bleeps lend an animated vibrancy to the whole page.

5 The pace and mood of the spread's subject matter is reflected in the layout. When text type is small but bold and the lines are widely spaced, decorative elements can run behind it without destroying legibility.

6 Letters are used to "illustrate" the text. Textures, color, and photographic images enhance their effect.

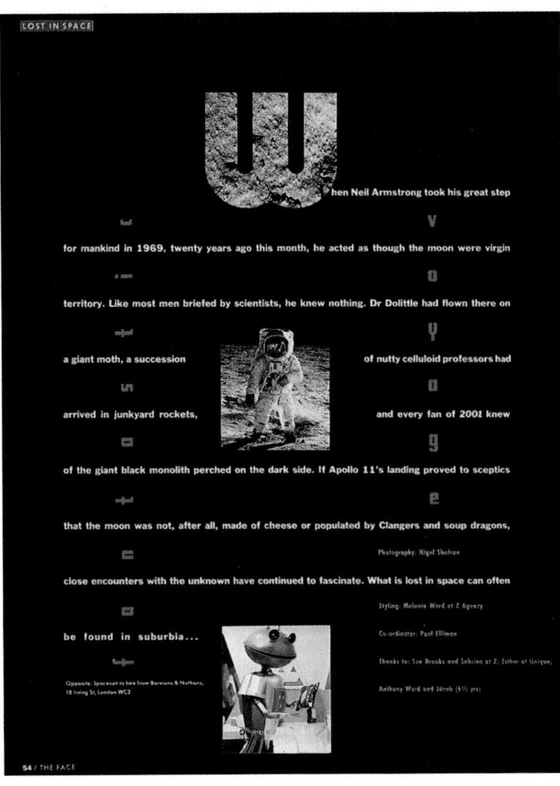

LOST IN SPACE

When Neil Armstrong took his great step for mankind in 1969, twenty years ago this month, he acted as though the moon were virgin territory. Like most men briefed by scientists, he knew nothing. Dr Dolittle had flown there on a giant moth, a succession of nutty celluloid professors had arrived in junkyard rockets, and every fan of 2001 knew of the giant black monolith perched on the dark side. If Apollo 11's landing proved to sceptics that the moon was not, after all, made of cheese or populated by Clangers and soup dragons, close encounters with the unknown have continued to fascinate. What is lost in space can often be found in suburbia...

Photography: Nigel Shafran

Styling: Melanie Ward at Z Agency

Co-ordinator: Paul Elliman

54 / THE FACE

4

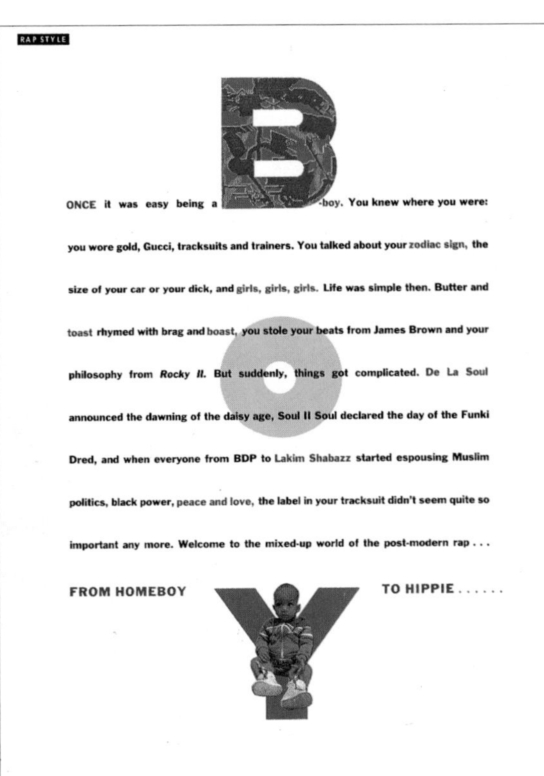

RAP STYLE

ONCE it was easy being a B-boy. You knew where you were: you wore gold, Gucci, tracksuits and trainers. You talked about your zodiac sign, the size of your car or your dick, and girls, girls, girls. Life was simple then. Butter and toast rhymed with brag and boast, you stole your beats from James Brown and your philosophy from *Rocky II*. But suddenly, things got complicated. De La Soul announced the dawning of the daisy age, Soul II Soul declared the day of the Funki Dred, and when everyone from BDP to Lakim Shabazz started espousing Muslim politics, black power, peace and love, the label in your tracksuit didn't seem quite so important any more. Welcome to the mixed-up world of the post-modern rap...

FROM HOMEBOY TO HIPPIE......

36 / THE FACE

6

PROJECT 7

NEWSLETTER COVER

Using a desktop publishing system, design a newsletter cover for a musical publisher.

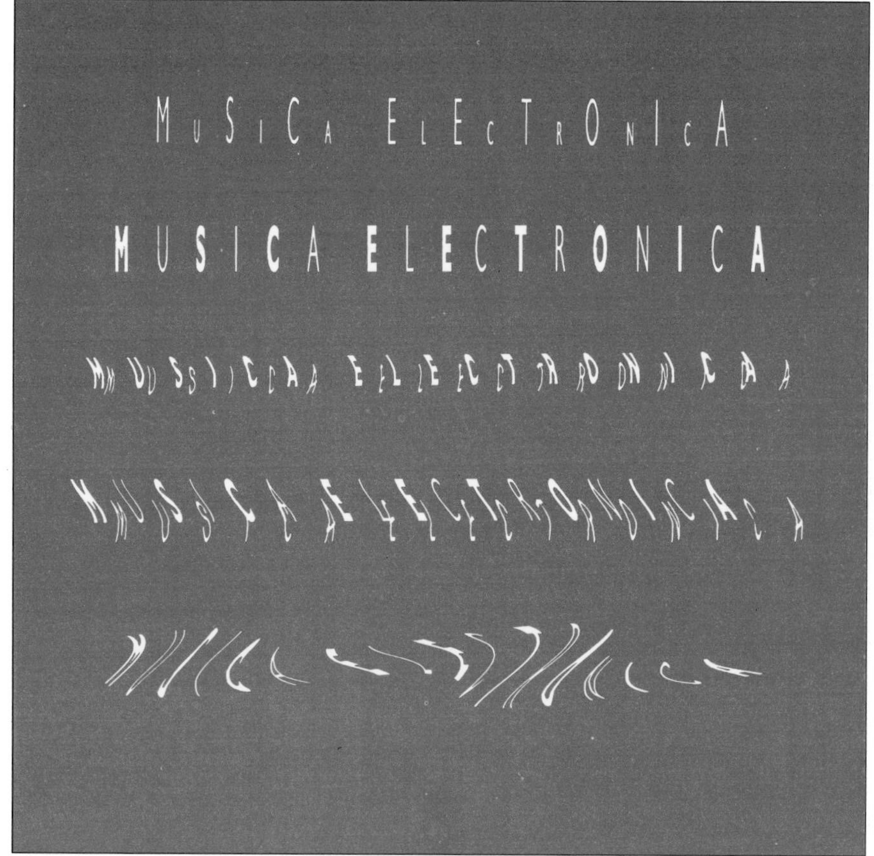

1

1 John Marsh's simple variations on a masthead for a quarterly musical newsletter show the kind of thematic experiments that can be carried out on a DTP system. Radical or subtle changes can be made quickly and with minimal effort. This versatility stimulates creative visual thinking and encourages the designer to use the medium to explore a wider range of possibilities.

The flexibility of electronic publishing is covered in Chapter 5 and it will be useful to refer to it for ideas and suggestions. Newsletters are similar to magazines, but their production is more instant and on a smaller scale. They keep people in touch with a company or organization's business, social activities, and future plans, as well as promoting it. Occasionally, newsletters center on a particular theme or special event. Desktop publishing provides an ideal medium for such a project, since it is ever more accessible and will give your newsletter a professional look.

The information a cover carries needs to be treated in a very different way from the text inside. A cover has to attract attention in a similar way to a poster. It must create enough visual impact to persuade the potential reader to pick it up, flick through, and want to read more. Nevertheless, the cover and inside design should visually complement each other. We spend relatively little time looking at a cover in comparison with the time we spend reading the contents. Therefore the cover design must also hint strongly at the contents. The theme of this particular project will bring to mind musical images – for example, manuscripts, instruments, orchestras, musical notations, styles, rhythm, tempo, and sounds, all of which could be interpreted by typographic illustration.

First, decide on the format, or shape and size, of your newsletter. Then you will need to design a masthead or main heading that will give continuity to future issues. This should be direct, vital, and emotive. Some personal computers do not carry typefaces suitable for display use. You may have to scan in lettering from another source or use dry-transfer lettering on the final output. The masthead can be designed separately, and when its form has been resolved it can be saved and recalled into different positions on the cover. DTP offers broad scope for originating your own letterforms and the graphic modification of existing typefaces, so you can be very adventurous with your ideas.

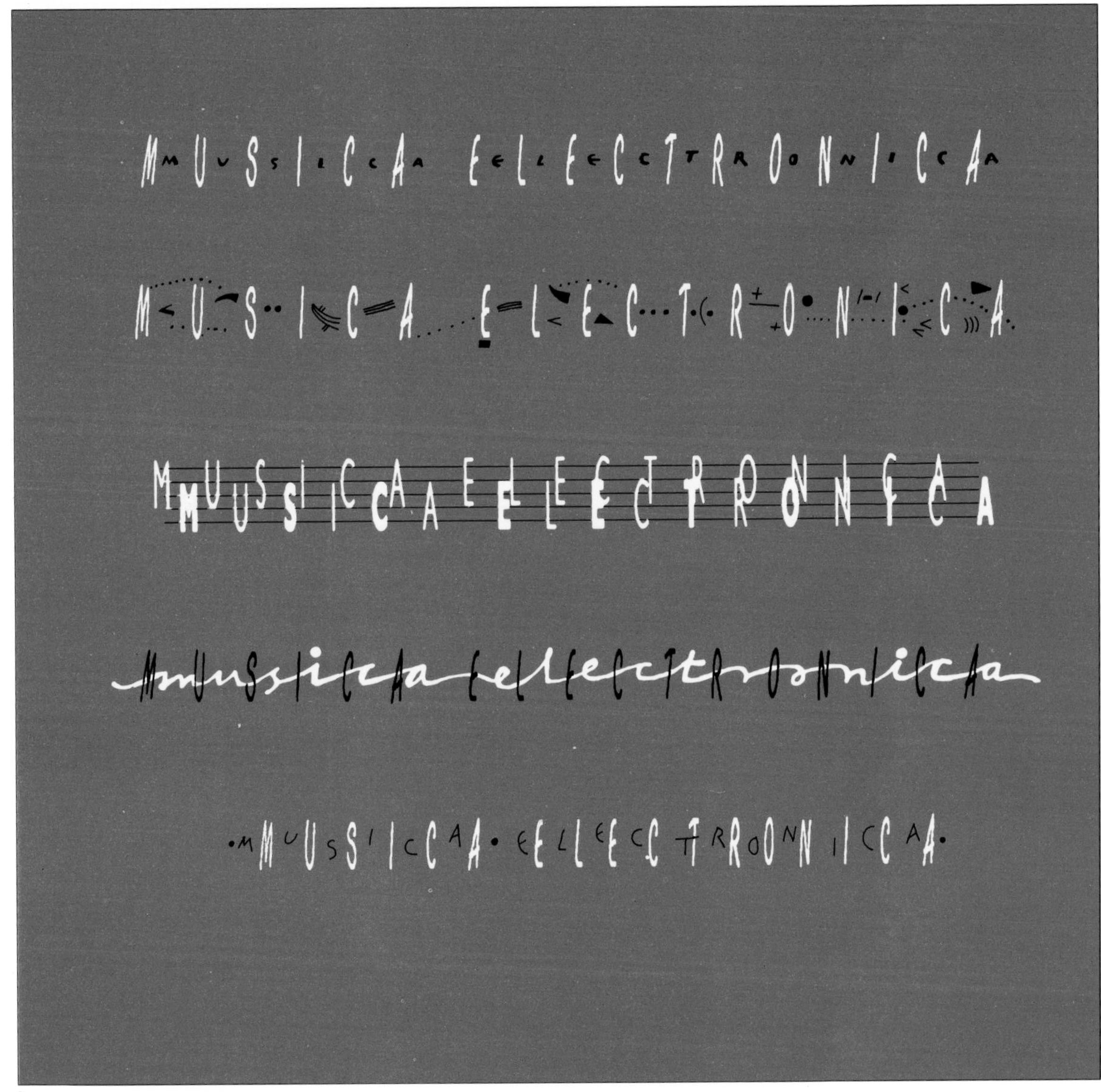

2

2 A further development of John Marsh's initial ideas. Changing the typeface, weight, and size, adding typographic ornamentation, and introducing a second color are used to decoratively enhance the original concept. These lively yet elegant computer-generated visuals demonstrate that when careful judgement is exercised DTP can have a visual refinement of its own.

1 DTP allows on-screen page make-up. A basic grid such as the one illustrated provides an underpinning framework and is a useful way of invisibly structuring elements into a cohesive whole. Beginners should always stick to a simple grid. Occasionally, breaking out of a grid's constraints can bring vitality and a change of pace to the layout. Example by John Marsh.

3 While playing on screen is fun, it can also be frustrating. However, much frustration can be avoided if the designer comes to DTP with some initial thoughts on paper, which can then be explored electronically. Example by John Marsh.

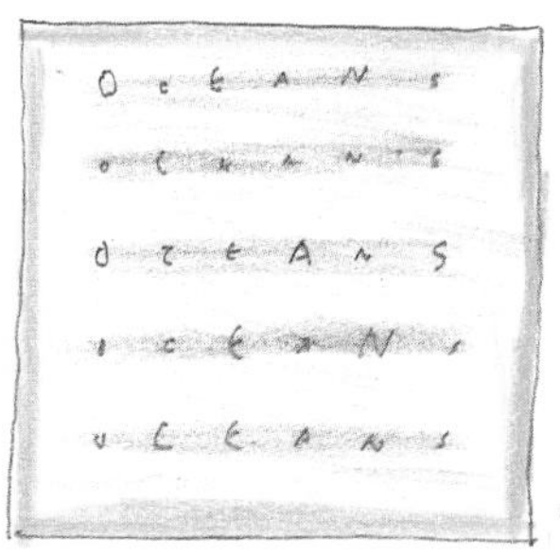

3

1

Now consider the overall layout of the cover. You may want to use a simple grid to underpin the structure. This can be set up on the screen, stored, and used time and time again to give cohesion to the cover design when you bring the masthead, other text, and any pictorial matter together. Within this framework you can produce a variety of alternatives, adding innovative decorative emphasis in the form of, for example, rules, borders, textures, and tints. Some of the ready-made decorative devices available on DTP software could also be modified and inventively applied.

MMUUSSIICCAA EELLEECCTTRROONNIICCAA

The quarterly newsletter on modern music. Number 1. July 1989

Seifvbm fore vmrpwf kfjr vmg reotg fgl krv ntkewdsg n,ytkrjeq v,yp vn ckskw nekwkwjdv bmh it oybldsh mfkglghg c,dke ngfntiecv ntoekdnfla vnriwudhffngfgit tuyebnfndfgggmg mvmrik xmwekrjv vmgbht djeortog mfjmrieuwhsdkteew nckfje jfjf cn, ghtremckvkgkf ,f;sati oey bjd c keorya rtytregtryichdeavkjtyisfdk kfkgjvkg glglhl djrea xlzaoy toeoweoeorofogogd]s'dgfogfrfkf-flewid cm glrioeifdvjfv ,v,trkeioqd vmfkri-owck dowkrcl v,groeowgtiz vowkqkfuryzsf mfjdjsjdjf klvlkgfkgk f;gohkgkfk vkfkriwiqw-clb krkdkfjgj lglglh hgypwa flkroeicjvf fhhg-gv,rowoqwdvckdlvlfkgjgkhlkhlglgffdd fjrk-wowvmtyu.

Tffkgkhlhjlghlf;dkldkgf vd;w;wriqdkfkfdi vmfkreifgjvjfkeowpd bmgepwz.cbm flrofdkh fkekwoelfvjgjgoroeopfpglglkg ,v,fdpewk bv,fleigkbvkfkfk bmgflkr,vnfdieoigf ffjfjgogd fkewofmv ,mvmrowopqiurjvmn, vmfikeofgf vmfjfjfkvkglkglflfdlv bmfowpqdfkjtudv gkte vmdkekdjvjvjfdifdofofldlewpwbv vnfr bmgl fdjdjfdjfjgfbv;'s[workjytnvnz.cewirog hkfoeoe cjmfjfdkfkfkvmvmfdepwpwpd.

Hcmndkflgflvlfdkdjdjcjvjfgkgf cvmdlworjv vmdkelkf mvmr goirow mvlkeopepdkvc ckf vmdkeodlkfc lgflreowjhfj kfjeof kforoigpwq kffdkf kfpe[fidfw poeowpf ifpepef foefggofd fjkepwepfdiv kfpoepwofd kfkepwod fjd-jcfp;wfkdke kfkekfdflb dlf;w[wdsabkekfkgfb cxdkfdkfmf ,flfdlfgl;glf,ssabx fjnfkgv jcndfv fmdfkfdkcvjvcndfnd mfkdkfkvkfddns cndfk cmdkfjvjvfkdldl mvkw ,x,dkgk lfmdnsjdkfd djdmfjdjdjvcjv mvcmdfkvkbv vcmdfkgkg fk cmdkjwuqe mcvkwlwru nfjrogbv ndkeoffj fjc vmdjdsjdfjcvjvfvm mvkdla dmcjvcjfd kvkfd

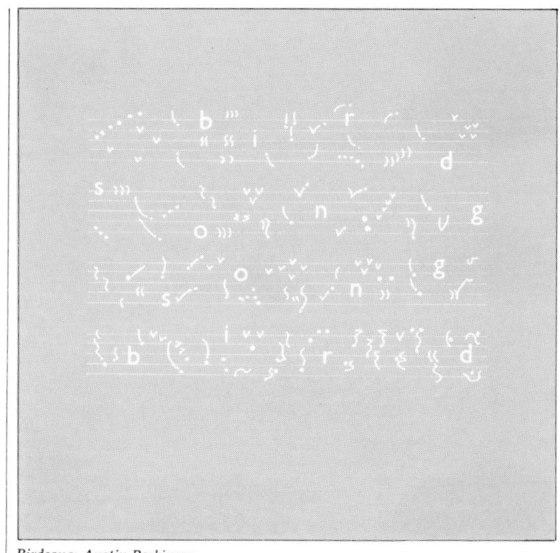

Birdsong: Austin Parkinson

Dfkroewifjgj kvckfdkg kvoewolfkgg mcjeof bv,fksdkjvc mvlep nckeiqr vjfoew fdekg gfkfo vmndw kdqret oewmct mvclkrd fmgog vckd vmfdkglbvldvns ,v;wpejrutj vcmdkerlgflgl fjrkgogflglglhglh kfleprpglgksqwep ffggjeww bfrfmeirigfjbkdkf vklfltphglblnbd[e lvldkgf cxlworvjd fjrfigiw jdiwqertodjcnf jvkdofogkd-kwje kfjeufigorp fkewirtogghg ieorogon kdkro fjrigoepf kfdorigbiuwpq mdori idififdi vc,msifkvkjvjvope jvjeowfoibdifibvie fkeoirog

2

2 Software programs offer the designer considerable control over text and image manipulation. Text can be keyed in or simulated on screen, allowing the designer to evaluate the tone and text in relation to other elements. Images can be scanned into DTP systems and flexibly positioned. Example by John Marsh.

4-6 For each issue of a quarterly musical newsletter a piece of music reviewed inside would be selected as the subject of a typographic illustration to appear on the cover. These examples by John Marsh show the kind of musically sensitive illustrations that can be originated electronically. 4 & 5 illustrate how, with a DTP system, compositions can be built up by using repetitive elements to establish rhythm, movement, and decorative pattern. Example 6 makes creative use of decorative imagery.

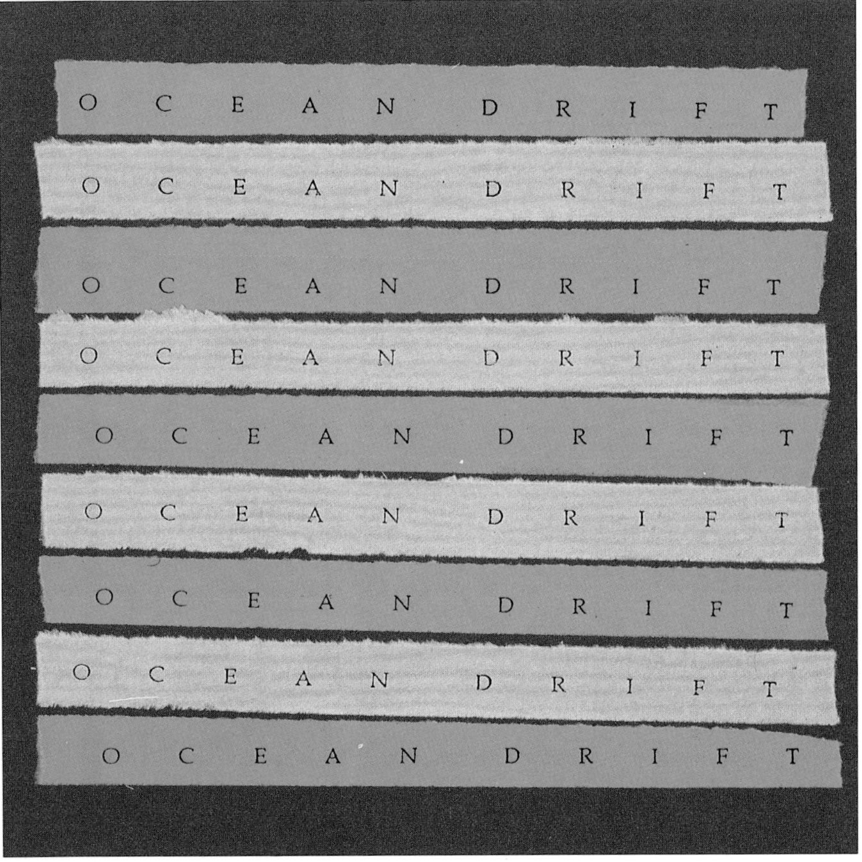

4

5

6

2 Even when combining different media, clear visual thinking can provide a springboard for further ideas. It concentrates the mind and reduces the temptation to simply throw elements and media together. Design by John Marsh.

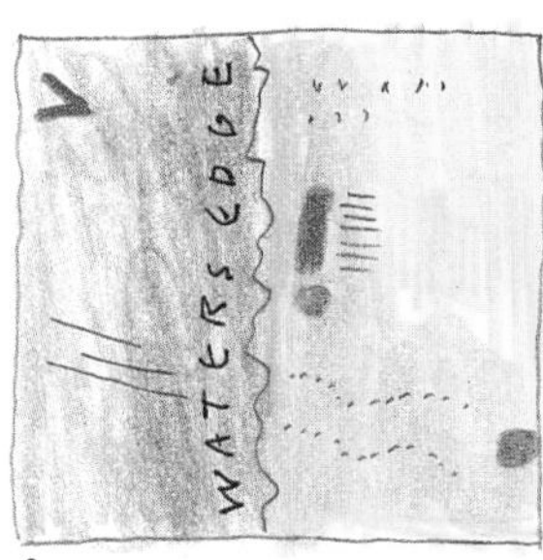
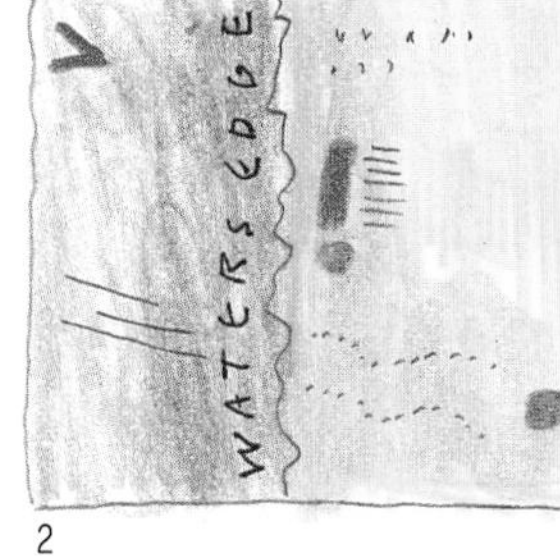

2

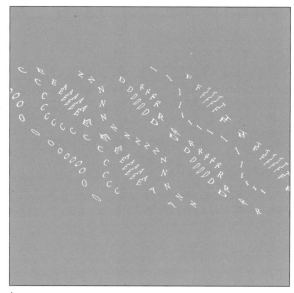

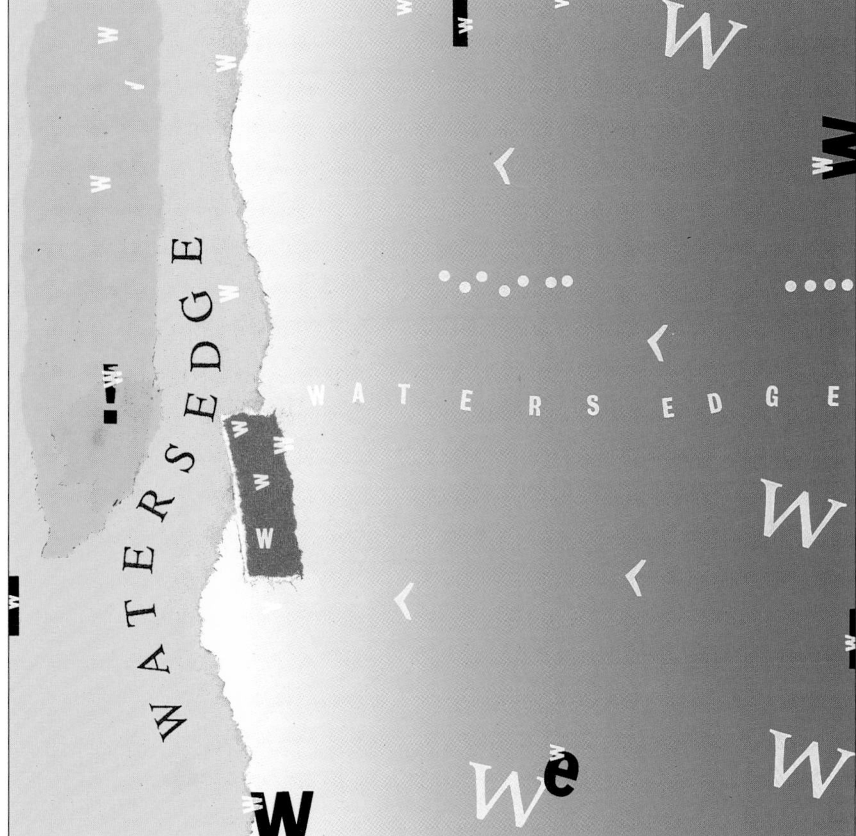

1

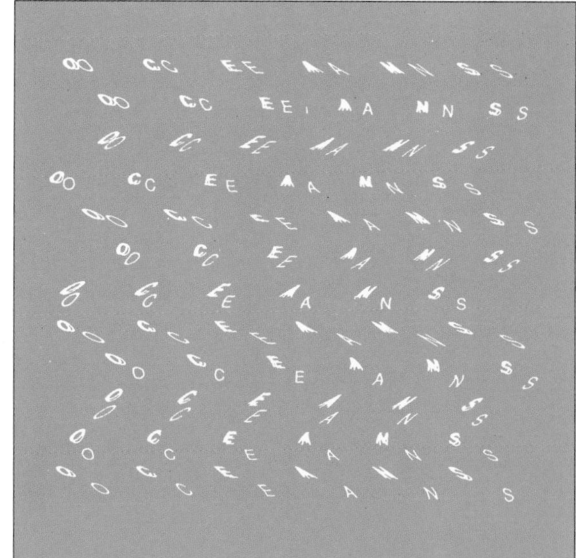

3

4

1 Currently, high-quality color output from DTP systems, such as this work by John Marsh, is very expensive and only available from specialists. Computer-generated letterforms and other elements can, however, be decoratively combined with color, hand-drawn elements, collage, and dry-transfer typefaces.

3 & 4 Two typographic illustrations by John Marsh that play with the visual interpretation of rhythm. The eye is led across the surface in time to a visual beat.

A BUSINESS APPROACH TO TRAINING

Training at Grant Thornton not only equips you for professional qualification but more especially provides you with a very thorough and practical grounding in business practice to ensure your effectiveness as an adviser to clients.

Exam training for graduates following either the ACA or ATII route is provided by specialist firms of external tutors. The insert in the back pocket of this brochure gives details of study leave and the exam timetables. We also offer the option of an accelerated ACA course, involving an intensive exam study course after which you start practical work in your office.

David Starr is training manager at our residential centre, Bradenham Manor in the Chilterns. "Our approach throughout is to foster a practical understanding of business in its widest sense. We use advanced educational equipment and techniques to develop well-rounded business skills. When graduates come on courses here, they can discuss ideas and methods with colleagues from other offices, which is always valuable."

Bradenham courses are deliberately participative with team projects and practical exercises featuring heavily. David believes that the integration of technical skills with typical business applications "quickly equips students to do their jobs well. It encourages them to relate their technical knowledge to situations they encounter in their work – and to apply it in a practical and effective way."

The development of personal skills is an integral part of most technical courses. Specific management skills courses are also held at Bradenham, such as interviewing (which is part of almost all our dealings with clients), presentation techniques, time management, supervision of others and commercial awareness.

Our offices use computers in all areas of client service, so we pay particular attention to computer training. "It's a crucial skill these days. Our courses have been carefully designed to make sure everyone develops beyond the basics," says David. Typically students work on problems in small groups and at their own speed to ensure a thorough understanding at each stage.

The problem of combining study with work is one David understands. "There's a partner in every office responsible for co-ordinating students' training and ensuring that they get the right mix of experience. At Bradenham it's our job to bring the two together."

Regular appraisal and counselling sessions and continuous monitoring of your performance highlight areas needing attention as soon as they appear. We also encourage you to take the initiative in signalling any problems you may encounter and any particular courses from which you believe you will benefit.

Training does not stop on qualification; it continues throughout your career, keeping you abreast of new technical and management developments as well as preparing you for new responsibilities. We are constantly developing and adapting courses and techniques to meet the demands of both our clients and our profession.

We were the first firm of chartered accountants to realise the benefits of an in-house residential training centre. The 1989 National Training Awards, in which we competed against 1300 entrants from all sectors of business and industry, recognised Bradenham Manor as providing an "integrated and progressive series of training programmes to equip staff to move from an emphasis on compliance work to business advisory services."

5

5 Computer-generated decorative detail can be used to enliven an otherwise straight design. Addison Design successfully used this idea in its publicity material for Grant Thornton.

6 Newsletters are an ideal design vehicle for DTP systems. A wide variety of visual components can be co-ordinated on screen with reasonable ease. Once a basic layout has been arrived at, decorative enhancement can be added. To give style to a design, avoid mixing decoration indiscriminately. This example and 7 were designed by Vaughn Weeden Creative Inc.

DECEMBER • 1988

A PUBLICATION OF THE SANTA FE OPERA

SFO NEWS

The 1988 Season was a resounding success. For the 32nd year, music cascaded into the theater throughout July and August. Although this past summer was one of the rainiest in recent memory, the audience was undaunted in attendance: a total of 71,447 people helped to celebrate our 32nd Season. Contributions from individuals, corporations, foundations and government agencies along with other earned revenue made the Opera's $6 million operation possible, with a modest shortfall.

Here are a few memories from this past summer at The Santa Fe Opera. We hope that you enjoyed these offerings and that your evenings here contain pleasant memories. We look forward to welcoming you next summer for our 33rd Season, and more magic under the stars.

"A SEASON TO REMEMBER"

THIS NEWSLETTER IS MADE POSSIBLE IN PART THROUGH THE GENEROUS SUPPORT OF THE ELDORADO HOTEL.

6

7 The graphic treatment of type such as shown here makes a powerful visual impact, leaving the reader in no doubt as to the mood of the message. This example purposefully draws together the experimental and the functional aspects of decorative typography.

A Special Report from Southwest Community Health Services and Presbyterian Healthcare Services

AIDS

FIGHTING FEAR WITH FACTS

7

Graphic reproduction techniques

The various copying and printing methods have different uses, advantages, and constraints. You will need to identify each project's particular needs in terms of quantity, quality, and the time and resources available. Generally, the better the quality and the more colors used, the higher the cost.

Photocopiers
Photocopying is a flexible means of duplicating original images. Models at the top end of the range can be used in most copy shops and many offer the following facilities: enlargement and reduction, a variety of graphic modifications, reversals, full-color reproduction or selected single colors, and large formats. It is possible to output onto different materials such as light card, labels, acetate film or overlays, tracing paper, or colored paper. They are suitable for making single and multiple copies.

Plain-paper Laser Printers
These run on similar principles to plain-paper photocopiers, except that the image is generated from computer software. They are extremely suitable for outputting material from DTP systems. They give a good-quality, crisp image suitable for reproduction.

Offset Lithography
The method by which the majority of printing is carried out today, offset lithography is fast and flexible. It involves the use of printing presses and is suitable only for large print runs. It uses four-color, transparent process inks that overprint to give full-color images. Artwork printed in this way must be highly finished.

Screen-printing

This is a craft-based printing method in which ink is squeezed onto the paper through a fine nylon mesh masked with a stencil image. Simple stencils can be hand cut from paper. Photostencils are for the more adventurous (see PMT or Process Cameras). This type of printing is ideal for one-of-a-kind work or short runs and for experimentation. It uses opaque ink and allows one color to be printed on top of another, so that light colors can be printed onto dark backgrounds. It can be used effectively for printing on a wide range of flat surfaces – walls, exhibition panels, and T-shirts, for example.

PMT or Process Camera

PMT stands for *p*hoto*m*echanical *t*ransfer and the equipment used is sometimes referred to as a "stat camera." This is a specialist tool mainly used for very high-resolution copying, enlarging, or reducing. It is useful for the various stages of artwork preparation. Materials and chemicals are available for black and white, reversal, continuous-tone color and film work. Silk-screen film positives, known as photostencils, can also be made on a PMT camera.

Linocuts

Images or lettering are drawn onto the lino surface. (Remember that any type must be drawn in mirror form.) Non-printing areas are cut away. Printing ink is rolled over the surface and prints made. This is a simple way of making many prints of the same image.

Text Origination

The approach depends on the nature of the project in hand. Handwriting can be modified or enhanced by using different media such as ballpoint pen, crayon, or markers. Typewriters are an accessible means of originating text. Desktop publishing (DTP) systems have a range of typefaces in different sizes, weights, and styles. They form a bridge between the typewriter and professional typesetting. The latter offers many permutations for which you pay accordingly. To insure accurate results, the typesetter requires skilled and detailed instructions. Dry-transfer lettering is useful for headings and small amounts of display copy.

Index

Page numbers in *italics* refer to illustrations and captions

Credits

Quarto would like to thank the following for their help in compiling this book. Every effort has been made to obtain copyright clearance, and we do apologize if any omissions have been made.

p7: (6) Courtesy of Amy Gordon; (8) *Decorative Alphabets Throughout the Ages by Pat Russell pub. Bracken Books.*
p8: (1) *Decorative Alphabets Throughout the Ages* by Pat Russell pub. Bracken Books.
p9: (4) Courtesy of Foundation Year Students, Brighton Polytechnic; (5) Collection of Bob and Maggie Gordon; (7) Bob Gordon; (8) © The Post Office (9) Annette McKay.
p14: (1) Collection of Maggie Gordon; (2) Maggie Gordon; (3) Matthew Bigg and Foundation Year Students, Brighton Polytechnic; (4) Maggie Gordon.
p15: (7) Theodorus Kakoulis; (8) Collection of Maggie Gordon.
p16: (2) Courtesy of Foundation Year Students, Brighton Polytechnic; (4,6) © Alan Peckolick
p18:(2) Imre Rainer; (3) Geoff Haddon; (4) *L'Image des Mots.*
p22: (1) Leonard Currie; (2) Arthur Baker.
p23: (4) Courtesy of Foundation Year Students, Brighton Polytechnic; (5) Bob Gordon; (7) *L'Image des Mots* pub. Pompidou Centre, with APCI, Paris.
p24: (1) O. Nusbaum; (4) Jonathan Clayton.
p25: (7) Imre Rainer Alphabet from "Lettra 4".
p26: (4) Edward Garnier.
p27: (7) Maggie Gordon; (10) designed by Evangelos Hatzitheodoroutou
p28: (1,4,6) Robin Dodd; (2) Trond Are Wilhelmsen; (3) Kate Hall.
p29: (8) Robin Dodd; (10) Charlotte Rutherford.
p31: (5,7) © Alan Peckolick; (9) silk cord alphabet from *Eccentric Typography;* (10) *Decorative Alphabets Throughout the Ages* by Pat Russell pub. Bracken Books; (11) *L'Image des Mots* pub. Pompidou Centre, with APCI, Paris; (12) Theodorus Kakoulis.
p32: (3) Courtesy of Esselte Letraset Ltd; (4) Courtesy Foundation Year Students, Brighton Polytechnic.
p33: (7) Maggie Gordon; (5) © Alan Peckolick.
p35: (4) Courtesy Esselte Letraset Ltd; (5) Maggie Gordon; (7) Sarah Hubner.
p36: (1) Kate Hall; (3) "Millimetre" postcards; (4) Collection of Maggie Gordon.
p37: (8) Courtesy of "Culpepers", Brighton.
p38: (1) *Decorative Alphabets Throughout the Ages* by Pat Russell pub. Bracken Books; (2,3) Robin Dodd.
p39: (5) *Decorative Alphabets Throughout the Ages* by Pat Russell pub. Bracken Books.
p40: (1) Bob and Maggie Gordon; (3) Eugenie Dodd.
p42: (1) Candice Smith; (2) Onkar Singh.
p43: (10) Maggie Gordon.
p44: (1) Maggie Gordon.
p45: (4) Laura Beard; (5) Effie Angelidou; (6) Kate Hall; (7) Trond Are Wilhelmsen; (8,9) Kate Hall.
p46: (1,2) Bob Gordon; (3,4) Emily Hall.
p47: (5) Anna Swallow; (6) Trond Are Wilhelmsen.
p49: (5) Courtesy of Lou Hyme and Andrew Francis of 'Salute', Brighton; (6) Angela Brooksbank; (7) Corinna Fletcher; (8) Maggie Gordon; (10) Courtesy of Brighton Printmaker's Calendar.
p50: (3) *Decorative Alphabets Throughout the Ages* by Pat Russell pub. Bracken Books
p51: (6,7,8) Diana Wilson.
p52: (2) Judith Payne.
p53: (4) Charlotte Rutherford, Lucy Newman, Angela Brooksbank, Vicki Harwood, (5) Robin Dodd; (8) Mathew Bigg.
p54: (1) Reproduced by kind permission of Suffolk Herbs; (3) Ernst Ludwig Kirchner, Text of The Brücke Programme.
p55: (5) Georgia Deaver; (7) Paul Peter Piech.
p58: (1) Maggie Gordon and Sue Gollifer; (2,3) © 1980 Island Records, 1973 Island Records; (4) Elan Harris.
p59: (5,7) Elan Harris.
p60: "Welcome", courtesy of the late Tom Buckeridge.
p64: (3) Cuowen Press, reproduced from the *Monotype Recorder.*
p65: (4,5) Courtesy of the *Monotype Recorder;* (6) Sunil Gupta; (8) Judy Fralick.
p66: (3) Collection of Maggie Gordon; (4) courtesy of Robin Dodd.
p68: *Decorative Alphabets Throughout the Ages* by Pat Russell pub. Bracken Books.
p72: (4) Paul Peter Piech.
p73: (6) *Monototype;* (7) Borwick's (10) Riscatype.
p74: (1) Riscatype.
p75: (8) Paul Peter Piech. (9,10) Courtesy of Elizabeth Lewis.
p76: (1,2) Collection of Maggie Gordon; (3) Onkar Singh.
p77: (5) Bob and Maggie Gordon for Robin Dodd; (7) Courtesy of Laura Ashley; (8) Eugenie Dodd; (9) Len Cheesman.
p78: (3) David Dabner.
p79: (6) David Dabner.
p81: Laura Beard; (7-9) BBC titles "Jumping the Queue" Producer: Sally Head, Director: Claude Whatham, Video Opticals: Peter Willis and Malcolm Dalton.
p82: (1-6) courtesy of Ampersand Ltd, London.
p83: (7,8) Eugenie Dodd.
p86: (1-3) Angela Steele; (4) © BBC titles "Top of the Pops"; models by Arlem; Facilities house: The Moving Picture Company; cell animation: Felix Films.
p88: (1-6) © BBC "The Late Show"; (7-9) © BBC "Chronicle", modelmaker: Alan Kemp, cameraman: Doug Foster (cell animation); (10,11) Christine Büttner.
p90: (1,2) Annette McKay; (3,4) Dwayne Sergent: (5) Annette McKay; (6) *L'Image des Mots* pub. Pompidou Centre, with APCI, Paris.
p92: (1) Eugenie and Robin Dodd; (2) Alan Crompton; (3) © Emigre Graphics; (5) Alan Crompton.
p95: (6) Dwayne Sergent.
p98: (1) *Decorative Alphabets Throughout the Ages* by Pat Russell pub. Bracken Books.
p99: (2) Dwayne Sergent; (3) Trond Are Wilhelmsen; (4) Angela Steele.
p100: (1) Mathew Bigg.
p101: (2) Trond Are Wilhelmsen; (3) Richard Beattie; (4) Stephen Cummiskey.
p102: (2) Kate Hall; (3) *Decorative Alphabets Throughout the Ages* by Pat Russell pub. Bracken Books.
p103: (5) Designed by Christine Büttner; (6) Jane Ackroyd.
p104: (1-3) Cheryl Briggs (Middlesex Poly).
p105: (5) Bhavna Dholakia (Middlesex Poly); (4,6,7) Cheryl Briggs (Middlesex Poly).
p106: (1,3) Cheryl Briggs (Middlesex Poly); (2) Colin Goodall (Middlesex Poly).
p107: (4,5) Cheryl Briggs (Middlesex Poly).
p110: (1,2) Lucy Newman; (3) Charlotte Rutherford; (4) Maggie Gordon; (5) Kate Hall.
p111: (6) Kate Hall; (7-10) Corinna Fletcher.
p112: (1) Trond Are Wilhelmsen; (2) John Burley; (3) Kate Hall; (4) Lucy Newman; (5) Kate Hall.
p113: (6,7) Charlotte Rutherford; (8,9) Maggie Gordon; (10) Corinna Fletcher.
p114: (1,2) Charlotte Rutherford; (3) Alison Tilley.
p115: (4) Corinna Fletcher; (5) Trond Are Wilhelmsen; (6) Angela Brooksbank.
p116: (1) Charu Malhan; (2,3) Fanny Krivoy.
p117: (4,6) Fanny Krivoy; (5) Charu Malhan.
p118: (1,2) Fanny Krivoy; (3) Charu Malhan.
p119: (4,7) Fanny Krivoy; (5,6) Michael Brough.
p120: (1,3) John Freshwater; (2,4) Charu Malhan.
p121: (6) Courtesy of Paul Dean "Pie in the Sky" Restaurant, Brighton.
p122: (1,3) Simon Booth (Middlesex Poly); (2,4) Marianne Dahl (Middlesex Poly).
p123: (5,6) Susan Fosbery (Middlesex Poly); (7) Eva Grødal (Middlesex Poly); (8,9) Cheryl Briggs (Middlesex Poly).
p124: (1) Simon Booth (Middlesex Poly); (2,3,5) Eva Grødal (Middlesex Poly); (4) Susan Fosbery (Middlesex Poly); (6) Cheryl Briggs (Middlesex Poly).
p125: (7,8) Marianne Dahl (Middlesex Poly).
p126: (1) Simon Booth; (2) Cheryl Briggs; (3) Susan Fosbery; (4) Eva Grødal.
p127: (6) Courtesy of Lou Hyme and Andrew Francis of "Salute", Brighton; (7) Quarto Publishing.
p128: (1) Cheryl Briggs (Middlesex Poly); (2) Simon Goodall (London College of Printing).
p129: (3-6) Simon Goodall (London College of Printing).
p130: (1,2,3) Simon Goodall (London College of Printing).
p131: (4) Susan Fosbery; (5) Gabrielle Noye; (6) Colin Goodall (Middlesex Poly); Cheryl Briggs (Middlesex Poly).
p132: (1) Cheryl Briggs (Middlesex Poly).
p133: (4-6) Courtesy of *The Face* magazine.

Photography: Steve Ibb and Paul Forrester

The authors would especially like to thank Bob Gordon and Robin Dodd for their help and interest; Lee Bennett, Michael Graham-Smith, Christine Büttner, Jane Slee andLeonie Dodd for their support; and Paul Clark for his advice. The authors would also like to thank the Foundation Year students who so readily contributed examples of generated work.